Great Sporting Eccentrics

Great Sporting Eccentrics

Weird and Wonderful Characters
From the World of Sport

GEOFF TIBBALLS

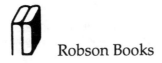

Robson Books

First published in Great Britain in 1997 by Robson Books Ltd,
Bolsover House, 5-6 Clipstone Street, London W1P 8LE

Copyright © 1997 Geoff Tibballs
The right of Geoff Tibballs to be identified as author of this work
has been asserted by him in accordance with the Copyright,
Designs and Patents Act 1988

British Library Cataloguing in Publication Data
A catalogue record for this title is available from the British
Library

ISBN 1 86105 122 0

Set in Times by Pitfold Design, Hindhead, Surrey.
Printed in Great Britain by Creative Print & Design Ltd.,
Ebbw Vale

Contents

Introduction

Our glorious sporting heritage is full of colourful characters, some of whose behaviour on and off the field of endeavour has been so idiosyncratic that it has overstepped the boundary rope into the realms of eccentricity. From the men of Hambledon who laid the foundations of cricket, the pioneers of soccer with their long beards and even longer shorts, and the daredevil drivers of the 1920s who risked their necks steering mighty racing monsters around the circuits of Europe, sport has always had its fair share of eccentrics. There was the Test cricketer who used to do bird impressions as he came in to bowl, the racehorse owner who was guided by the stars and the bad-tempered golfer who once threw himself into a water hazard.

For some reason, certain sports seem to lend themselves to eccentricity more than others. Cricketers and golfers, in particular, have always appeared prone to curious behaviour. Perhaps the relatively gentle pace of the respective games allows more scope for individualism than the hurly-burly of other sports – it must be difficult to be too eccentric while driving a Formula One racing car at 200 mph. Certainly where soccer is concerned, the true oddballs are usually goalkeepers, providing further evidence to support the theory that all of that breed are crazy. Down the years, there have been wonderful characters between the posts such as 'Fatty' Foulke, who buried an opposing centre-forward head-down in the penalty area; Albert Iremonger, who used to rush out to take throw-ins; and, more recently, Rene Higuita, of the famous 'Scorpion' save.

Eccentricity is very much in the eye of the beholder. It is a difficult term to define. Actions which seem perfectly normal to some may appear eccentric to others. Therefore the people included in this book represent a personal choice. To those who think it is standard practice to kneel down at the crease and pray before the start of each innings or to sing opera at the wheel of a Grand Prix car, I humbly apologize.

And eccentricity is by no means indicative of incompetence. Some of the leading practitioners in their field have displayed eccentric traits – WG Grace, Brian Clough, Walter Hagen, Bill Tilden, Max Baer, Tazio Nuvolari, Dickie Bird. Others, like Eddie 'the Eagle' Edwards, made a career out of eccentricity.

Within these pages, you will find the famous and the obscure, from world champions to the humblest 'rabbits'. All have one thing in common – they have, albeit sometimes unwittingly, brought a touch of colour and humour to their chosen sport. At a time when the pressures of modern sport dictate that there are fewer and fewer characters, it is a pleasure to be able to recall the likes of French racing driver Raymond Sommer who, in a bid to get his car started, once siphoned petrol by suction, in the process swallowing a considerable amount of fuel. Somehow it is difficult to envisage Michael Schumacher going to such lengths.

Geoff Tibballs, 1997

Acknowledgements

The author would like to thank the following for their help in the preparation of this book: The British Newspaper Library, the library services of Westminster, Nottinghamshire, Derbyshire, Leicestershire and Merseyside, *The Times*, the *Daily Mail*, Graham Jones of the *Faversham Times*, Zak Waters, *Total Football* magazine and Jeremy Robson and Kate Mills at Robson Books.

Acknowledgments

1 Cricket

The Man Who Thought He Was a Bird

Leslie O'Brien Fleetwood-Smith was known to his friends as 'Chuck'. A left-arm spin bowler, he was considered good enough to represent his native Australia at Test level on ten occasions between 1935 and 1938. Although he performed with some degree of success on the international stage, his brief career has largely been forgotten except by those who were fortunate enough to witness him in action. For Fleetwood-Smith was without doubt the most eccentric cricketer ever to play for Australia.

Team-mate Bill O'Reilly attributed Chuck's bizarre behaviour to the phases of the moon. 'When the moon was high,' said O'Reilly, 'Chuck would go crazy, calling out various stupid chants . . . God had given him everything required of a bowler, except a brain-box. He was definitely a screw loose.'

Fleetwood-Smith was at his finest if the game was becoming boring. In such circumstances, he would feel compelled to liven things up on the field, his *piece de resistance* being the call of the magpie. Sauntering in to bowl, he would start making loud cacking and coo-cooing noises, baffling the batsman to distraction. If he was fielding close to the wicket, he would lapse into the bird calls between deliveries, rendering all around him helpless with laughter. In addition to the screech of the magpie, his repertoire included the whoop of the whipbird, a sound which, for added authenticity, was accompanied by

1

the raising of his head skywards. It was a sight to behold.

These ornithological interludes did have their benefits. During the 1938 tour of England, there was an awkward moment at Northampton following the controversial dismissal of one of the county batsmen. Fleetwood-Smith promptly eased the tension by treating all present to an impromptu impression of a kookaburra on heat, complete with flapping wings and frenzied hops. On the same tour, the crowd at Worcester were baffled as he suddenly began chanting 'Lord Hawke, Lord Hawke' for no apparent reason. This was by no means his only fielding chant. He was particularly partial to 'Up Port Melbourne, Go Port Melbourne' in honour of his favourite football team.

Fleetwood-Smith had given early notice that he would be no conventional cricketer. As a youngster, he had always bowled right-handed until, convalescing at home following a bout of influenza, he began bowling left-handed in the family backyard when his right arm grew weary. He soon discovered that he preferred bowling with his left arm and in school matches would sometimes mix right and left-arm deliveries in the same over, just to confuse the opposition. He remained ambidextrous and, even in his first-class career, continued to bat and throw right-handed.

He made his mark in his own inimitable way on his very first appearance at Sydney Cricket Ground. Arriving, he was dismayed to see that his name-plate on the famous scoreboard had been reduced to 'F-Smith'. Seeking out the scoreboard attendants, he demanded that his name appear in full or not at all. The attendants reluctantly agreed to repaint his name-plate, somehow managing to cram together all the letters.

His first big game was for Victoria against the South African tourists when he took six wickets in the first innings. On that occasion, he wore a tatty singlet which had seen many better days, and in the belief that the garment had brought him good luck, he proceeded to wear it thereafter for all major matches (naturally, he declined to waste its powers on minor engagements). Even though it was soon virtually held together by threads, it was always the first item he packed when off on tour. Given that Fleetwood-Smith recorded figures of 1 for 298 – the worst in Test history – when England ran riot at The Oval in 1938, it is possible that his faith in the magic singlet was not altogether justified. His other lucky charm was a threepenny bit which he always kept in his right pocket while bowling. It had been given to him by his first wife.

A Clark Gable lookalike, Fleetwood-Smith was a rampant womanizer and enjoyed living up to his movie star image. At the start of a session, he would come out to field sporting a fat Havana cigar in his mouth. Only if the ball was hit towards him would he eventually stub it out. When patrolling the boundary, he could often be heard warbling 'I'm in the mood for love' and other romantic ditties. Keith Miller remarked how Chuck would wander round the field, chortling to himself. Playing to the crowd at every conceivable opportunity, he would suddenly start practising his golf swing, miming his joy at getting an imaginary hole-in-one. In truth, he was no mean golfer but, characteristically, found it impossible to take the game seriously. His favourite ploy was to tee the ball up (preferably at a hole out of view of the clubhouse), step back a few paces, trot in and hit the ball on the run!

Not renowned for his dedication – he revelled in being considered the worst batsman in the world – Fleetwood-Smith surprised many by taking positive steps to address the problem of his expanding waistline before the 1937-38 season. The method he chose was typically unorthodox: he took up wrestling. Dressed in bright-yellow tights, he toured gymnasiums and clubs in the Melbourne area, searching for suitable opponents. After one particularly strenuous bout, he turned up for a Victoria cricket training-session barely able to move his neck. Not surprisingly, his antics did not always endear him to the authorities. During the 1938 tour to England, he crept off one Sunday morning and went for a ride in a glider over the hills of the Peak District, a stunt which directly contravened Australian Board of Control rules. He simply shrugged off the subsequent reprimand.

For all his absurdities, Chuck Fleetwood-Smith was essentially a generous soul. Another contemporary, Arthur Mailey, believed him to be the only player he knew who genuinely applauded a six hit off his own bowling. When congratulating the batsman, Fleetwood-Smith would affect an upper-class English accent and enthuse: 'Great shot, old man.' Mailey was in a better position than most to pass judgement on Fleetwood-Smith since it was those two, together with Bill

Ponsford, who, on tour in England, went fishing one night off Brighton Pier dressed in their dinner jackets.

After his retirement from cricket, Fleetwood-Smith went downhill fast, at one point ending up amongst the down-and-outs on the Melbourne streets. He eventually died in 1971 at the age of sixty-three, a sad end for such a remarkable character.

His Lordship Entertains

Lionel, Lord Tennyson, grandson of the poet, brought an aristocratic air to the day-to-day business of county cricket when he captained Hampshire in the years following the First World War. He was assisted in this respect by Walter Livsey who, in addition to being the Hampshire wicket-keeper, was also Tennyson's personal manservant. Tennyson's instructions to Livsey when the latter was packing his cricket bags summed up his philosophy to the game – make sure there were sufficient bottles of champagne to celebrate victory or drown defeat. Livsey was supremely loyal to his captain and master. On one occasion when Tennyson's appeal against the light had been rejected by the umpires, Livsey, the next man in, called out on approaching the wicket: 'Where are you, my lord? I can hear you but I cannot see you.'

Watching from the pavilion, Tennyson liked to keep in touch with his batsmen, and when umpires began objecting to the constant flow of messages to the men in the middle, he resorted to sending his instructions by telegram. One Hampshire batsman, struggling to lay bat on ball, was alarmed to see a boy in a blue uniform trotting out with a small orange envelope. The contents revealed a terse inquiry as to what the recipient thought his bat was for.

Tennyson's unique brand of man-management showed itself on numerous occasions. One morning, he found himself stranded in London when required for a home game. He took a taxi to Southampton, whereupon he ordered his secretary to pay the fare. In order to do so, the poor secretary was obliged to go round the turnstiles and gather together all the admission money. For the game with Warwickshire at Edgbaston in June 1922, Tennyson travelled up from Southampton in the company of a young amateur batsman, Harold Day. As was his wont, his lordship paused for refreshment at a number of inns en route, with the result that the pair did not get to bed until dawn. 'Don't worry,' said Tennyson reassuringly, 'I'll win the toss.' Sure enough he did and duly put the opposition in. But in reply to Warwickshire's total of 223, Hampshire were skittled for just 15 in half an hour. At the end of that first day, the Warwickshire captain, the Hon. FS Calthorpe, was naturally in bullish mood and suggested to Tennyson that since the match was bound to finish early, they should have a game of golf. Tennyson took exception to this proposal and, apparently in language not appropriate to his social standing, bet Calthorpe £10 that Hampshire would win the cricket match. Other bets on Hampshire were placed at long odds and this optimism was rewarded when their second-innings total of 521 was followed by a Warwickshire collapse to 158 all out, earning the visitors an unlikely 155-run victory. The Hampshire players returned south considerably wealthier.

Three months later, on 10 September at Trent Bridge, Tennyson, who liked to juggle his batting order around as the fancy took him, was involved in another curious encounter when he sent off his own bowler Jack Newman. Anguishing long and hard over field placings before switching to bowling around the wicket, Newman had incurred the wrath of a section of the crowd. When he deliberated once more before the start of the next over, Tennyson took him off and ordered him to the pavilion. Reacting angrily to this dismissal, Newman kicked down the stumps. Tennyson explained later that Newman's offence had been the use of 'objectionable language'. He forced the errant bowler to write three identical letters of apology – to the president of Nottinghamshire, to their captain and to Tennyson himself – then decided to give Newman £5. Even by Tennyson's standards, this was curious behaviour.

In view of his cavalier attitude, it was something of a surprise when Tennyson was named captain of England against the visiting Australians in 1921. Indeed, nobody was more shocked than Tennyson himself. Receiving the telegram prior to the third Test at Headingley, he read it, rolled it into a ball, threw it at the ceiling, caught the rebound and exclaimed: 'Good heavens, they've asked me to captain England!' He certainly played a captain's innings. After injuring his left hand in the field, he went out to bat one-handed with England in dire straits. Eight wickets were down and ninety-two runs still needed to avoid the follow-on. Furthermore, England were already without Jack Hobbs who was absent with appendicitis. Wielding the bat like a tennis racket, Tennyson proceeded to batter the Australians for 63 in just over an hour, including ten fours, thereby saving the follow-on. In the *Manchester Guardian,* Neville Cardus wrote: 'Tennyson showed us that a man can drive one-handed if he will get quickly into the right position for driving. He rose high on his toes to the fast bowler's bumpers and played them down with a left elbow beautifully up. Tennyson returned to the pavilion at the end of his fine adventure to the wildest cheering one has heard on a cricket ground for many a long day.'

Although still incapacitated, he made another 36 in the second innings (including a six) and took a catch. In spite of these heroics, England lost the match by 219 runs. The Hon. Lionel went on to lead touring XIs to South Africa and Jamaica during the 1920s. He died in 1951.

The Short-Sighted Umpire

Former Leicestershire cricketer Alec Skelding was a mass of contradictions, someone who seemed to have spent his life doing the wrong jobs. Whatever he tackled, he looked like a square peg in a round hole.

As one who wore glasses and composed poetry, he was an unlikely fast bowler. Yet appearances were deceptive, for Skelding could certainly look after himself. Once when a member of the crowd became boisterous to the point of rowdy, Skelding hopped over the boundary fence, knocked the offender out cold and calmly returned to his place at third man.

He was one of the county's least able mathematicians and so was ill-equipped for the job of operating the Leicestershire scoreboard. Indeed, he once got into such a mess trying to keep track of play that an angry mob gathered beneath the scoreboard to vent their disgust.

Hearing the commotion, he poked his head out and called to the nearest protester: 'Do us a favour, cock. Get us an evening paper and let's have the right score.'

Upon his retirement from playing he became an umpire, another role to which he appeared eminently unsuitable. He officiated in first-class matches from 1931 to 1958 but was considered too eccentric to handle a Test match. Seeing his thick-lensed glasses perched on a red nose beneath a shock of white hair, players used to ask him where his guide dog was. England batsman Joe Hardstaff recalled going out to bat and being told by Skelding that there would be no lbw decisions because he was wearing his reading-glasses by mistake. He used to carry a flask in his pocket, which, he maintained, 'keeps out the cold and helps me to see straight.' Skelding, who had a known aversion to dogs – another potential minefield for an umpire – also developed his own system of umpiring signals. Having previously worked on a racecourse, he sometimes decided to give signals to the scorers in tic-tac! All in all, there was a certain irony in the fact that Alec Skelding became one of the men in white coats.

Big Bad Bill

Few relationships in cricket have been as turbulent as that between fast bowler Bill Bestwick and Derbyshire. Born at Heanor in 1875, Bestwick made his debut for the county at the age of twenty-three. His broad shoulders, fashioned by his years down the mines, made him a hostile bowler, but his work at the coal-face had also given him an unquenchable thirst and it was this which was to prove his undoing.

The problem first surfaced in 1907 when Bestwick was involved in a drunken brawl at Heanor with a man named William Brown. When Brown was later found stabbed to death, Bestwick was charged with manslaughter. However, the inquest ruled that he had acted in self-defence and so charges were dropped and he was released. His drinking got worse and two years later Derbyshire sacked him, even though he had taken over 900 wickets for the county.

Amazingly, after a spell with Glamorgan, he returned to the fold in

7

1919 at the age of forty-four, but this time Derbyshire were determined to curtail his drinking sessions. Whenever the team was playing away, one of the players – usually Arthur Morton – was appointed to accompany Bestwick at all times (presumably an exception was permitted for calls of nature). But Bestwick was a wily old fox and used to give his minder the slip by entering a shop by the front door and sneaking out the back. The alcohol soon took its toll once more. A report of the 1921 fixture with Gloucestershire stated: 'Bestwick occasionally suffered from a "thirst" and as a result was unable to bowl or field much in Gloucestershire's second innings.' The next game was at Cardiff against Glamorgan. Bestwick was again much the worse for wear on the Sunday evening and so, in an inspired move, Derbyshire decided to have him open the bowling for Glamorgan's second innings. With the red mist before his eyes, he demolished the home batting, taking all ten wickets (seven clean bowled and finishing up with three in four balls) in the space of nineteen overs for just forty runs. Rarely has a finer performance been given under the influence.

Even so, Bestwick's drinking continued to be very much a mixed blessing. The following season, he went absent at Worcester and later turned up, horribly drunk. Furthermore, he proceeded to barrack his own team from the stand!

Bill Bestwick retired in 1925, having taken 1452 wickets for the county. He died in 1938.

Amazing Grace

As the finest cricketer in the land, Gloucestershire and England's Dr William Gilbert 'WG' Grace (1848-1915) considered himself to be above the laws of the game. Consequently, he used to bully umpires and bend the rules to suit his own needs. He told one official who had the audacity to give the great man out: 'They've come to see me bat, not you umpiring.' With that, Grace calmly replaced the bails and continued with his innings. On another occasion, he lofted the ball towards the boundary, only to see a fielder perfectly positioned to take the catch. Before the fielder could do so, Grace declared the innings closed and forced the umpire to give him not out, on the grounds that the ball had been caught after the declaration.

He tried a similar tactic during a Gentlemen versus Players match at Lord's. Yorkshire's Schofield Haigh had asked Grace for permission to leave the field early on the last day in order that he could catch a train back to Yorkshire. Permission was granted, but as the time for Schofield's departure (and Grace's century) drew near, the doctor hit what seemed to be a certain catch in Haigh's direction. As Haigh waited for the ball to drop into his hands, Grace shouted: 'Take the catch and you miss the train!' Wishing to preserve his travel arrangements, Haigh wisely allowed the ball to hit the ground.

Grace did not always get his own way. Batting at Bristol, he got a bottom edge and the ball lodged in the top of his pad. Seizing the opportunity to add to his score, he waddled to the boundary with the ball intact and, on crossing the rope, demanded four runs. To his barely-concealed annoyance, the umpire refused. Grace met his match in Middlesex's Irish Baronet Sir Timothy O'Brien. Batting against Gloucestershire, Sir Timothy was making such rapid progress that the good doctor endeavoured to slow the run rate by bowling a succession of very wide deliveries. O'Brien responded by thrashing the ball backhanded through the slips (a kind of reverse sweep with menaces), a manoeuvre which nearly decapitated Grace's brother EM, who happened to be fielding there. Immediately adopting the high moral ground, WG informed O'Brien: 'If you do that again, I'll take my men off the field.' But O'Brien was not one to be intimidated and promptly repeated the feat. Grace was as good as his word and Gloucestershire marched off. A monumental row broke out, during which WG threatened to summon the police, before order was finally restored.

Grace's bowling was deceptive to say the least. Sir Arthur Conan Doyle said of him: 'He would lumber up to the wicket and toss up the ball in a take-it-or-leave-it style, as if he cared little whether it pitched between the wickets or in the next parish.' One of his favourite ploys before coming in to bowl was to point at a non-existent flock of birds flying across a bright sun and then bowl while the batsman's eyes were still dazzled. To put it mildly, he had gamesmanship down to a fine art.

He was, of course, delightfully unpredictable. In an 1893 match, he shocked his team-mates by suddenly declaring the innings closed with his own score on 93, just seven short of a century. He later explained that 93 was the only score between 0 and 100 that he had yet to make. He was a splendid all-round sportsman. In 1866, having scored 224 for All England against Surrey at The Oval, he absented himself from the field, nipped down to Crystal Palace and won the 440 yards at the National Olympian Association's championships. At the crease, the doctor could cope with all manner of adversity. At Bristol in 1885, he made 221 against Middlesex despite having spent the night at the bedside of a patient. Eleven years earlier, he had taken a team to play F Townsend's XI at Cheltenham. While the rest of the players used more conventional implements, Grace, as a concession to his greatness, agreed to bat with a broomstick and still succeeded in making 35, the second highest score.

This bearded colossus was regarded with such reverence that when he died on 23 October 1915 of natural causes, the propaganda-conscious Germans tried to claim him as an air-raid victim. Such was his value to the nation.

Keeping it in the Family

Whilst WG has always stolen the headlines in terms of family eccentricity, his elder brother EM, known as 'the coroner' because of his profession, displayed alarming idiosyncrasies of his own, many of which manifested themselves on the cricket field. Edward Mills Grace was of the belief that the individual player was bigger than the game – provided that the aforementioned individual bore the surname Grace. He was the archetypal petulant schoolboy who was not averse to storming off with his bat and ball if things were not going his way. Indeed, as a youthful cricketer at Long Ashton, he was so incensed by a borderline lbw decision that he promptly marched from the field, carrying the stumps under his arm. In doing so, he followed in the footsteps of his grandfather George Pocock, who, as organist at the Portland Wesleyan Church at Kingsdown, near Bristol, had become embroiled in a bitter feud with the deacon. Pocock responded by resigning on the spot and taking the organ with him.

EM's disdain for umpires was legendary. Bowling for Thornbury against Weston-super-Mare, he was hit for four successive sixes by FA Leeson-Smith. When the umpire called 'over', Grace snapped: 'Shut up, I am going to have another.' And so Grace bowled a seventh delivery, off which the unfortunate Leeson-Smith was stumped.

On more than one occasion, Grace's behaviour created a scene which all but required his alternative services as a coroner. Bowling against the United South team at The Oval in 1865, he persisted in attempting to remove the obstinate Harry Jupp by pitching lobs high into the air so that they landed on top of the stumps. When the tactic worked, Jupp and the crowd took exception. The match was stopped and the players tore up the stumps, ready to use them as weapons. Grace himself was taking no prisoners and declared: 'The first man who touches me will get the middle stump on his head.' Happily, common sense prevailed before any serious damage was done, but needless to say, Jupp was forced to sacrifice his wicket. The Graces were not exactly renowned for backing down. After the 1896 Australian tourists had routed Gloucestershire in double-quick time, Grace challenged the visitors' Harry Donnan to a single-wicket match. As EM ran up to bowl, a drunk in the crowd yelled abuse. EM saw red, turned on the miscreant and charged at him, in the words of one witness, 'like a rhinoceros'. The chase continued out of the ground and away across Ashley Down. When EM eventually returned and was timidly asked what he had done with the heckler, he replied: 'He's still running.'

Despite his brushes with authority, spectators and other players, the autocratic Grace, a familiar sight with his handkerchief stuck in the strap at the back of his cricket trousers, clearly loved the game. Indeed, if a clash occurred between his coroner's work and a game of cricket, there would only ever be one winner. He would simply announce that a post-mortem was needed and then go off to play cricket. And because he was a Grace, few people ever dared to question his ruling.

A Question of Timing

Nottinghamshire batsman George Gunn, who scored over 35,000 runs for the county between 1902 and 1932, took the art of clock-watching to faintly ridiculous lengths. But then George Gunn was no ordinary cricketer. An exceptional batsman whose technique was based on a sound defence, he would surely have won many more than his fifteen England caps had he not been considered such a maverick. In every sense, he was his own man.

Nowhere was this better demonstrated than in a match against Hampshire at Southampton. Gunn was at the non-striker's end as the clock reached 1.30pm. Assuming that it was lunch, he removed the bails and headed off towards the pavilion, only to be summoned back by the umpire who announced, 'Not yet, George. We're taking lunch at two o'clock today. Back you go.' Without uttering a word, Gunn retraced his steps, replaced the bails and took guard to face the next over. Receiving a straight ball, he calmly stepped aside and allowed the ball to hit the wicket, whereupon he tucked his bat under his arm and made off once more for the pavilion, informing the stunned audience as he departed: 'I take my lunch at 1.30.'

For a game against Yorkshire at Leeds, the Notts attack was severely depleted as a result of a car crash and so on winning the toss, the county captain AW Carr decided to pile up a big score in the hope that some of his bowlers might recover in time. He told the ageing Gunn to stay in until tea, but Gunn replied: 'I'm sorry, Mr Carr, but I can't hold out that long. My legs are not what they used to be.' Carr remained adamant and Gunn promised to stay at the crease until at least 3.30, even volunteering to hold out longer if he were to be paid an extra £1 an hour. In the event, he hung on until 5.30, making forty runs, and stunned Carr by submitting a claim for time-and-a-half on account of the extra length of his innings. At the end of the day, George Gunn was £5 10s better off.

Gunn enjoyed watching matches in the company of his wife. Sometimes when he saw her arrive at a ground, he would quickly land a six near where she was sitting to indicate that he would soon be joining her. Sure enough, shortly afterwards he would deliberately contrive to get himself out. On going out to open for Notts, he would sometimes tell the number three, Willis Walker: 'Get your pads on, Willis. I'll not be long.'

Despite this willingness to surrender his wicket from time to time, Gunn could dig in when the occasion demanded. However, his efforts were not always appreciated. Batting in difficult conditions against Yorkshire at Trent Bridge in 1913, he spent six hours compiling a century. Some of the club members did not approve of his slow play, and caustic comments were hurled in his direction. Gunn became so annoyed that in the second innings, he hit another century – this time in just ninety minutes. He was once barracked for slow play by a burly miner in a game against Derbyshire. After half an hour of listening to this taunting, Gunn lost his patience, stalked over to the man, offered him his bat and gloves and challenged him to do better. For the rest of the day, the heckler was remarkably subdued. Gunn did, however, have the good sense to leave the ground swiftly at the close of play in case the miner was waiting for him.

Often he appeared to be toying with the bowling, indulging in his own peculiar flights of fancy. He would treat a rank long-hop with the utmost reverence, playing it quietly back to the relieved bowler, but would then thrash the next delivery, one of perfect line and length, for four. He liked nothing more than marching four or five yards down the pitch, even to fast bowlers. But once he got there, he would invariably greet the ball with the deadest of bats. He simply had to do things his way.

Then there was the occasion when Gunn was challenged to a single-wicket match by a cocky amateur who suggested a purse of £100. Gunn politely declined, but the amateur persisted. Eventually Gunn relented, but only if the stakes be reduced to £5. The match was played each evening on the practice ground at Trent Bridge from five o'clock to seven thirty. Gunn batted first, and by the end of the second evening had amassed 620 runs. At this point, the amateur cheekily suggested that Gunn might like to declare. Gunn preferred to play on but did allow his opponent to bowl at the 6ft-wide heavy roller instead of at the stumps. The amateur must have fancied his chances as Gunn took guard in front of the roller, but even with such a large target at which to aim, he made no headway. After a further ninety minutes on the third evening, Gunn's total had risen to 777. At this point, the challenger decided he'd had enough, threw down the ball and stormed off. He was never heard of again. George Gunn was not always prepared to sacrifice his wicket.

Hell Hath No Fury

The name of Mrs Iris Clarke may not feature prominently in *Wisden* but in 1983 she certainly made her mark on the Hampshire second XI. It was on 11 August that year that Robin Smith, batting in a second-XI fixture, had the misfortune to hit the ball through the window of Mrs Clarke's flat which overlooked the Southampton ground. The next thing the players knew, sixty-two-year-old Mrs Clarke had marched onto the pitch and was demanding an apology from Smith. Hampshire pointed out that the flats were all insured against damage from cricket balls, but the argument escalated when Mrs Clarke flatly refused to hand the ball back. Still unrepentant several hours later, she told reporters: 'They told me I was holding up their game. I said that if they could break my windows, I could spoil their silly cricket. They are not getting their ball back.'

The Batsman With Inflatable Pads

Born into a wealthy East Midlands family, furniture magnate Sir Julien Cahn (1882-1944) was a cricket fanatic, and between 1923 and 1941 his team of country-house cricketers played over 600 matches, including tours to Jamaica, North and South America, Canada, New Zealand, Denmark and the Far East. Sir Julien himself had unusually fragile bones and commissioned a pair of inflatable batting-pads to protect his legs. The pads, which were inflated with a bicycle-pump by his chauffeur before each innings (often while Sir Julien was dictating a business letter to his secretary), looked decidedly cumbersome but proved useful run-getters, since any ball that pitched off-line was shinned away by him for leg-byes. The only problem with the pads was that they were uncomfortable to walk in for any length of time, and so Sir Julien often summoned a bath chair to transport him from the pavilion to the wicket and back again.

His opinion of his own batting was as inflated as his pads. He used to practise in the nets with Nottinghamshire's John Gunn, elder brother of George. Gunn would deliberately bowl slowly to him and tell him how well he was batting; Sir Julien would take the bait and wager five shillings on his wicket. Gunn would wait for the stakes to be raised to £1 a wicket before upping the tempo. Suddenly, Sir Julien would see his stumps flattened by three successive deliveries, leaving the bowler £3 richer. Gunn would then turn and say: 'You must have lost your concentration, Sir Julien.'

At its most hostile, Cahn's bowling was gentle and, as such, heavily punished. It was said that at any ground, one could tell when Sir Julien was bowling because there would be a faint whistling in the trees from the ball being hit there. For all his punishment, he always had one supporter since his personal barber travelled with him all around the world. He thus perfected the art of the late cut.

Sir Julien's home, Stanford Hall near Loughborough, boasted a golf course, tennis and squash courts, bowling and putting greens, a swimming pool, a lake and even a performing seal pond! Visiting teams usually stayed at the mansion and availed themselves of the facilities. Cunningly, he housed them in the wing of the house situated directly above his 350-seater theatre, the pride of which was a mighty Wurlitzer organ. To ensure that his team's opponents did not get much sleep on the night before a match, Sir Julien would practise on the organ in the small hours.

He was a deeply superstitious man. He liked to turn round three times before passing through a doorway and always put on his right batting-pad first. When a wicket fell unexpectedly, these operations would take place simultaneously, giving rise to a performance which one observer likened to 'an ostrich doing a courtship dance'.

Joker in the Pack

Few cricketers of modern times have carved their personality on the game to the extent of Nottinghamshire and England's Derek Randall.

His perpetual fidgeting, boyish enthusiasm, infectious grin and improbable athleticism endeared him to spectators across the world. Going out to bat, whether facing a humble county bowler or a Test superstar, Randall would shuffle and twitch at the crease as if he were a bag of nerves. Before virtually every delivery, he would go through a series of mannerisms, including tweaking his cap and the top of his left pad. Every bowler must have fancied his chances of getting him out, but as the majority discovered, where Derek Randall was concerned, appearances could be deceptive.

Not everyone appreciated Randall's antics. His habit of whistling Simon and Garfunkel tunes in the field had occasionally been known to distract batsmen. His finest hour was in the 1977 Centenary Test at Melbourne where he made a brilliant 174 (for which he was sent 174 pork chops by a Nottingham butcher). In the heat of the battle, Randall turned somersault to evade a wicked bouncer from Dennis Lillee and ended up on bended knee, doffing his cap at the bowler. Lillee was not amused, later describing Randall as a 'bloody pain in the arse'. Coming from Lillee, maybe it was a veiled compliment.

With Derek Randall, it had always been thus. As an eighteen-year-old playing in the Bassetlaw League for Retford, he fidgeted so much while watching a tight finish that team-mate John Cook, a policeman, dragged him to the toilet and handcuffed him to the cistern before returning to watch the remainder of the game. Randall was only freed when everyone went home. When he turned professional, the Nottinghamshire players bet him a pint of bitter that he couldn't stand still for half an hour. Randall gave up after thirty seconds, saying he wasn't thirsty.

With Randall, the only thing that was expected was the unexpected. As a youngster on his first MCC tour, he enlivened a pompous official reception in India by suddenly turning a cartwheel. The faces of his hosts were a mixture of amusement and amazement. When handed caviar on the same tour, he remarked: 'The blackcurrant jam tastes of fish to me.' A journalist calling at his house in the middle of winter was greeted by Randall answering the door wearing a brand new set of cricket pads. He explained that he was breaking them in. During a close encounter with Yorkshire, he was fielding in the deep when John Hampshire lofted a ball from Notts spinner Bob White towards him. Randall positioned himself beneath the ball, but at the very last minute he appeared to bow his head and allow it to fall behind him. The umpire duly signalled a six and White was on his way to remonstrate with the fielder when Randall mischievously produced the ball from behind his back. Apparently, he had thought it would be a bit of a wheeze to try and catch the ball with his hands behind his back. Luckily for him, it worked – but it did little for his team-mates' blood pressure.

Randall, who dressed up as the Fairy Queen for the England team's traditional Christmas Day lunch in Australia, was a willing participant in touring pranks. One of the most memorable took place in Adelaide where he visited a bar in the city's busiest shopping street in the company of Ian Botham. As the pair studied the locals, they were intrigued by the arrival of a mini-skirted girl who happened to be about the same height as Randall. Seeing the opportunity for a bet, Botham wagered Randall £5 that he could not swap clothes with the girl. Randall accepted, slipped the girl a couple of pounds and changed into her skirt. Still not satisfied, Botham bet him another fiver that he would not dare to go out into the street dressed like that. By now, Randall was game for anything; he minced outside in his mini-skirt and loitered by the kerb. Before long, a car drew up and offered him a lift. To get one up on Botham, Randall climbed in and immediately set about explaining to the driver that he was really an England cricketer and that this was the sort of thing they got up to on their days off. Unfortunately, the driver didn't believe him. 'He thought it was some sort of come-on,' said Randall later. 'I had to deal several blows with my handbag before being able to get out of the car and retreat back to the bar.'

A Century Before Breakfast

Founded in 1897, the Early Bird Cricket Club was made up of butlers, valets, footmen and sundry servants from the large houses owned by the gentry of Victorian London. These doughty fellows used to rise before daybreak and start practising at 5.30am every Tuesday on playing fields at Battersea Park, the idea being that they could then dash back to work in time to rouse their masters from their slumbers. Within a few years, they were playing dawn matches against other teams of early risers and even travelled further afield to take on sides composed of the staff of country estates.

A Fair-Weather Player

Herbert Tremenheer Hewett (1864-1921) was an aggressive left-handed batsman who channelled much of his venom into a hatred for rain. Captaining Somerset against the Australian tourists in July 1893, Hewett watched from the pavilion as rain wiped out play for the first day. The second day saw more rain, but the weather gradually improved and play was able to begin, resulting in victory for the visitors in a low-scoring game. In truth, the decision to play at all was that of the Somerset committee – the umpires and Hewett had deemed the conditions unsuitable. So outraged was Hewett by the decision to play that he resigned the captaincy.

In September 1895, Hewett was chosen to lead an England XI against Yorkshire at the Scarborough Festival. Once again, the start was delayed because of rain and when the reluctant Hewett finally led his men out, he was subjected to abuse and derision from the crowd, a scene described by *Wisden* as 'a most unseemly demonstration'. This was too much for the temperamental Hewett, who promptly stormed off the pitch, out of the ground and indeed out of first-class cricket! For the remaining twenty-six years of his life, he never again lifted a bat in anger. And all because of a couple of rainy days.

The Fanatical Pope

Dr Rowley Pope was one of the unsung heroes of Australian cricket – a diehard supporter who, at his own expense, accompanied the team on numerous overseas tours in the 1920s and 1930s, during which he acted as general helper and dogsbody.

His pre-tour preparations were more thorough than most of the players'. Determined to be prepared for all eventualities in a foreign land, he took with him everything bar the kitchen sink (and few would have been surprised if one of those had been secreted somewhere in his luggage). Before departure, he itemized the contents of every bag and recorded them in a filing system which he kept at all times in one of his inside pockets. The amount of luggage he took on tour was legendary and grew to such an extent that restrictions had to be placed upon him for fear that he might overload the ship. On the 1932 tour to the United States and Canada, Pope was limited to thirty-six bags which contained everything a cricketer could need, from, in the words of Australian captain Vic Richardson, 'a fish hook to a feather duster'. When Richardson asked the good doctor whether, amongst his cases, he had any information about the United States which could prove useful in an official speech, Pope produced three books – a history of the US, a history of Canada and a tome devoted to North American cricket.

Pope prided himself on being able to respond to any demand. Bert Oldfield once asked for a tiny screw with which to fit an earpiece to his sunglasses, and Pope immediately came back with three different types of suitable screw. During a 1926 tour, Pope was asked for a button-hook and once again rose to the occasion within minutes. Given his apparent infallibility, it was only natural that certain players would do their utmost to catch him out. Victoria skipper Edgar Mayne got the better of him by asking for a bicycle pump. Of course, Mayne had no need for such an object but he just wanted to see Pope's reaction on realizing that he didn't have one. Pope was predictably distraught, but he wouldn't make the same mistake twice. Thereafter, he always made sure that he packed a bicycle pump in his tour luggage.

Capped for Incompetence

The second XI from Churt CC in Surrey were such abysmal fielders during the 1939 season that anyone dropping a catch had to wear a special red hat until the next chance went down. Even if the wearer redeemed himself in the meantime by holding a blinder, he was not allowed to pass the hat on until the next catch went to ground. He rarely had long to wait.

Let Us Pray

The association between cricket and men of the cloth dates back to the very origins of the game, but none have combined the two disciplines with such fervour as the Leicestershire and England batsman Albert Knight. At the start of each innings, Knight, a deeply religious man who was a lay preacher, would go down on his knees at the crease to pray for help from above. When he played at Middlesex, this must have brought a new meaning to the Lord's Prayer.

So as to leave nothing to chance, he also prayed loudly at home on the night before a match that he might make a century the following day. This led to an unholy row with the irreverent Derbyshire fast bowler Bill Bestwick, who was staying as Knight's house guest. Hearing Knight's prayers, Bestwick responded by praying that he would shatter his host's stumps for nowt. Sure enough, the next day the scorebook read 'Knight b Bestwick 0'. Apparently their friendship suffered, Knight considering that he had been out-supplicated by a novice.

In spite of sundry complaints about his pre-innings ritual – Lancashire fast bowler Walter Brearley moaned to one umpire that Knight was receiving unfair assistance – Knight prospered in the early years of the twentieth century. His earthly reward was a career total of 18,142 runs and three England caps.

Catcher in the Rye

The cricketers from the moorland hamlet of High Farndale in North Yorkshire boast one of the world's most bizarre pitches. Whilst the wicket itself is manicured to perfection, the rest of the ground is an uncut meadow used by a local farmer to graze his herd of cattle. The result is that bowlers and fielders alike find themselves stumbling through two-foot high grass, taking care to avoid rabbit burrows, badger sets and numerous cow pats. Thus the familiar sound of willow upon leather is interspersed with the odd cry of anguish. The land is owned by house builder Sir Lawrie Barratt, who rents it to farmer Gilbert Weldon. He in turn allows the cricketers to use it free of charge. High Farndale player Andy Fawbert admits: 'Most teams like to play us early in the season when the grass is shorter, but they know what to expect and it's only the outfield that can cause problems. Cow muck can be a bit messy and when one chap fell down a badger hole, we had to bring the boundary in.'

Baited Bowlers

A great-grandson of Charles II, Lord Frederick Beauclerk (1773-1850), took gamesmanship at cricket to extraordinary lengths, this despite the fact that he was the vicar of St Albans. A perpetual cheat who bribed both players and scorers (in one year he claimed to have made £600 from fixing matches), he would con teams unfamiliar with his tactics by pretending to be disabled or, at the very least, badly injured. He created this illusion by lurching from the pavilion, either with a fake limp or with a mass of padding stuffed up the back of his shirt. To those teams with experience of his deceptions, he would demonstrate his contempt for their bowlers by hanging a valuable gold watch from the top of his middle stump. It is not recorded how frequently he had to send it for repairs.

His other great passion in life was horse racing, although he always rode under an assumed name for fear of incurring the wrath of his bishop. He even preached from a saddle fitted into his pulpit.

A Man of Many Parts

Charles Burgess 'CB' Fry (1872-1956) was, quite simply, just about the finest all-round sportsman in the land. As well as representing

England at both cricket and soccer around the turn of the century, he also held the world long jump record for twenty-one years. Indeed, he would have gone to Athens for the 1896 Olympics had he known they were taking place.

Oxford-educated Fry was a larger-than-life character in the mould of the Graces, and he shared with them an air of superiority which bordered on the regal. As a footballer, he had his own dressing-room and bath! Inevitably, this loftiness sometimes brought him into conflict with those whom he considered to be lesser mortals. Whilst playing for Sussex, whom he joined from Oxford in 1894, he once took considerable umbrage at being no-balled for throwing. Back in the pavilion, he proceeded to tie his bowling arm in a splint and to cover the apparatus by buttoning down the sleeve of his shirt. He was all set to embarrass the umpires by bowling with the straightest of arms until his captain, the Australian Billy Murdoch, intervened and put a stop to the charade. Nor did he always react well to criticism from spectators. In 1912, he captained England to victory against Australia at The Oval, but in the course of the match he had been booed by a section of the crowd for refusing to restart play after rain. Fry felt that to have done so would have been to the Australians' advantage and the result completely vindicated his decision. As England celebrated victory – one which also clinched the rubber – the crowd's jeers turned to cheers. But Fry stubbornly refused to step forward and acknowledge them. His friend and team-mate KS Ranjitsinhji, the Jam Sahib of Nawanagar, urged him: 'Be your noble self.' To which Fry replied aloofly: 'This is not one of my noble days.'

Fry, who used to practise his strokes with an umbrella, edited a number of periodicals in his time, including *CB Fry's Magazine*, where he imposed a rule that no sentence should exceed twenty-five words. However, Fry himself broke the rule on such a regular basis that the contributors rebelled. He resolved the situation by offering a dispensation to those who had also enjoyed a classical education, because they 'understood how to frame subordinate clauses'.

He made several unsuccessful attempts to enter Parliament as a Liberal, but he did have the distinction of being the only opening batsman ever to be offered the throne of Albania. This came about in

1920 through his association with Ranjitsinhji, who by then was a member of the Indian delegation to the League of Nations and had appointed Fry as his personal adviser. At the time, Albania was a newly independent state. An Albanian bishop called on Ranji and Fry and hinted that if someone, preferably an Englishman, were to be found who was prepared to spend £10,000 a year in Albania, the crown would be his. With Ranji's help, the money would have been no problem and it is believed that Fry was seriously tempted by the offer. But in the end the matter fizzled out, with Ranji clearly reluctant to lose Fry's services. CB Fry would have to settle for a more modest stage.

A Prince Amongst Players

For both Sussex and England, the name of CB Fry is inexorably linked with that of the Indian prince Kumar Shri Ranjitsinhji (1872-1933). Ranji's batting is said to have possessed an almost mystical air, his prowess first manifesting itself in his days as a Cambridge undergraduate when he managed the extraordinary feat of hitting three centuries in a day . . . in three different matches. He began by hitting 128 for Cassandra before lunch on the second morning of a two-day match against Saffron Walden on Parker's Piece. After lunch, he wandered over to a game on an adjoining pitch featuring the Basinelles Club. Finding them a man short, he immediately offered his services and struck a swift 132. He then returned to his original match but discovered that his side were still batting, steadily building on the foundations which he had provided. Spotting him at a loose end, the Long Vacation team seized the opportunity to stiffen their batting line-up for the game with Christ's and Emmanuel. Ranji duly obliged, hitting 150.

Sometimes batting came too easy to Ranji. Partnering Percy Fender for Sussex against Australia at Hove in 1912, Ranji suggested between overs that it might be 'interesting' to nominate in advance which strokes he intended to play. He told Fender: 'I'll send the first ball down to Kellaway's left hand at long leg and the third ball to his right – he's always slow to get back. We'll run two each time.' Sure enough, two of Ranji's famous leg-glances ensured that the plan was accomplished, and each time as they crossed, Ranji reminded Fender to run two. In another over, late cuts to Bardsley at deep third man brought two runs to the fielder's left, then two more to his right. Throughout the innings, Ranji always fulfilled his predictions.

He was the most immaculately dressed of cricketers with his silk shirt neatly buttoned at the wrists. The only thing which ever ruffled his sartorial elegance was the British weather. The summer of 1912 was generally wet and cold and the Scarborough Festival of that year was definitely a place for only the hardy. The wind whipped off the North Sea with such force that each day, Ranji, recently returned from tropical India, went shopping to buy another layer of clothing. First it was another vest, then a woollen waistcoat and so on. Onlookers were convinced that he was putting on weight by the minute and *The Times* wrote: 'Had the cold lasted, he certainly would not have been able to pass out of the dressing-room door.'

In 1915, he lost his right eye in a shooting accident in Yorkshire, an injury sustained ironically while he was home from the war on sick leave. After that, he wore a glass eye but still managed a career total of 24,567 runs at an average of 45, including seventy-two centuries.

One Man and his Dog

One of the most bizarre encounters to go under the name of cricket took place at Harefield Common, near Rickmansworth, on 21 May 1827. On that occasion a local farmer, Francis Trumper, and his sheepdog succeeded in defeating 'two gentlemen of Middlesex' at cricket. The day was won by the dog's agility in the field. According to *The Times*, spectators from Uxbridge and the surrounding villages were 'much astonished at the dog's dexterity'. *The Times* went on: 'The dog always stood near his master when he was going to bowl, and the moment the ball was hit he kept his eye upon it, and started off after it with speed; and, on his master running up to the wicket, the dog would carry the ball in his mouth and put it into his master's hand with such wonderful quickness that the gentlemen found it very difficult to get a run even from a very long hit.'

Lemon Entry, My Dear Watson

Spectators were often puzzled as to why Charles Newhall, who played for the United States' Philadelphia XI in the nineteenth century, always went into bat carrying a lemon. Investigation revealed that the lemon served two purposes – to be sucked before each stroke and also to enable Newhall to spit into the wicket-keeper's eye if the latter appealed too vigorously for his dismissal!

The High Chief's Temper Tantrum

In 1908, Ratu Lala was the High Chief on the Fijian island of Taveuni. As befitted a man of his status, he went into bat first for Cakaudrove in an inter-state match with neighbouring Bau. The custom on Fiji at the time was for every batsman to receive a trial ball, after which play began in earnest. However, as the Bauan team were to discover to their cost, it is not advisable to bowl out the High Chief at the start of his innings. Alas, his stumps were shattered by the first proper delivery he faced. There was a stunned silence, broken only by the sound of Ratu Lala pulling up the stumps and ordering his team from the ground. The match was thus abandoned after just one ball and furthermore, the cheerless Chief banned cricket from his lands for many years to come.

Dickie Bird – Worrier Incarnate

Wherever cricket is played and the relative merits of umpires are discussed, the one name guaranteed to be on everyone's lips is that of Harold 'Dickie' Bird. A modest opening bat, first with his native Yorkshire and then with Leicestershire, Bird was just another of the journeymen cricketers who ply their trade in the county game year after year. But when he turned his attention to umpiring, he became a colossus on the world stage, a household name. He is treated with a universal fondness usually reserved for someone like the Queen

Mother. Even people who have never met him always seem to know a story about Dickie Bird. A few of these tales have been embroidered over the years by the man himself in his guise as a popular after-dinner speaker, but the majority are completely authentic. For things happened to Dickie Bird that didn't seem to happen to other people. Where this unassuming little man in a white coat was concerned, truth really was stranger than fiction.

Right from his days as a young cricketer with Barnsley, Dickie Bird was an incorrigible worrier. Although the locals did not realize it at the time, there were some illustrious names at Barnsley in those days. Future broadcaster Michael Parkinson used to open the batting with him and when Dickie was star batsman, a boy by the name of Geoffrey Boycott first played for the club. Parkinson recalled how Dickie was always so nervous before an innings that he once inadvertantly buckled his pads to each other and fell flat on his face as he went out to bat.

It was said that Bird suffered so much with his nerves that he used to try and chew his fingernails through his batting gloves. He was also incredibly superstitious. If he had a bad run with the bat, he would immediately give away all his cricket gear. This habit was cured when he did it once too often and his team-mates, who had previously always returned his gear when asked, made him buy it back. For a Yorkshireman, that was a terrible punishment.

He has always had a morbid fear of being late for anything, an idiosyncrasy which has resulted in him arriving for appointments hours ahead of schedule. The first county championship match he was given to umpire was Surrey versus Yorkshire at The Oval in 1970. Naturally, on such an important occasion in his life, Dickie made sure he arrived in good time. To be precise, he turned up at 5.30am, nearly six hours before play was due to begin. Needless to say, the gates to the ground were still locked but, in an inspired move, he decided to scale them. Unfortunately for him, he was spotted by a passing policeman who, suspicious of what anyone might be doing climbing the gates of The Oval at that time of the morning, promptly arrested him. There was much explaining to be done before Dickie was able to resume his pre-match preparations.

Invited by the Queen for lunch at Buckingham Palace, he arrived at breakfast time and had to while away the intervening five hours in a nearby coffee shop. For a Sunday lunch date with John Major at Chequers scheduled for noon, Dickie turned up at 9.30am. Happily, the cricket-loving Prime Minister knew all about Dickie's eccentricities and had him sent through straight away.

In the course of the build-up to a match, Dickie Bird would go to the toilet three or four times to calm his nerves. Even when out in the middle, he was still a picture of agitation – a shuffle here, a twitch there. Yards of wool would be wrapped around his waist in the form of deposited sweaters, and from time to time he would receive more unusual requests. During the 1974 series between England and India, the wind at Old Trafford kept blowing Indian captain Sunil Gavaskar's hair into his eyes. In the middle of a session, Gavaskar asked Bird whether he had such a thing as a pair of scissors, because the flopping hair was impairing his vision. Dickie didn't have any scissors but he produced a razor blade from his pocket and halted play to cut off the offending locks.

His infectious good humour and popularity with the players made him the recipient of many strange objects. The tale of Allan Lamb's mobile phone (which Dickie was obliged to answer) has been well documented and on another occasion, on a particularly fiery wicket, Derbyshire batsman Ashley Harvey-Walker handed his false teeth to umpire Bird.

Dickie would sometimes become so involved in the play that he forgot himself. In his first season as an umpire, he was standing at square leg for the fixture between Hampshire and Lancashire at Southampton. When he saw Lancashire wicket-keeper Keith Goodwin set off for a potentially suicidal second run, Dickie shouted: 'No, Goody, no, get back.' As Goodwin failed to make his ground and umpire Bird was obliged to raise his finger, the Hampshire fielders creased up with laughter.

For all his strange mannerisms and the misfortunes which befell him, nobody should jump to the conclusion that Dickie Bird was either a pushover or a fool. He was a highly-respected umpire and one who was a stickler for the rules. Usually he was spot on, but he did get himself into an almighty tangle during a 1984 Benson and Hedges Cup tie between Scotland and Yorkshire at Perth. New rules for the competition had brought about an alteration to the timing of the tea interval in the second innings. Whereas previously tea had been taken after twenty-five overs, the new regulations meant that it was now to be taken at the end of the thirty-fifth over instead. But Dickie had forgotten about the change and took the teams off after twenty-five overs. When he was informed that he had made a mistake, he insisted on attempting to rectify the error by taking the teams off again ten overs later! Watching the players troop off for a second time, the Scottish public-address announcer commented: 'Aye, they sure do like their tea, these English lads.' It was the sort of adventure which could only have happened to Dickie Bird. No wonder Ian Botham once described him as: 'Great bloke, completely bonkers.'

A Quiet Word from the Captain

The Germans have never exactly been renowned for their cricketing expertise, but in the years leading up to the Second World War their approach typified the ruthless efficiency which Hitler tried to instil into the nation's youth. One of the most fearsome captains operating in the Berlin cricket league during the summer of 1936 was a man by the name of Thamer, to whom anything short of perfection constituted a mortal sin. At the start of one match, he found himself a man short. Appalled by the unreliability of a colleague, Thamer refused to allow play to commence until he had a full team and set about searching for a replacement. He eventually managed to enlist the services of a raw recruit – a callow youth who had never played cricket before. The lad was duly given a pair of flannels and sent to field out in the wilds at deep mid-off, as the captain himself opened the bowling with his demon off-breaks. Thamer reasoned that if he despatched the youth to such a distant outpost he would rarely be called upon, but in the captain's very first over the poor lad dropped a skier. Worse was to follow. In Thamer's next over, the youth spilled another lofted catch. This proved too much for the irate Thamer, who promptly stormed over to deep mid-off and felled the hapless fielder with a right hook to the chin. When it was subsequently pointed out at a dinner given for a

British touring team that such an assault would scarcely encourage the youth of Germany to play the game, the *Reichsportsfuhrer* replied: 'Yes, I have heard about the incident, but I understand it was a very simple catch . . .'

The Search for Perfection

Albert Trott of Middlesex and Australia had one major aim in life – to be the first player to hit a ball over the pavilion at Lord's. Trott, whose older brother Harry was the Australian captain, had prepared himself for the feat for some months, and to this end had armed himself with an extraordinarily heavy bat, weighing over three pounds. The match in which he finally chose to attempt the record hit was between MCC and the Australians on 31 July 1899. Playing for MCC, Trott set about the bowling of MA Noble with a vengeance. One blow landed just short of the pavilion rails, the next pitched on the seats. After these two sighting shots, he finally achieved his goal, sending the ball soaring over the Lord's pavilion to land in the garden of the ground's dressing-room attendant Philip Need.

After that, Trott's reputation as a big hitter went before him. In the same season, he scored 164 for Middlesex against Yorkshire. He offered just one chance during the innings – a lusty blow to long-on – but the fielder, after losing the ball in flight, suddenly saw it bearing down on him at a frightening pace and opted to leave it! Yet ultimately, Trott's record hit was to prove a mixed blessing, for he became increasingly obsessed with carrying pavilions wherever he played and this relentless pursuit ended up ruining him as a batsman.

By 1907, he was in dire straits financially. The only bright spot on the horizon was his benefit game against Somerset, but by a peculiar twist of fate, he contrived to take four wickets in five balls so that the match finished a day early, thus depriving him of much-needed gate receipts. He said afterwards: 'I'm bowling myself into the workhouse.'

In 1914, at the age of forty-two, Trott committed suicide by shooting himself at his seedy London lodgings. When he died, his room was littered with empty beer bottles. He left his worldly possessions – his clothes and £4 in money – to his landlady.

Chose His Own Rules

A forceful batsman, Fuller Pilch was one of the stalwarts of the Kent side of the 1830s and 1840s. In 1854, aged fifty-one, he retired to become an umpire, in which capacity he employed his own highly individual interpretation of the rules. Basically, Pilch, who always puffed on his pipe before giving decisions, detested the lbw law. Thus any bowler who appealed to him for lbw was told gruffly: 'None o' that. Bowl 'em out. Bowl 'em out.'

The Clown Prince of Lancashire

As a crafty right-arm slow bowler, Cec Parkin (1866-1943) was one of the mainstays of the Lancashire attack in the years after the First World War. In the space of four seasons, his variations in pace and flight earned him nearly 1,000 wickets, yet it is as one of the game's most colourful characters that he will always be remembered.

There was rarely a dull moment when Parkin was around. He once went as the opposing speaker to a serious cricket debate, but when he arrived, he agreed entirely with the first speaker and did card tricks instead! On the field, he was forever the clown. He delighted in pretending to make catches and throwing an imaginary ball in the air. The poor batsman was often halfway to the pavilion before he realized that the stroke had really gone for four. On other occasions, Parkin would substitute an orange for the ball. There was the time when, with an orange concealed in the palm of his hand, he pretended to make an impossible pick-up and splattered the fruit into the gloves of wicket-keeper George Duckworth.

He was invariably working at some piece of 'business' designed for the amusement of his colleagues. Fielding in the covers, he would amble towards a gently rolling ball, and without bending down or breaking stride, flick it off his boot and into his hand. When batting, Parkin, who was a tall, dextrous man, used to torment the opposing fielders by appearing to attempt suicidal runs yet, by virtue of his long reach, always leaving his bat touching the inside of the crease. Sensing a run out, fielders would take hasty shies at the wicket, often leading to overthrows. Parkin was once batting with the portly and less agile Richard Tyldesley when the pair found themselves running alongside each other. As the ball whistled past for yet more overthrows, Parkin slung his bat over his shoulder and marched back to the crease whistling 'The British Grenadiers'.

When it came to bowling, Parkin utilized every ounce of his cunning. He used to experiment with different bowling techniques in the nets with his wife batting, often sending her home with chipped fingers and bruised thighs. He liked to deliver every ball differently, to keep the batsman on his toes. In the same over he would mix up fast-medium away swingers; high, slow full-tosses; leg breaks and off breaks. The story goes that he was even known to bring his right hand over empty and instead bowl a lob with his left hand. As he began his run-up, he would often sing 'The sky is blue and I love you', accentuating the 'you' at the moment of delivery. Another favourite ploy was to stop dead in his tracks three yards behind the bowling crease and suddenly propel a high, slow donkey-drop. He did this in the 1919 Roses match and, to the delight of the Old Trafford crowd, trapped a bemused George Hirst lbw. When the next wicket fell (he took fourteen in the match), Parkin threw the ball high over his head and caught it one-handed behind his back without looking. Fittingly, when he died he had his ashes spread on the wicket at Old Trafford.

A Saw Point

When the volatile Majid Jahangir of Glamorgan and Pakistan was bowled for 28 by Derbyshire's Ian Buxton in August 1968, he stormed to the pavilion and immediately sawed his bat in half. When asked to explain his actions, he answered: 'I was getting a bit fed up with it. I haven't made many runs with it lately.'

A Curious Collection of Bats

During the 1880s, one of the most popular fixtures of the Surrey club cricket season was the annual match between the Coachmen and the Gardeners at Upper Caterham. The Coachmen were captained by a Mr Munday, who wielded an enormous bat, nearly a foot wide, which was painted bright scarlet with pictures of saddles and stirrups on the back. The Gardeners were led by the appropriately-named Mr Garlic, who boasted a similarly large bat, painted green and with pictures of vegetables, spades and hoes on the back. Sportingly, he also had a hole in the middle of his bat to give the bowlers a chance. Neither of these cricketing worthies is believed to have ever scored a run in the history of the fixture.

Match Abandoned

In August 1981, Mrs Mildred Rowley was granted a decree nisi because of her husband's excessive devotion to Stourbridge Cricket Club. She was granted the divorce at Wolverhampton two months after her husband Mike, aged forty-six, left home to live in the club pavilion.

The fifty-one-year-old nursing sister lamented: 'Cricket was not just a hobby. It was a total obsession – I'd just had enough of it. I don't mind the game; at first I used to go and watch. But I object to it being the be-all and end-all in my home. Mike could tell you who scored what years ago, and what the weather was like at the time. But he could not remember my birthday unless I reminded him.'

At the time, Mr Rowley was working as a sales manager for a steel company in Smethwick. He had been the club's scorer for twenty-one years and had missed only one match – when he went to Headingley to watch England play Australia. He conceded that Stourbridge CC was the main reason for the divorce. 'Cricket is the only life for me,' he explained. 'I don't blame Mildred.'

Mr Rowley was not in court to hear the termination of his seventeen-year marriage. He was in Devon with Stourbridge who, under their touring name of Worcestershire Marauders, were playing Torquay Cricket Club.

Loyal to His Boots

An accomplished batsman and smart slip-fielder, Jack Crapp played for Gloucestershire from 1936 to 1957, during which time he won seven England caps. On retiring from the playing side, he enjoyed a further twenty-two years as a first-class umpire, and throughout his forty-three-year career he always wore the same pair of cricket boots. The hand-made boots, for which he had paid five guineas to Bristol shoemakers Stubbs and Burt, travelled with him all over the world. They became famous in their own right. He once lent them to the local boy scouts, who put them on show at a jumble sale under the invitation: 'See the boots that Jack Crapp wore – 5p.'

The Gambler Who Lost

Surrey and England wicket-keeper Edward Pooley was known to be fond of a bet. But he overstepped the mark on the 1877 tour to Australasia, when he ended up in a New Zealand jail.

Before England's match with a Christchurch XXII, Pooley bet a local gambler by the name of Ralph Donkin that he could correctly nominate the individual scores of each of the Christchurch players. Donkin offered him odds of 20-1 in shillings so that for every right score, Pooley would receive £1, but for every incorrect score, he would have to pay a shilling. The rules settled, Pooley then bet that every batsman would score a duck – a shrewd move, since many of these teams of twenty-two usually contained a fair proportion of no-hopers. As it turned out, nine did indeed fail to score, which should have left Pooley nearly £9 richer. But Donkin felt that he had been tricked and welshed on the deal. The resulting argument deteriorated into a brawl and both men were jailed pending a trial. By the time Pooley was acquitted, his depleted team-mates (Pooley was the only keeper in the party) had travelled to Australia and lost the first Test by forty-five runs. However, it was not all doom and gloom for Pooley. The Christchurch people had been so touched by his plight that, upon his release, they collected £50 for him and presented him with a watch.

Pooley was a fearless wicket-keeper. He stood up to all bowlers – slow and fast – with the result that in his career he broke both thumbs and every finger. At Lord's one day, he staggered into the pavilion with three teeth knocked out. There he bumped into the celebrated prize-fighter Jem Mace, who told him: 'Pooley, I would rather stand up against any man in England for an hour than take your place behind the stumps for five minutes.'

But the one thing Pooley was unable to conquer was his gambling addiction, which took such a toll on his finances that he eventually died in the workhouse.

Old Timers

Certain cricketers seem to improve with age, and down the years a select few have carried on playing long after qualifying for their bus passes. London club cricketer Charles Absolon took 209 wickets in a season at the age of seventy-six, and in 1897 he still managed 100 wickets even though he was eighty. Frederick Lester was playing for Yoxall in Staffordshire at the age of eighty-seven in 1957. His sons Frederick and Christopher had long since retired from the game – 'They couldn't last the pace,' he said. But both Absolon and Lester were mere youngsters compared to William Adlam, who in 1888, at the age of 104, played in an old-timers' match at Taunton. He scored three . . . with the help of a runner.

Dead Ball

The funeral of former Derbyshire opening batsman Harry Bagshaw in 1927 was a curious affair. For in accordance with his wishes, the deceased was buried dressed in his umpire's coat and clutching a cricket ball. His headstone depicted broken stumps, dislodged bails and an umpire's hand with the index finger raised skywards, signalling 'Out'.

Aubrey Goes to Hollywood

Born in 1863, the son of a Brighton doctor, C Aubrey Smith was educated at Charterhouse and Cambridge. There he displayed an aptitude for cricket which led to him joining Sussex, whom he captained for two seasons from 1887. It was not exactly the most distinguished period in the county's history, although the captain did attract a degree of attention for his unusual bowling run-up, which earned him the nickname of 'Round-the-Corner' Smith. WG Grace wrote of his approach to the wicket: 'When Smith begins his run he is behind the umpire and out of sight of the batsman; and I can assure you it is rather startling when he suddenly appears at the bowling crease.' Sometimes he would start his run-up from an area around mid-off – it appears that, as with most things in his life, he varied matters as they took his fancy.

He also captained England in his solitary Test appearance, before concentrating on his blossoming career as an actor. Eventually, at the age of sixty-three, he moved to Hollywood where he played the archetypal crusty Englishman in a host of films, including *The Prisoner of Zenda* and *The Life of a Bengal Lancer.*

But his love of cricket never deserted him and in the 1930s he endeavoured to popularize the game amongst the film moguls by founding the Hollywood Cricket Club. Among those he recruited were Errol Flynn, David Niven, Basil Rathbone and Boris Karloff. A contemporary photograph shows Sir Charles (he was knighted in 1944 for improving Anglo-American relations) batting, with Karloff keeping wicket. It was indeed a brave batsman who was not unnerved by the immediate presence of Frankenstein. . .

Sir Charles's status in Hollywood was such that he could dictate the rules of the game and incorporate his own brand of aristocratic eccentricity. In one encounter, he was fielding in the slips when he dropped a catch. He immediately stopped the match and demanded that his butler be brought onto the pitch. 'Fetch me my glasses,' ordered Sir Charles. Several minutes later, with play still awaiting resumption, the dutiful butler returned to the middle bearing the spectacles on a silver tray. A few balls later, Sir Charles fumbled another slip catch and bellowed at his butler: 'Damn fool, you brought me my reading glasses!'

On the Wrong Track

The most eccentric travel arrangements of recent times probably belonged to the Reading British Rail engineering department team who, in September 1989, caught the wrong train for a match against their Banbury counterparts. They boarded an Inter-City express confident that it was bound for Banbury but, unforgivably, they had failed to take into account timetable alterations which meant that the train in question no longer stopped there. Thus the Banbury players could only watch aghast from the platform as their opponents sailed through the Oxfordshire town and continued on towards Leamington Spa. After an hour-long detour, the Reading boys finally made it back to Banbury where their hosts were still waiting patiently. In the circumstances, it was hardly surprising that when play did get under way, Reading lost by eight wickets.

Disputed Decision

During a cricket match in Karachi, the hot-headed Prince Aslam was given out lbw. He did not agree with the decision but was forced to return to the pavilion. Obviously the injustice continued to gnaw away at him, because a few minutes later he returned to the field brandishing a loaded revolver which he fired above the head of the offending umpire. As umpires and players alike fled for their lives, it was wisely decided to abandon the game.

The Umpire With One Arm

When Frank Chester gallantly lost an arm in the First World War, it finished his career with Worcestershire at the tender age of eighteen. But eight years later, in 1922, he embarked on a new cricketing career as a first-class umpire.

The first match at which he officiated was between Essex and Somerset at Leyton and beforehand, he went into his garden and dug up six stones which he would use as his counters. Remarkably, he kept the same six stones for the remaining thirty-three years of his umpiring career, storing them in a matchbox during the winter. They became a familiar prop on the county circuit, particularly as he used to toss them into the air in an exaggerated manner to mark each delivery. He was essentially a serious man, although when fielding at square leg he liked to talk about horse racing to nearby fielders, and he did have a few highly individual mannerisms, including a particularly melodramatic way of signalling leg-byes.

When standing at the bowler's end, he liked to crouch down so that his head was level with the bails. This helped him to judge lbw decisions. However, he felt obliged to abandon this position following an unfortunate incident during a match between Surrey and Sussex, when Surrey's Freddie Brown drove a half-volley straight back into Chester's false arm, the force knocking it out of its socket. There was an awkward silence as the arm lay on the grass. Unruffled, Chester left the field and got the arm refitted, but when he returned, instead of standing right over the stumps, he made a point of standing several yards behind them, an action which immediately broke the ice.

He was a widely-respected umpire, although his tendency in later years to start rejecting appeals in an Australian accent led to suggestions of bias against the tourists. He retired as an umpire in 1955 and died two years later.

The Saga of Bobby Peel

In his day, Bobby Peel (1857-1941) was just about the finest exponent of slow left-arm bowling in England. His sterling performances for Yorkshire with both bat and ball won him twenty caps for his country between 1884 and 1896. A quiet man, he had a reputation for being a master of line and length and was not one to buckle under an attempted onslaught from an opposing batsman. In addition to his bowling, he had twice hit unbeaten double-centuries for Yorkshire, making him seemingly indispensable to the side. But Peel had an Achilles heel. For his left hand was equally adept at holding a beer mug as a cricket ball.

By 1897, Peel was the senior professional in the Yorkshire dressing-room. His captain was the noted disciplinarian Lord Hawke, who had already overseen the departure of a number of the old guard. Peel would often turn up for matches decidedly the worse for drink – one *Wisden* report described him as 'having to go away' during a game.

Matters came to a head in August of that year when Yorkshire were due to entertain Middlesex at Bramall Lane, Sheffield. For Peel, it marked a return to the side after a month's absence, the result of being 'indisposed' on the last day of the previous game. *Cricket* magazine diplomatically described the Middlesex match as 'his first appearance after a long illness'. On the morning of the nineteenth, the first day of the fixture, the drunken Peel staggered down to breakfast at the team hotel, where his physical state attracted the attention of team-mate George Hirst. Diagnosing that Peel was in no condition to play, Hirst physically persuaded him to return to bed to sleep it off. In the meantime, Hirst sought out Lord Hawke and explained to him that Peel had been taken 'very queer in the night and won't be able to turn out this morning.' A firm but fair man, Lord Hawke expressed his concern and promised to visit Peel at the close of play.

Middlesex won the toss and elected to bat, but Lord Hawke's compassion for his sick colleague quickly evaporated as a red-faced Peel suddenly joined the team as Hawke led them out. Puzzled by the unexpected recovery and only too aware that Yorkshire now had twelve men on the field, Lord Hawke approached Peel and immediately realized that he was drunk. 'Leave the field at once,' ordered Hawke, but Peel stood his ground. Precisely what happened next remains open to debate. Some sources state that Peel had lost the plot so completely that when given the ball, he began bowling at the sightscreen in the mistaken belief that it was a Middlesex batsman. Others claim that he proceeded to urinate on the wicket. Maybe he did both, but what is not in dispute is that Lord Hawke was compelled to lead him bodily from the field – and out of Yorkshire cricket.

Ignoring pleas from his colleagues, Peel refused to apologize. He was convinced that the side could not function without him. But Lord Hawke knew that no one man was bigger than the team and was left with little option but to sack him. Upon his enforced retirement from cricket, Peel not surprisingly pursued the other great love in his life and became the landlord of a public house. Perhaps the most remarkable thing about Bobby Peel is that he lived to the age of eighty-four.

A Wet Outfield

When the feeling takes them, a group of foolhardy cricket enthusiasts indulge in a game on just about the most bizarre pitch in the world – a sand-bar called Bramble Bank in the middle of the Solent, the stretch of water between Hampshire and the Isle of Wight.

Bramble Bank only surfaces twice a year for about an hour at a time when the water is at its lowest at the spring and autumn equinox. The result is a sandbank measuring some two acres, liberally dotted with pools of water.

It was first used as a cricketing venue in the early part of the century, but when yachtsman Uffa Fox organized a game there in 1954, it was the first such encounter since 1922. Employing oars as bats, Fox's men scored 29, thus defeating a team from Parkhurst prison (principally officers) by seven runs. Parkhurst were somewhat handicapped by the fact that only seven of their team were able to land. A more recent match took place in 1984 when the Royal Southern Yacht Club from Hamble challenged the Island Sailing Club from Cowes. The players waited eagerly in a flotilla of boats for the moment when the island emerged from beneath the sea. They then took the field wearing wellington boots and whites. Island Sailing Club lost by eight wickets, the winning hit being a six and lost ball.

The Hands of God

When Rev John Charles Crawford died in 1935 at the age of eighty-five, his obituary in *Wisden* revealed that he used to bowl very fast right-handed and slow with his left. It added that he was capable of being an extremely hard hitter against weak bowling, but that sometimes he took pity on the opposition and batted left-handed.

Waltzed Back to the Pavilion

Batsman Ernest Killick, who played for Sussex between 1892 and 1913, loved music. When he heard a good tune, he couldn't get it out of his head and could think of nothing else. This did prove a problem when his mind was supposed to be on other matters – such as cricket. At one county match, he had just settled down at the crease when the band struck up a waltz. Unconsciously, he started to move his feet in strict time to the music and was instantly bowled with his feet nowhere near the pitch of the ball.

A Tragic Hypochondriac

Arthur Shrewsbury of Nottinghamshire and England was a splendid batsman and one of the earliest experts at padding away potentially dangerous deliveries. Off the field, he was a studious soul who worried incessantly about his health and appearance.

He was particularly sensitive about the fact that he had gone bald by the age of thirty, and throughout the 1887 tour to Australia he wore an ill-fitting wig. He was equally self-conscious about the wig and so insisted upon eating all meals with a hat on his head. Soon he was never seen in public without either a cap or a hat.

As the years progressed, he became increasingly convinced that he was suffering from some incurable illness. His morbid imagination took such a hold that in 1903, aged just forty-seven, he took his own life by shooting himself. His obituary in *Wisden* stated: 'Illness which he could not be induced to believe curable, together with the knowledge that his career in the cricket field was over, had quite unhinged his mind.' The sad irony was that Arthur Shrewsbury was, in fact, remarkably healthy.

A Model of Disorganization

There have been few more exciting sights in post-war cricket than that of Denis Compton in full flow. His timing of the ball was exquisite. Yet the timing of his off-field activities bordered on the chaotic and landed him in numerous embarrassing situations.

When his old Middlesex and England colleague John Warr retired from his job in the City of London, Compton arrived at the Stock Exchange at 5.30 on a Tuesday afternoon when the farewell party had been arranged for 4.30 at the Royal Exchange the following day. He once managed to get himself billed to appear in two charity cricket matches, a long way apart, on the same day. In the event he appeared at neither, turning up instead for a pro-am golf tournament to which he hadn't been officially invited. Whenever he realized the error of his ways, he was, of course, extremely apologetic.

At times, he was equally disorganized on the field. In 1934, the sixteen-year-old Compton was selected to play for the MCC against Suffolk. On arriving at the ground at Felixstowe, he discovered that he had left his cricket bag at Lord's. Trying to help out the youngster, George Brown, the former Hampshire player, offered Compton his flannels and boots. The only problem was that Brown was seven inches taller and took boots that were two and a half sizes bigger. So when Compton eventually took to the field for his MCC debut, he was wearing boots stuffed with paper and trousers which had room for his batting partner. Scarcely able to move about the batting crease, it was little surprise that he failed to trouble the scorer.

When he was able to run, things were only marginally less muddled. His running between the wickets has entered cricketing folklore, and Compton himself calculated that he had been involved in no fewer than 275 run-outs. In fairness, it ought to be pointed out that in one or two of these he may have been the innocent party. Many of his batting partners have expressed their views on his ability to create mayhem when going for a quick single. John Warr claimed that Compton was the only batsman in the history of the game to have called his partner for a single and to have wished him luck at the same time. Warr always said that Compton's first call was an opening bid – a tentative statement of policy – and the second merely a basis for negotiation. It was after that that the serious business started (in the unlikely event that it was not already too late). Trevor Bailey remembered batting with Compton in the 1954 Old Trafford Test against Pakistan: 'I set off for a run when Denis called me, and I was a third of the way down the pitch when he yelled "Wait!" Then he said "No" as we passed each other. So you might say I was a victim of the three-call trick.'

On many occasions, Compton's chaotic lifestyle forced him to play with a borrowed bat, and he had even been known to arrive for the start of play wearing last night's dinner-jacket. And just occasionally, there was the suspicion that his mind was elsewhere, such as the occasion when he advanced down the ground at the height of a Test match to enquire after the result of the 2.30 race at Ascot!

The Club Chair-Man

David Harris, a member of the pioneering Hambledon side, was so stricken by gout in his later years that he ordered an armchair to be carried out to the wicket whenever he was bowling. After successfully delivering each ball, Harris would sit in the chair for a rest until required again.

A Heavy Drinker

Before he became captain of New South Wales, Reg Bettington played for Oxford University. An accomplished leg-spinner, he was an amiable fellow who suffered constant teasing about his ample girth. He once responded by picking up fourteen-stone Greville Stevens, his fellow leg-spinner in the University team, and throwing him out of the dressing-room window.

It appears that Bettington was often unaware of his own strength. On the night of the 1920 Boat Race, he and a group of friends tried to gain admission to a classy restaurant but were prevented from doing so by an officious commissionaire. In the mild jostling which followed, Bettington gave the commissionaire a playful push which sent him reeling into the potted palms. Charged with being drunk and disorderly, Bettington listened as the lengthy catalogue of the evening's consumption was read out, ranging from Martinis (several) to port and brandy. At this point, Bettington disputed the evidence: 'Naow port,' he protested. When he sobered up, he went on to become an eminent surgeon until his death in 1969.

The Laws According to Harry Weigall

Gerry Weigall of Cambridge University and Kent was one of the game's great philosophers. He had an aphorism to suit every cricketing situation and was only too keen to impart these words of wisdom to less experienced team-mates.

Each maxim was illustrated with either a walking stick or an umbrella, lest the listener be unable to comprehend the precise meaning. A favourite was 'Never run to cover on a fast wicket'. It could be that he learned this one the hard way after running out three partners, including his captain, while making 63 in the 1892 Varsity match. Other rules to be obeyed included 'never cut in May', 'never play back at the bottom end at Canterbury' and 'never hook until you have made 84'. Quite how he arrived at that particular figure remains something of a mystery.

His advice was not only confined to the field of play. 'Never eat pie at a cricket lunch', he always insisted, perhaps a wise precaution in the days before refrigerators. Since down the years everyone within earshot had been treated to these sayings, people naturally expected Weigall to abide by them. Thus when MCC played Bradfield and lunch was steak and kidney pie followed by apple pie, all eyes turned to Weigall. He had no option but to refuse both and thus had to make do with a meagre lunch of salad and cheese and biscuits. He who lives by the sword . . .

Handy Hanif

Pakistan Test player Hanif Mohammad bowled four right-handed deliveries and two with his left in the last over before lunch against Somerset at Taunton in July 1954. He chose to repeat this bizarre feat after tea.

Captain Curious

Born in Sydney, Sammy Woods boxed with the local Aboriginal champion as a boy before being sent to England at the age of thirteen to be trained as a 'proper gentleman'. At Cambridge University, he developed into a fine all-round sportsman instead. In 1888, he was picked as a fast bowler for Australia, even though he had never played a first-class game there. Seven years later, he won the first of his three caps for England! In between times, he also represented England thirteen times at rugby, rising to the position of captain in 1892.

At cricket, Sammy Woods also captained Somerset where he liked a breakfast of champagne and lobsters and adopted a team-selection process which owed very little to convention. When challenged as to why he had picked one particularly inept player, Woods replied: 'Oh, he is not much of a bat, he doesn't bowl and he can't field – but, by George, what a great golfer he is!' On another occasion, he was about to lead Somerset on a journey north when he realized that the team was three players short. After hastily enlisting the services of two of his godsons, he struck up a conversation with a fellow passenger on the train – a man who said that he had made big scores in club cricket. Without a moment's hesitation, Woods made him the eleventh man. The decision to include a complete stranger was to backfire somewhat, as Woods himself admitted: 'He made nought and nought, and it turned out he hadn't played since he was ten but wanted to get a close view of the game for nothing.' But, by way of justification, Woods added: 'He was a very good whist-player.'

Before going out to bat, Woods always drank a double whisky and smoked a cheroot, but he was forced to retire from the game in 1910 through arthritis. Further misfortune followed during the war when he damaged his back after a camel bolted from beneath him. He went on to serve Somerset in an administrative capacity and was willing, nay eager, to help out on the medical side. He could often be seen attempting to wrench a dislocated shoulder back into place – invariably with disastrous results. A regular spectator at home matches, Woods could be heard mercilessly haranguing anyone who happened to wander in front of the sightscreen at a crucial moment. He also had a curious tendency to applaud when nobody else did. Right up until his death in 1931, Sammy Woods lived in local pubs and drank a bottle of whisky a day. Without doubt, he was one of Somerset's earliest and finest characters.

Big John

Standing 6ft tall and weighing in at fifteen stone, Nottinghamshire paceman John Jackson presented a formidable sight to opposing batsmen, at least one of whom decided that discretion was the better part of valour. Struck on the foot by a fearsome delivery, a batsman by the name of Ludd hobbled around in agony while Jackson appealed for lbw. When the umpire ruled 'not out', Ludd said: 'Mebbe not, but I'm a-goin'.' And with that, he retired to the safety of the pavilion.

In Ludd's defence, Jackson did appear to derive inordinate pleasure from causing injury to batsmen. Lamenting the fact that he had never taken all ten wickets in an innings, he suddenly remembered a game for the North versus the South. 'Ah bowled out nine of them and lamed Johnny Wisden so's he couldn't bat, which was just as good, wasn't it?'

Whenever he took a wicket, Jackson blew his nose, a habit which earned him the nickname of 'The Foghorn'. He always insisted on being paid in cash, which he used to keep in the pocket of his trousers while playing. In the middle of one match, the pocket gave way under the weight of sovereign coins and the contents fell to the ground.

Team-mates with dubious motives rushed over and offered to retrieve the coins, but Jackson brusquely waved them away. None were prepared to argue with him.

Jackson played for Nottinghamshire from 1855 to 1866 when his tempestuous career was cut short at the age of thirty-three, ironically through injury. He died in 1901.

German Know-How

As has been stated earlier, the Germans were slow to pick up the rudiments of cricket. A story from the *Cologne Post* of August 1922 illustrates the point: 'At a cricket match the other day, a batsman went in with only one pad on. Noticing it adorned the right leg, the fielders assumed he was a left-hander and altered their positions accordingly. But he turned out to be right-handed after all, so the wicket-keeper pointed out to him that he had the pad on the wrong leg. "Nothing of the sort," was the reply. "You see, I thought I was going in at the other end."'

A Kindly Gesture

Following his troubles with the bat on the 1996-97 South African tour, England captain Mike Atherton was promised help from an unlikely source. For the captain of Britain's worst cricket team, the Applecross Allstars, offered Atherton a place in his side. The inappropriately-named Allstars, who play in the Scottish highland village of Applecross, have recorded just one victory in eight years. 'We thought it might give Mike a chance to regain his touch,' said a team member. At the time of going to press, it is thought that prior commitments may prevent Atherton from taking up the offer.

A Bad Impression

A forceful batsman with Kent and Middlesex in the latter half of the nineteenth century, Charles Inglis Thornton once hit upon the idea of playing an innings 'ball by ball, in the manner of certain well-known batsmen'. It was an ingenious exercise but one which foundered all too swiftly. For the master mimic was out first ball when, according to contemporary sources, 'leaving the ball alone in the customary manner of a certain defensive player'.

Thornton's hitting became the stuff of which legends are made. He is reputed to have hit a ball from Tom Emmett into the sea at Scarborough; and when playing at The Oval in the early 1870s, he struck a delivery from Surrey's James Southerton so far that the wicket-keeper Edward Pooley exclaimed: 'So 'elp me God, Jimmy, I believe it's gone on to Brixton Church.'

Thornton began his cricket at Eton. Fielding at long leg in a schoolboy match and feeling hungry, he called out to a vendor with his cart of ices, cakes and buns and proceeded to eat a jam-filled bun on the field. This act earned him the none-too-original nickname of 'Buns'.

Some of his most memorable moments took place at Scarborough, although there was one which, unlike his mighty blow into the North Sea, he probably preferred to forget. As he strode out to the middle, he could hear a band playing in the background. Disregarding any enjoyment the music may have provided for holidaymakers, Thornton did not wish to be distracted from his art and immediately ordered the band to stop playing. The command was obeyed but Thornton was out for a duck anyway. Hours later, he was still blaming his dismissal on the band.

Butler Barnes

When he was omitted from the Australian Test team to face South Africa in 1953, Sidney Barnes asked whether he could be twelfth man for New South Wales against South Australia in Adelaide. At the drinks interval, Barnes strode out to the square wearing a grey suit with a red carnation and carrying a tray with a scent spray, portable radio and cigars which he then offered to players and umpires alike.

A Style All of his Own

Richard Tyldesley, the portly Lancashire leg-spinner of the 1920s, could be the most deceptive of bowlers. The manner in which he slowly lumbered up to bowl, as if the merest mobility was placing an intolerable strain on his limbs, invariably lured the batsman into a false sense of security. A fine but stationary slip fielder who was known to wear three sweaters on a cold day, Tyldesley was also the most painstaking of appealers. If the ball hit the batsman's pads, he would lean to one side, peer down the pitch and, shaking his head knowingly, say: 'No, that weren't out. No.' As Neville Cardus put it: 'He implied that he would not have accepted a decision in his favour even if the umpire had proffered one.' Then suddenly, when he had seemingly convinced himself of the futility of an appeal, he would turn to the umpire and exclaim: 'How was it?' Sensing that the batsman had already been tried by judge and jury, umpires frequently answered in the affirmative. It was an admirable ploy.

An Unhappy Medium

With Lord's covered in hailstones for the June 1968 Test against Australia, the ground received a call from a mysterious woman claiming to be responsible. The caller declared: 'I have occult powers so far as the weather is concerned. Several years ago, I used these powers to break the drought in Australia. The Australians have not yet paid me for my services. My spell over their matches will continue until they pay their debts.'

Australian fast bowler Graham McKenzie took a similar call during the tourists' rain-affected game at Leicester, and so journalistic sleuthing was employed to unmask the meteorological mystic. Newspapers reported the caller as being Mrs Doris Munday, a forty-nine-year-old psychic. Mrs Munday later admitted: 'It was three years ago when the Australians asked me to break up their seven-year drought, and when I did it, they gave all the credit to the Aborigines. They also promised to take up a collection for me and didn't. Not that I wanted the money, but I was annoyed. So I started off by smashing the Brisbane Test in 1966 and I've been bashing them ever since.'

In view of the fact that the Australians have managed to play a great deal of cricket over the past twenty-nine years, it must be concluded that an amicable agreement has been reached between the two parties.

The Batsman Who Did the Splits

Hampshire's George Brown was playing against Warwickshire at Southampton when his bat split. Most batsmen would have sent for a spare, but Brown gamely ripped off the loose section, handed it to the umpire and batted for the remainder of his innings with half a blade. As one observer later remarked of Brown: 'He wasn't half a good bat!'

A Bad Traveller

With his ginger hair and mutton-chop whiskers, George Parr (1826-91) was a familiar figure at county cricket grounds in the nineteenth century. But rather like an early Denis Compton, he was none too adept at making travel arrangements.

In 1846, at the start of his career with Nottinghamshire, Parr was living at Radcliffe-on-Trent. Staying with him was his team-mate Alfred Mynn, and the pair were due to be at Southwell to play in a benefit match for county captain William Clarke. Unfortunately, Parr gravely miscalculated the time needed to travel from Radcliffe to Southwell (a journey which had to be made via the river) and the two arrived late. Clarke was so angry that he put one over Parr by refusing to pick him for the rest of the summer.

Parr's travel troubles resurfaced thirteen years later when he was selected to captain a representative England XI on a tour of the United States. To combat sea-sickness on the voyage across the Atlantic, he drank copious amounts of gin and water. Even when the party reached dry land, the going was tough, principally because they had to transport Fred Lillywhite's portable yet cumbersome scoring-booth with them wherever they went. There was also the matter of the weather, which by the time the tour ended in October was bitterly cold. For the final match – a game against a combined Canada and US team – Parr took on the role of umpire since he had been injured in an earlier encounter. But he soon decided it was too cold to stand around umpiring and retired to hot gin and water in the pavilion. He left his team-mates to field in overcoats and gloves. On the second day, there was no play because of snow and so the teams played baseball instead.

Back in the warmer climes of England, Parr eventually returned to umpiring. His advice to young players came perilously close to suggesting outright bribery of an official and was clearly designed more for his own benefit than that of the players. 'When you play in a match,' he wrote, 'be sure not to forget to pay a little attention to the umpire. First of all, enquire after his health, then say what a fine player his father was, and finally, present him with a brace of birds or rabbits. This will give you confidence, and you will probably do well.'

Silent Protest

Forty-four-year-old Mr George Smith of Coventry lay down on the wicket of the Coventry and North Warwickshire ground for fifteen minutes in 1989 to protest at a ball being struck through the window of his sitting-room.

A Bizarre Dismissal

James Southerton was known as 'the man of many counties' after playing for three in one season during the 1860s. A week after playing for Sussex against Surrey, he turned out for the men from The Oval. It was at that ground in 1870 that he featured in one of the most curious incidents in the history of cricket. Playing for Surrey against the MCC, he cut a ball hard into the ground from where it bounced into the hands of WG Grace at point. Grace, never usually one to miss a trick, did not appeal and neither did the umpires or any of the fielders think that Southerton was out. But Southerton marched off to the pavilion and nothing could induce him to return. He was listed in the scorebook as having 'retired, thinking he was caught'.

The Emperor Caldecourt

Born in 1802, William Caldecourt became a ground boy at Lord's when he was nine and a practice bowler at the age of fifteen. A man ahead of his time, he had the distinction of being the first person to bat at Lord's wearing gloves, but his pride and joy was a bowling machine, the catapulta, which he patented and introduced to the practice nets at Lord's. He made his name as a forceful batsman for Hampshire before turning to umpiring in the 1830s and was arguably the most extrovert official of his time. Nicknamed 'Honest Will Caldecourt' because he fearlessly no-balled all overarm deliveries, he used to wear a Napoleonic hat with one arm tucked into a huge great-coat. This arm would emerge solely for the purpose of signalling wides and no-balls.

Barnes-Stormer

Billy Barnes played for Nottinghamshire between 1875 and 1894, during which time he represented his country twenty-one times. What makes these otherwise ordinary statistics remarkable was that Barnes sometimes turned up for county games the worse for drink and indulged in spectacular outbursts – verbal and physical – against authority.

He had no time whatsoever for captains, in particular his Notts leader Arthur Shrewsbury who, to Barnes's undoubted chagrin, also became the England captain. The pair fell out on a regular basis and matters came to a head in the third Test of the 1884-85 series in Australia when Barnes refused to bowl after being requested to do so by Shrewsbury.

Two years later, the irascible Barnes missed the second Test in Sydney with a hand injury, reputedly sustained when he took a swing at the Australian skipper Percy McDonnell, missed and hit a brick wall.

When his form eventually dipped, a decline encouraged by his alcohol intake, the Nottinghamshire committee seized the opportunity to sack him.

Battle of the Sexes

On 16 July 1888, Paddington Recreation Ground in London staged a theatrical cricket match between teams of men and women. The male thespians batted with broomsticks and were only allowed to bat and field left-handed, the penalty for picking up the ball with the right hand being three runs to their opponents. The ladies won by thirty-seven runs, scoring 60 to the gentlemen's 23.

Way-Out East

At a time when there were fewer and fewer characters in the county game, Essex slow left-arm bowler Ray East was a worthy exception. He played for Essex from 1965 to 1984 and earned a justifiable reputation for being the finest clown on the county circuit.

Fielding out on the boundary, East engaged the crowd in constant banter. A favourite performance was to act like a stringless puppet which was out of control. He would then tell the spectators that they should be ready to stop the next ball because he was dizzy from being moved around so much by his captain. Always keen to improvise, he found the perfect opportunity one year at the Scarborough Festival where, in mid-afternoon, a mock gun-battle was being fought on a nearby lake. As East ran up to bowl, the sound of cannon fire reverberated across the ground, at which he collapsed in front of the umpire as if he had been shot.

Going out to bat against Lancashire on a fiery pitch, East decided to have a quiet word with fast bowler Ken Shuttleworth on the way to the crease. He told Shuttleworth that if he pitched the next ball up and kept it straight, the bat would not prevent it hitting the stumps. Sensing an easy wicket, Shuttleworth duly bowled a half-volley on middle and leg. Possibly just to look convincing, East gave an almighty swing but instead of missing the ball, he sent it soaring over the ropes for six. To say the least, Shuttleworth was not amused and East knew he was in for a torrid time. So as the next ball came down, he threw away his bat, dived to the ground and lay flat on his stomach with his hands on his head. The anticipated bouncer flew harmlessly by.

In 1980, when several Essex players were struck down by a flu virus, East paraded up and down outside the dressing-room, carrying a placard saying 'Unclean'.

Not all of East's comic moments were intentional. As coach to the Essex second XI, he was sitting in the dressing-room watching his team batting when the phone rang. The call was for one of the fielders patrolling the boundary. Leaning out of the window, East mimed that the fielder was wanted on the phone. Moments later, the two Essex batsmen arrived in the dressing-room. 'Lunch already, lads?' inquired East. 'No,' said one, 'we've declared, haven't we? Wasn't that you waving us in?'

East's antics soon spread to other members of the team and the Essex boys became known as a bunch who enjoyed a good laugh, on and off the field. There was the time when Keith Pont, weary through having to field at third man from both ends, grabbed a nearby bicycle at the end of the next over and pedalled around the boundary to his new position. And in a match with Cambridge University, paceman John Lever bowled the batsman a vicious half-volley with an orange which disintegrated as it hit the bat. Cec Parkin would have been proud of him.

Three-Fingered Jack

Among the Epsom team of the early nineteenth century was a unique character by the name of Long Robinson, who stood some 6ft 6in tall. He was known to all in the village as 'Three-Fingered Jack' on account of having lost two fingers on his right hand in an encounter with a cricket ball. But the injury did not prevent him from playing the game he loved, although he was forced to bat virtually one-handed thereafter. In fact, he used a bat with a specially-grooved handle and had a screw fastened into his right hand so that he could hold the bat. He pioneered other equipment too, and was believed to be the first batsman to wear pads. But the ones he wore were wooden and attracted such ridicule that he decided to dispense with them. He must have presented a strange sight with his screwed-on hand and his wooden pads . . .

2 Soccer

A Goalkeeper Extraordinary

Even allowing for the fact that all goalkeepers are crazy, William 'Fatty' Foulke (1874-1916) was crazier than most. Born at Blackwell, Derbyshire, Foulke was the heaviest player in the history of professional football. He stood 6ft 2½in tall and as his career progressed, he expanded from fifteen stone to a massive twenty-five stone. He wore size 12 boots and his shirts took 24in collars. Despite his size, he was remarkably agile. He was also blessed with a terrible temper.

He could punch the ball from his own goal to beyond the halfway line and, when the mood took him, was capable of inflicting similar damage upon opposing forwards. In the course of a career which encompassed Sheffield United, Chelsea, Bradford City and England, Foulke was involved in a number of unseemly incidents. In the 1898-99 season, playing for Sheffield United, he picked up the Liverpool centre-forward George Allan, turned him upside down and stood him on his head in the penalty-area mud. The resultant penalty turned the course of the game and afterwards Foulke apologized to his team-mates for his moment of madness, before adding mischievously: 'I made a right toffee-apple out of him, didn't I?'

The 1902 FA Cup Final was decided by a controversial late goal. Sheffield United lost 2-1 to Southampton in a replay amid claims that the winning goal was offside. At the end of the game, Foulke was still fuming and, having torn off his kit in the dressing-room, went searching for referee Tom Kirkham. Luckily, another official saw the unforgettable sight of twenty stone of naked flesh pounding the Crystal Palace corridors and told Kirkham to lock his door before the aggressor could get to grips with him.

In 1905, Foulke was transferred to Chelsea but his temper showed no signs of improving. Playing at Burslem Port Vale, he grabbed a home forward around the waist and hurled him into the back of the net. Referee TJ Homecroft had no choice but to award a penalty. Afterwards he said of Foulke: 'He did not try to save the shot but stood glaring at me. I kept a reasonable distance until the close of the game, and then made my way quicker than usual to the dressing-room. If Foulke had put one of those large hands on me, I might have been short of some part of my anatomy.'

Foulke's sheer bulk created unexpected problems. He once stopped a game by snapping the crossbar, and if he was injured, it needed at least six men to carry him off as no stretcher was able to bear his weight. He used to say: 'I don't mind what they call me, as long as they don't call me late for lunch.' As if to underline the point, he once sat down at the dinner table before his Chelsea team-mates had arrived, and proceeded to eat the food intended for the whole team.

When his career was over, he set up a penalty-kick business on Blackpool beach, charging a penny a shot and offering threepence back for each goal scored against him. Few youngsters would have got rich at the expense of 'Fatty' Foulke.

A Cunning Disguise

A tricky inside-forward with excellent vision, Jimmy Seed was the star player with Welsh team Mid-Rhondda. So when the supporters heard that Tottenham Hotspur manager Peter McWilliam was showing more than a passing interest in their hero, they tried to warn the Spurs man off, going so far as threatening to lynch McWilliam if they found him in the vicinity of their ground.

But McWilliam was a canny fellow who was determined to get his man. So one afternoon in February 1920, heavily disguised in spectacles and a false beard, he crept unnoticed into the Mid-Rhondda stand to spy on his target. He was so impressed that he signed Seed immediately after the game for £350.

McWilliam, who had two spells in charge of Spurs sandwiching another with Middlesbrough, was a distinctly agitated manager. Sometimes he couldn't even bring himself to watch his team in action – a feeling with which many managers can identify – but in his case it was down to nerves rather than the quality of performance on the pitch. Yet curiously, in his playing career as a left-half with Newcastle, he had enjoyed a reputation for being the most laid-back of individuals. In fact, he was so relaxed that he would often take a half-hour nap just before kick-off.

The Coach who Dropped his Trousers

Paulo Mata, coach with the Brazilian club Itaperuna, was so incensed at a referee allowing a late goal against his team, then sending off three of his players, that he rushed onto the pitch and ran towards the official. En route, Mata removed his shirt before three policemen, sensing a full-scale streak, halted him in his tracks in an attempt to prevent further embarrassment to television viewers. Denied access to the referee, Mata was determined to proceed with his protest and, with his back to the TV cameras, dropped his trousers.

Explaining the March 1997 incident, Mata said: 'I went naked because I'm tired of working honestly only to be scandalously robbed. Football in Rio de Janeiro is a disgrace.' It remains to be seen whether any English managers copy this latest South American trend.

A Man of Contrasts

Leicester City striker Steve Claridge is generally regarded as the scruffiest player in English football. With his hunched shoulders, shirt hanging out and socks around his ankles, he is hardly a picture of sartorial elegance on the field. He is also renowned for being an appallingly lazy trainer and has incurred fines of varying severity for turning up late.

Yet Claridge, who has also played for Bournemouth, Cambridge United, Luton and Birmingham, has a surprisingly meticulous side to his nature, as demonstrated by his pre-match ritual. When the team stays in a hotel before games, Claridge always has to have a room on his own, and the first thing he does is to remove the hotel sheets from the bed and replace them with ones which he has brought from home.

However, his favourite pre-match meal is more in character. His former Birmingham skipper Liam Daish revealed: 'Steve likes Rice Krispies and baked beans – sometimes together.'

Raising a Tenor

Eager to build a new sports and community centre at their Ryde headquarters, Isle of Wight Saturday League team Oakfield FC applied for £75,000 from National Lottery funds. When the application was refused, the club, reasoning that much of the lottery money appeared to go to the arts, declared itself an operatic society in a bid to obtain a grant. In August 1995, their name was formally changed to the Oakfield Operatic Society. Manager Mark Cass admitted: 'It's crazy, but you have to be innovative. And we'll give the singing a go. Who knows, we may find a budding Pavarotti among our ranks.'

The High-Scoring Goalkeeper

Paraguay's charismatic goalkeeper Jose Luis Chilavert reckons he is the best in the world. He is certainly more than capable, but what really makes him stand out is his remarkable ability to score goals.

By no means the first South American custodian with a tendency to go AWOL from his own penalty area, Chilavert enjoys nothing more than racing upfield to take free-kicks and penalties. In 1996 alone, he scored eight goals for his club, Velez Sarsfield of Argentina, plus one for his country. Among his most spectacular efforts was a sixty-yard free-kick in a league game against River Plate, taken quickly after he had spotted the opposing keeper German Burgos off his line. The two men met again for a World Cup qualifier in Buenos Aires in September 1996. Chilavert, who was less than complimentary about Burgos, boasted that he would score again. So when Paraguay were awarded a free-kick some twenty-five yards out, there was only one man to take it. Photographers behind the goal claimed that Burgos was trembling as Chilavert lined up his shot. He managed to get both hands to the ball but allowed it to slip from his grasp and over the line.

That goal has added to the Chilavert phenomenon. The man who wears the image of a snarling bulldog emblazoned on his goalkeeper's jersey has become a cult hero. T-shirts featuring the bulldog have sold like the proverbial hot cakes and the Paraguayan football association even staged a competition among Asuncion pet owners to find the bulldog bearing the closest resemblance to the one on Chilavert's shirt.

The Clown Prince of Soccer

Sunderland inside-forward Len Shackleton was known throughout the land as 'The Clown Prince of Soccer'. From the moment he made his debut for the club on 5 October 1946 and scored six goals against Newport County, Sunderland fans knew he was something special.

Supremely confident in his ability, Shackleton was the consummate ball-player. He indulged in frivolous back-heels and taunted leaden-footed opponents with his artistry. He really began to turn on the entertainment in the closing stages of a game, provided his team were comfortably ahead. He had been known to wait for a high ball with his hands on his hips and then trap it dead with one foot. He would then stand there with his foot on the ball, casually brush the hair from his forehead and make a point of consulting an imaginary watch. Seemingly bored to the point of distraction, he would then call to the dug-out and ask how long there was to go. He once dribbled around several opponents plus the goalkeeper, but when faced with the empty net, he stopped the ball on the goal-line. From this vantage point, he looked around and shouted out to the goalkeeper, still desperately trying to scramble back: 'It's not over the line yet!'

Like so many mavericks, Shackleton had little time for those in authority. In his book on football, he famously included a chapter titled 'What The Average Soccer Director Knows About The Game'. There followed two blank pages. His outspoken approach undoubtedly contributed to the fact that such a talented player won only five England caps.

The Venerable Barrie

Barrie Williams was a football manager with a difference. Not for him the tired old cliches about taking each game as it comes and a game of two halves. He was never 'over the moon' or 'absolutely gutted', and he would probably rather have appeared on *Noel's House Party* than admit to being 'sick as a parrot'.

For this former English teacher, who guided non-league Sutton United to their famous FA Cup giant-killing act at the expense of First Division Coventry City in 1989, had a penchant for quoting Shakespeare, Kipling and seventh-century English theologian the Venerable Bede in his programme notes. He succeeded in harnessing his gift for poetry with his knowledge of the coaching manual, and composed stirring poems to rally his troops before each match in that great Cup run.

Following the victory over Coventry, little Sutton were drawn at Norwich in round four. Before the tie, Williams returned to the classics, quoting the motto of the Benedictine order: 'See everything, adjust a little, be grateful for the burden.' Realistically, Williams knew that Sutton had little chance at Carrow Road, and to prepare his players for the possibility of defeat, he quoted a line of Kipling to them: 'Face triumph and disaster and treat those two imposters just the same.' He was wise to issue such advice: Sutton lost 8-0.

The Doctor Who Didn't Know Best

Dr Bob Mills-Roberts was a fearless goalkeeper for Preston North End and Wales, winning a total of eight caps for his country. However, sometimes his courage bordered on the foolhardy, as on the occasion in 1897 when he passed himself fit and insisted on playing for Wales against England at Sheffield, even though movement was virtually impossible because his arms were in splints up to the elbows. In the circumstances, it was a minor miracle that Wales only lost 4-0.

A Load of Tosh

Fulham winger Trevor 'Tosh' Chamberlain was one of the great characters of the late fifties, and could always be relied upon to do the unpredictable. He once snapped a flag in half when he mistimed a corner kick, and was almost booked by the referee after having a major row with team-mate Johnny Haynes. Sometimes if a bad tackle on him went unpunished, Tosh would refuse to get to his feet, saying that he would sit the game out 'until that bleeding ref apologizes'.

One of his most scatterbrained moments came in a match at Craven Cottage when he nearly scored a spectacular own goal. He suddenly hit a ferocious shot from all of forty yards towards his own goalkeeper Tony Macedo, who had to dive full length to his right to tip the ball over the bar. As the inquests began, spectators debated whether Tosh had accidentally over-hit a back pass or, because he had been mucking around with the ball on the halfway line, had simply forgotten which way Fulham were kicking.

The Oldest Winger in Town

Long after most footballers have hung up their boots, seventy-one-year-old Fred Rosner was still turning out each week on the left wing for Downham FC in Division Four of the Hackney and Leyton

League. In 1995, he was said to be the oldest regular footballer in Britain by six years and what made his feat all the more remarkable was that Downham, the amateur team he founded back in 1948, are not a veterans' team. 'That would be too slow for me,' he said, preferring to mix it with lads half his age. 'Sometimes players think it's going to be a piece of cake being marked by me – until I tackle them.'

As a Jew raised in Vienna, Fred learned his football the hard way and remembered being chased out of the park with his ball by members of the Hitler Youth. In all his years on Hackney Marshes, he had only three visible rewards – Hackney and Leyton League Division Five winners' medals 1953-54 and 1956-57, and League Cup runners-up medal 1956-57. His other memories were more painful – three broken noses and a blood clot in his leg.

His name only went in the referee's book once, when he was sent off at the age of sixty-eight. The decision still rankled three years later. 'The referee was a woman and I think it was her first game. When she blew for offside at a corner, I said to her quietly: "You can't be offside direct from a corner." All I was trying to do was explain the rules, but she just sent me off.'

Fred was not contemplating retirement. 'Far from it,' he said. 'To be frank, I think I have got to train more. One game of football a week is really not enough for me . . .'

The Goalkeeper Who Prayed

At the start of each match, Isidore Irandir, goalkeeper with the Brazilian club Rio Preto, would kneel down in the goalmouth and say his prayers, hoping no doubt that the Lord would protect him from swerving free-kicks and viciously inswinging corners. He went into his usual routine just as opponents Corinthians kicked off in a match at the Bahia Stadium, but had reckoned without the celebrated left foot of Roberto Rivelino. Receiving the ball on the halfway line, Rivelino, who was all too aware of Irandir's ritual, blasted a shot towards the Rio Preto goal. It sailed into the back of the net after just three seconds' play, whistling past the ear of a startled Irandir, who was still on his knees concluding his beseechments to the Almighty. As Corinthians celebrated, Irandir's brother ran onto the pitch armed with a revolver and pumped six bullets into the ball.

Wash-Day Souvenir

Football supporters are notorious for collecting unusual items of club memorabilia, but few can rival fifty-five-year-old Reading schoolteacher Dave Downs. For he is the proud owner of the water used to wash the Reading team kit after they beat Luton Town in the 1988 Simod Cup final.

Dave had hoped to get one of the players' shirts as a souvenir but when that failed, he approached the groundsman's wife who washes all the kit. 'I asked her if she would keep me a bottle of the water used in her washing machine to clean the Wembley kit, and she did. It's in an inscribed milk bottle at home in my display cabinet, with all the sediment collected at the bottom. I also have the Division One play-offs shirt-wash next to it in a plastic coke bottle.'

Dave has arranged with the club for his ashes to be buried under the centre spot at Elm Park. 'I originally asked for them to be buried under the goal Reading were attacking, but it was pointed out that this would mean someone digging me up every game and moving me from one goal to the other at half-time.'

A Way With Words

The team-talks of Sunderland manager Johnny Cochrane, who was in charge at the club from 1928 to 1939, became legendary. Cochrane adopted such a laid-back approach to management that he never bothered about the opposition.

Raich Carter recalled: 'Just before a game, this man wearing a bowler hat, smoking a cigar and drinking a whisky would pop his head round the dressing-room door. He'd ask, "Who are we playing today?" We would chorus, "Arsenal, boss." Johnny would just say, "Oh, we'll piss that lot," before shutting the door and leaving us to it.'

Peterlee Make A Stand

In a bid to get around the non-league Pyramid ruling which states that all grounds must provide covered accommodation for at least 200 spectators, Northern Leaguers Peterlee (average gate 25) recently tried handing out umbrellas to fans.

The Son of God

For many years in the 1980s, David Icke was a familiar face on British television. The former Coventry and Hereford goalkeeper, whose playing career had been cut short by arthritis, had successfully carved out a new niche as a BBC television anchorman. Clean-cut and personable, he seemed the most straightforward individual imaginable. But his relaxed on-screen persona hid a fervent zeal which would subsequently manifest itself in a most unusual way.

In 1984, he moved to the Isle of Wight and began spending hours poring over railway timetables. He announced his intention of writing the history of steam on the island and, to this end, joined the Isle of Wight Steam Railway Society. According to members, his enthusiasm for the project went way beyond that of the standard trainspotter. John Loe, one of the society's founders, remarked: 'He was in and out in less than a year. In view of what later happened, I am very relieved that we got off so lightly.'

Icke then turned his attention to the environment. He formed the Isle of Wight Green Party and went on to become national spokesman for the Green Party, a move which reportedly resulted in the termination of his contract with the BBC.

But it was Icke's book, *The Truth Vibrations*, published in April 1991, which really catapulted him into the headlines. He was dubbed the Son of God after predicting the imminent destruction of the planet. He began wearing turquoise and announced that his wife was to be known thereafter as Michaela (after the archangel Michael). Her real name was Linda. He claimed to have been Socrates (the philosopher, not the Brazilian defender) in a previous incarnation, and said he had been told by a medium that he was 'a healer who is here to heal the earth'.

For months, the self-styled prophet was scarcely out of the newspapers, but gradually media interest in him waned. The world hasn't ended and David Icke hasn't returned to presenting the snooker on television – which is probably just as well, because turquoise would clash dreadfully with the green baize.

The Supreme Enthusiast

Workington-born John Burridge is one of the game's great enthusiasts. Now aged forty-six, he has kept goal for over twenty clubs including Blackpool, Crystal Palace, Wolves, Sheffield United and Newcastle, and in each case his dedication to duty has been outstanding. Indeed, it is no exaggeration to say that Burridge lives, eats and sleeps football, for he has been known to take a ball to bed at night and to watch *Match of the Day* in his full goalkeeping kit, complete with jersey, gloves and boots.

A Confusion Over the Rules

The very first Scottish Cup tie took place in October 1873, with Kilmarnock meeting Renton at Crosshill, which was then the home of Queen's Park. The tie was also just about the most bizarre in the history of the competition, simply because Kilmarnock thought they were playing rugby! The *Glasgow Evening News* reported that the Kilmarnock team was 'not thoroughly conversant with Association rules. On account of this, the Renton club kept the ball well up to the goal posts of their opponents as they received several free-kicks in succession thro' some of the Auld Killie's men persistently using their hands.' Not surprisingly, Kilmarnock lost 3-0.

Distressed of Leicester

A group of Leicester City fans claimed they were so distressed after the award of a controversial penalty against their team that they had to take time off work; and following consultation with solicitors, they announced their intention to sue the referee at the centre of the storm for lost earnings.

They were upset when referee Mike Reed gave Chelsea a match-winning penalty near the end of extra-time in an FA Cup fifth round replay in February 1997. Television replays supported the view that it should not have been a penalty.

After the incident, John Regan, editor of the Leicester fanzine *Where's the Money Gone?*, reportedly had to take a day off from his job as a window salesman because of the 'extreme distress' caused by the penalty award. He spoke to a solicitor who advised him that he could claim for lost earnings.

Others swiftly followed suit, one fan putting in a claim for £140 plus expenses. 'He had to have two days off work,' explained Mr Regan. 'He's a timid lad. Something has to be done to protect fans from these sort of incidents.'

Rochdale supporters were believed to be consulting solicitors to ascertain whether distress could be back-dated to cover the past thirty-five years. 'We could be sitting on a gold-mine,' said one.

The Fiery Frank Barson

It could be argued that 'eccentric' is not the right word to describe Frank Barson, the oft-suspended centre-half who did time with a number of clubs between the wars – but any player who is reputed to have pulled a gun on his manager has to be someone out of the ordinary.

A former blacksmith from Sheffield, Barson began his career with Barnsley who suspended him twice, for a total of three months, after two sendings-off. Then he moved to Villa, where he received two further bans for breaches of club discipline. It was there that he is said to have reacted so badly to punishment that he brandished a gun at the manager. Nevertheless, while he was with Villa, he won a Cup winners' medal in 1920 and also earned his sole England cap in the same year.

In 1922 he joined Second Division Manchester United for a fee of £5,000, with the promise of a public house if he helped United to promotion. Within two years, they did reach the higher grade and Barson was duly given his hostelry. But surprisingly for one who relished a battle on the pitch, he was put off by the surge of customers and abandoned the idea.

Age did nothing to mellow him. Joining Watford, he was banned for seven months after being sent off and getting involved in a fracas with the police. Wigan Borough also suspended him for three months. He was no better behaved in non-league football where he was repeatedly dismissed and suspended. Fittingly, he was sent off in his last ever game.

Revenge is Sweet

From 1994 came the story about the convict goalkeeper who deliberately let in fifteen goals so that he could settle an old score with the team coach.

Paul Morgan, a twenty-one-year-old who was serving two years for wounding, was keeping goal for Prescoed open prison in South Wales. But somehow he didn't seem to be trying too hard. 'It was the fifth goal that really gave it away,' said one spectator. 'Morgan just lifted up his leg and allowed the ball to go under it. When the instructor asked him what he was doing, Morgan replied: "I told you I was going to get you back one day."' Prison governor Nicolas Evans said Morgan held a grudge because he had been disciplined for swearing.

Morgan's inactivity resulted in a 15-5 defeat and a fight in the team van on the way back to the prison. He was later moved to Cardiff prison to escape the wrath of his team-mates. Governor Evans added: 'The lads here take their football very seriously.'

A Manager in Nappies

Some footballers disparagingly refer to a rookie manager as still being in nappies, but in the case of Romanian club Sadcom FC, it was actually true. For in January 1997, Aurel Rusu, the Sadcom president, was so dismayed because his team were languishing in the country's bottom division that he appointed his son Lucian as the new manager. Lucian was just six months old.

The Oldest Hooligan

In October 1980, eighty-two-year-old Samuel Phillips was banned by the Herefordshire FA from attending Ledbury Town home games for the rest of the season because of his unruly behaviour. At the end of the club's home game against Lye in August, he was alleged to have grabbed the referee by the shirt in protest at the award of a penalty against Ledbury. But the artful pensioner got round the ban by watching Ledbury through a hedge from an adjoining cricket pitch. Mr Phillips, who had supported Ledbury for nearly fifty years, said defiantly: 'No-one is going to stop me watching my team.'

Home and Away

As manager of Sheffield United in the 1938-39 season, Ted Davison hit upon a novel method of securing promotion to Division One – he treated United's last three home games as away matches. All season, United's away form had been excellent but their chances of promotion were being threatened by indifferent results on their own Bramall Lane ground, where they had drawn too many matches. So Davison came up with his master-plan. On each Saturday morning before the last three home games, the players were driven by bus from Sheffield to Derbyshire, where they had lunch. It was just like an away game. Then they returned to the city for the match. The curious psychology worked: United won two and drew one of those vital games to win promotion at the expense of neighbours Sheffield Wednesday.

Pig-Out

Footballer Dave Clark was banned from playing for Worthing United in February 1997 after nailing a pig's head to the opposing team's dug-out before a game. Clark, a butcher by trade, was reported to the Sussex FA, although he insisted that the stunt was just part of a long-running joke.

Pym's Number One

A former Devon fisherman, Dick Pym underwent a career change which meant him keeping things out of a net. He kept goal with distinction, first for Exeter City and then with Bolton Wanderers, with whom he won three England caps in 1925 and 1926. When he switched to football, he took with him a few superstitions probably gleaned from old sea-dogs. One was that he would refuse to travel if the numbers on his train ticket added up to thirteen. Another was that he always carried a lump of coal in his pocket, even during matches. Presumably he took care not to land on it when diving across the goalmouth.

Life's A Drag

In 1989, five Newport County supporters were arrested after they turned up for a match at Kidderminster Harriers in drag. Before the game, forty County fans had trooped into an Oxfam shop and bought women's clothes. 'I don't know whether this is a new style or what it is,' said a perplexed superintendent Peter Picken.

The Mad Doctor

Wrexham-born goalkeeper Dr Leigh Richmond Roose won twenty-four caps for his country between 1900 and 1911. He played for ten different clubs (among them Stoke City, Everton, Sunderland and Arsenal), on each of whom he stamped his quirky personality.

Dr Roose was an amateur and, as such, filled in a weekly expenses form. Like most goalkeepers, he suffered a few pre-match jitters and thus his claim for reimbursement always began: 'Use of toilet . . . twice . . . two pence.' He preferred to travel in style. Living in London, he sometimes did not relish the prospect of accompanying the rest of the team north on a scheduled train for an away match, so instead he would hire a special train and charge it to the club. Since Roose did not enjoy hanging around for long periods, he usually booked a train which would get him to the ground just a few minutes before kick-off – by which time most of his colleagues were nervous wrecks, convinced that he wasn't going to turn up at all. Having said that, his team-mates were probably glad of the excuse not to travel with him, since he was, to say the least, a curious companion. Seated in his carriage at the start of the journey, he would ask the station porter to feed his dog which, he said, was in the guard's van. The obedient porter would then walk the length of the train, armed with a selection of dog biscuits, only to find, on reaching the guard's van, that there was no dog. The poor man would then retrace his steps to relay the news, only to find that there was no Roose either. He had scurried off elsewhere – it was his idea of a joke.

The doctor's peculiar sense of humour was evident again in an international against Ireland in Belfast. He arrived for the game with one hand heavily bandaged. He said that he had broken a couple of bones but was sure he was fit enough to play. The Welsh officials hailed him a hero and press photographers were invited to record for posterity the moment that the wounded warrior went into action for his country. With the photo session over, it was time for the serious business to begin. But as the referee blew his whistle to start the game, a grinning Roose removed the bandages to reveal a perfectly healthy set of fingers. He hadn't been injured at all – it was another of his elaborate practical jokes. Fortunately for him, Wales won.

Roose's principal superstition concerned the shirt which he wore under his goalkeeper's jersey. He was adamant that to have this undershirt washed would bring him bad luck, so throughout his career it never went to the laundry. The lack of hygiene probably helped to ensure that opposing forwards were reluctant to challenge him!

Needless to say, his goalkeeping technique owed little to any manual. If there was insufficient action for his liking, he would sit down next to the goalposts and chat to the crowd. He was much happier when there was plenty going on – indeed, in one international he fulfilled two roles. The Welsh full-back had suffered an injury, reducing the team to ten men. In such circumstances a forward is usually moved back into defence, but Roose was having none of that and insisted on playing in goal and at full-back simultaneously, to avoid disrupting the team pattern. The sight of him charging between the two positions must have been worth the entrance money alone. Sadly for Welsh football, this remarkable player was killed in the First World War.

Crazy About Everton

So obsessed was Harry Boswell about Everton that he named his home Goodison Park and painted the house all blue. His wife, who had suspected the worst when he wore blue pants on their wedding night, divorced him, claiming that he loved Everton more than her. (At least he didn't come out with the line that he loved Liverpool more than her . . .) Six months later, Harry remarried, wearing blue suit, socks and scarf to the ceremony, after which he rushed home to watch Everton on TV. He insisted that his new bride understood him.

'Punch' Drunk

As Arsenal coach, James 'Punch' McEwan had been placed in charge of the team dressing-room at the 1927 FA Cup final against Cardiff. It was a match which Arsenal were expected to win comfortably, and in anticipation of victory they had ordered a case of champagne to be delivered to the dressing-room. But as the Gunners slid to a shock 1-0 defeat, McEwan decided to drown his sorrows and drank the lot before the players had trooped off the pitch.

A Close Encounter of the
Third Division Kind

Michael Knighton, the chairman who likes to demonstrate his ball-juggling skills on the pitch before big games, achieved another claim to fame in November 1996 as the man who talked to aliens.

According to newspaper reports, the chairman and chief executive of Third Division Carlisle United made his claims about contact with aliens at a conference of UFO experts in the town. He allegedly said that in 1977 he was driving with his wife Rosemary on the M62 when he saw strange lights in the sky. Under the headline 'KNIGHTON: ALIENS SPOKE TO ME', the *Carlisle News and Star* reported him as saying: 'The bright dot became a triangle and shot down from the sky at an incredible speed. It then turned into a glowing disc which hovered above a petrol station at about the height of Nelson's Column.' He said he watched for about thirty minutes. He was then quoted as saying that before the shape sped off, he heard a voice inside his head which told him: 'Michael, don't be afraid.' He reportedly said: 'I was so excited. It was just the most incredible experience. For seven years after that, I spent time UFO-spotting. I just wish I could come in contact again.'

Knighton was upset over the tone of the story and threatened to resign, prompting one fan to say: 'I'm pretty sure we would be the only club in history to lose a chairman to aliens.'

The Dope in Black

A Tanzanian soccer match was postponed in January 1978 after the referee was arrested on the pitch and accused of smoking marijuana just before the kick-off. It is not known whether he had time to say goodbye to all 44 players and the two pink elephants behind either goal.

The Dapper Struth

The Glasgow Rangers team of the 1920s swept all before them. Their driving force was manager Bill Struth, who took over in 1920 after his predecessor William Wilton had drowned. Struth liked to be as smart off the field as his team were on it, and always used to keep half a dozen double-breasted suits in his office. It was not unusual for him to change two or three times a day.

Saved By the Bell

In March 1995, a new member was added to the crazy goalkeepers' union in the shape of Alan Bond, custodian for Gwent amateur side Newport Civil Service. Bond achieved fame for being the first goalkeeper to answer a phone call while facing a penalty!

Newport Civil Service were playing local rivals Hamdden in a cup tie when the latter were awarded the penalty. As the Hamdden striker began his run-up, the tense silence was broken by the sound of a phone ringing. To the amazement of players and spectators alike, goalkeeper Bond shouted 'Hang on a minute' and turned to answer the mobile phone he had left in a corner of the net. The penalty-taker skidded to a halt and the game was put on hold while Bond chatted on the phone to his babysitter. When twenty-five-year-old Bond came off the phone, he was booked by referee Alan Carvell for 'ungentlemanly conduct', but he had the last laugh. For when the penalty was eventually taken, he saved it.

The bizarre incident took place after Bond was brought on as substitute for the original goalkeeper who had been sent off. In the rush to get onto the pitch, he forgot to switch off his mobile phone.

After the match, which Newport Civil Service lost 1-0, Bond, a driver for a plastics company, attempted to justify his eccentric behaviour: 'I couldn't ignore the ringing – it might have been an important call. The penalty-taker cursed me, and the Hamdden fans were screaming blue murder, especially when I saved the kick. It's a miracle I saw the ball at all, I was laughing so much.'

Even referee Carvell sympathized: 'I couldn't believe my eyes when I saw the goalie chatting away on his mobile phone. I told him that if it happened again, he would be sent off. I can see the funny side now though, particularly since he was apparently waiting for a call from his babysitter. Fortunately, it's not the sort of thing that's ever likely to happen at Wembley.'

Jack's Spats

Jack Tinn, who managed Portsmouth from 1927 to 1947, was the most superstitious of men. The diminutive Geordie guided Portsmouth to three FA Cup finals and attributed his success to his lucky spats. Throughout the 1939 Cup run, which ended in a 4-1 victory over Wolves at Wembley, Tinn wore the magical spats, which were religiously put on for him by the same player before every match.

A Pre-Match Sweetner

Before playing for the Rest of Europe against Britain in 1947, French goalkeeper Julien Darui chose to calm his nerves with several glasses of wine, each of which contained around twenty lumps of sugar. The Rest lost 6-1.

Food For Thought

Soccer fanatic Andy Marwick has travelled to over 700 different grounds in Britain. But he doesn't only go for the football, because Andy is the country's number one pieman.

The thirty-three-year-old security adviser from Surrey never visits a ground without tasting the pies, and logs all new pies and new grounds in his various Football Pies notebooks. He awards each pie a percentage for meat value, gristle content, pastry weight and pastry flavour, with additional comments on heat, texture, quality and the all-important ratio of kidney to beef.

His love of pies is well known amongst his friends. On Andy's wedding day, his best man swapped the wedding cake for a huge steak and kidney pie. It wasn't real, but it fooled Andy for a while and unnerved the bride.

A Sporting Giant

As befitted one who kept goal for the Corinthians, Howard Baker was the fairest of sportsmen. Indeed, in keeping with the Corinthian ideal, he would make no attempt to stop a penalty and would leave the goal empty so that the other team could score. He said: 'I would stand beside one of the goalposts while they tapped the ball in.'

The 6ft 3in Baker, who also held the British high jump record between 1921 and 1947, went on to play for Chelsea and Everton. At Chelsea, he delighted in lobbing the ball over the heads of opposing forwards, basketball-style, to the accompaniment of chairman Gus Mears shouting instructions from the directors' box through a loud-hailer. Baker confessed: 'I couldn't help being a little bit spectacular.'

So famous was he by the end of his career that he was able to command the London express train to make a special stop at his local station at Mossley Hill, outside Liverpool, so that he could get home a little earlier.

The Longest Christmas

For the past twelve years, the Lord John Russell public house in Portsmouth has had a tradition of not taking down its Christmas decorations until Pompey are knocked out of the FA Cup. In most seasons this means they can be dismantled before twelfth night, but in 1997 they had to stay up until the middle of March. Apparently, if Portsmouth actually win the Cup, the decorations will remain up the whole year round. It seems unlikely that the fairy will need to worry about overtime just yet.

Ate Referee's Notebook

When Bristol amateur footballer Mike Bagley was booked for bad language during a game in December 1983, he was so incensed that he seized the referee's notebook and ate it. Besides the resultant indigestion, he was banned by his league for six weeks.

El Loco

Long before it became fashionable for goalkeepers like Manchester United's Peter Schmeichel to dash upfield for last-minute corners, Peruvian international goalkeeper Ramon Quiroga had perfected the art of being an extra outfield player in moments of crisis.

Christened 'El Loco' ('the crazy one') by his team-mates, Quiroga kept goal for Peru in the 1978 World Cup finals and could often be seen encouraging his colleagues from well outside his penalty area. He was at his most eccentric when Peru were struggling to pull back a 1-0 deficit against Poland. With two minutes remaining, Quiroga suddenly appeared on the halfway line to tackle a Polish player and instigate another attack. Moments later, he thwarted another Polish breakaway by popping up well inside the Poland half. Unfortunately, on this occasion his rugby-tackle on Poland's Grzegorz Lato earned him a booking.

Quiroga, who to the consternation of his team-mates liked to juggle the ball on his feet in the most dangerous of situations, also had an unusual penalty-saving technique which proved mightily effective against Scotland. As Don Masson ran up to take the kick, Quiroga just stood there with his hands on his hips but at the last second he sprang into action, coming a yard off his line and plunging to his right to save. This nonchalant approach to penalty-saving would later be copied by the likes of Bruce Grobbelaar, but the pioneer was the man they called 'El Loco'.

The Jack Walker of Faversham

We all know how Victor Kiam liked the razor so much that he bought the company; well here is the Saudi Arabian millionaire who bought the club so that his son could play for it.

In the spring of 1996, Saleh Aisawi announced his intentions of paying £250,000 to buy impoverished Faversham Town, who at the time were at the bottom of the Winstonlead Kent League with an average gate of 33. Mr Aisawi, a forty-two-year-old former Saudi international, was one of the few regular spectators at Faversham and trained each week with the youth team, of which his fourteen-year-old son Karim was a member. And thereby hangs the tale. For Karim wanted to become a professional footballer, but with Faversham facing bankruptcy, his father knew the chances were slim.

Club secretary Vernon Willis admitted he thought it was an April Fool's Day joke when he first heard about the offer, but Mr Aisawi said: 'I just want to do everything I can to help Faversham and my son. I love football and I don't think I am wasting my money.'

The takeover has not been without its teething troubles. At the start of the 1996-97 season, lines of communication appear to have been crossed when a team of London-based players were brought in by chairman Aisawi to replace the existing side. The eleven 'old' Faversham players were about to get changed for the opening match against Herne Bay, only to discover they were surplus to requirements when the eleven from London suddenly appeared in the dressing-room. Led by manager Hughie Stinson, the old boys walked out, leaving the newcomers to crash 3-0.

A Novel Solution

Arriving at Middlesbrough railway station in the late 1940s, the Bolton Wanderers entourage were horrified to discover that the players' shinguards were missing. They had been left behind in Lancashire. Bolton trainer Bill Ridding, who later went on to manage the club from 1951 to 1968, came up with the perfect solution – he went to a local bookshop and purchased twenty-two paperback romantic novels as temporary replacements.

Elephant in Penalty Shoot-Out

When Sanger's Circus toured the country in the 1890s, one of the chief attractions was a penalty-taking elephant. Using an outsize ball, the elephant proved a formidable opponent, both at taking penalties and at stopping them. It led the circus to boast that the elephant was unbeatable.

On arriving in Leicester, the circus proprietor saw the publicity value in challenging the professional footballers of Leicester Fosse to take on the beast in a penalty-taking competition – four shots from each player and four from the elephant. A quartet of Leicester players put their reputations on the line, but the gamble backfired as the first three failed miserably. The club's honour was left in the hands of the last man, William Keech.

Faced with such a mammoth goalkeeper, Keech knew that his only hope was to get the elephant to commit itself. Clearly it was impractical to expect it to dive, not least because such action would have demolished the Big Top. So instead, Keech opted for the more subtle approach of a little shimmy to one side. As the elephant raised its leg in anticipation of the shot, Keech cleverly placed the ball in the other corner. Using these tactics, Keech held the elephant to a 2-2 draw before winning the rematch 3-2. It was one day that the elephant was unlikely ever to forget.

The Life of Brian

There have been a number of 'personality' managers over the last few decades – Bill Shankly, the canny Scot who, as a birthday present, took his wife to watch Rochdale reserves; Malcolm Allison, the supreme showman with the cigars and fedora; Tommy Docherty, a wisecrack for every occasion; and Ron Atkinson, who wears more jewellery than Liz Taylor. But there has only been one true eccentric in those years – Brian Clough.

Clough is living proof that greatness and eccentricity can go hand in hand. He would probably dispute that he is eccentric, but anybody who has ever worked with him would be forced to admit that at the very least, he is different.

How many managers would pay £1 million for a player and put him in the third team? How many managers would have their players searching the hedgerows at the training ground for mushrooms? How many managers would encourage their players to drink alcohol on the night before a big game? And how many managers would include, as part of training, a contest to see how many of their players would fit into a five-a-side net? Clough did all of these things – and more.

Even as a young player at Middlesbrough, Clough was something else. He was supremely arrogant. His job was to score goals and he wouldn't allow anyone to get in his way, especially his own team-mates. He would yell 'Out of the way' at colleagues as they were shaping to shoot, and then steal the ball from them and score himself. He once actually barged a team-mate, Arthur Fitzsimmons, off the ball before running on to score. When challenged about it later, Clough answered: 'I'm better at it than he is.' What made it more galling was that he was right.

As a manager, he tackled transfers with a style of his own. When he and his partner Peter Taylor were in charge at Derby County, they were anxious to sign a promising centre-half, Roy McFarland, from Tranmere Rovers. Late one night, they went to the house on Merseyside where McFarland lived with his parents, and almost dragged him downstairs in his pyjamas. 'Take as much time as you want,' said Clough at two o'clock in the morning, 'but we're not leaving this house without a decision.' McFarland duly signed. In

1979, by which time he had taken over at Nottingham Forest, Clough made Birmingham City youngster Trevor Francis Britain's first £1 million footballer. Lest Francis grow too big for his boots, Clough had him clean them – as well as those of his team-mates – and initially consigned him to the third team.

Another Forest striker, Garry Birtles (whom Clough once memorably described as being second best to the half-time Bovril on the day he watched him at Long Eaton United), incurred the manager's wrath for complaining about an early start. So Clough dumped him off the team coach in the middle of nowhere and said: 'Find your own way.' Yet within an hour Clough, unnerved by an abortive take-off, had dragged the Forest players off a plane bound for the Middle East, saying: 'I couldn't care less what happens to the match-guarantee.'

Clough was a winner, and he wanted people around him who were winners too. It was rumoured that while he was at Derby he sacked a couple of tea ladies who were overheard laughing after a defeat.

His pre-match preparations could be equally bizarre. Very occasionally he would skip games altogether, announcing that he preferred to tend the roses in his garden. No other manager could have got away with it. He certainly believed in getting his players to relax before a big game – even if it meant getting them drunk! But there was method in his madness. Before the second leg of a vital European Cup tie at Anfield in September 1978, Clough watched his players down a few bottles of Chablis at lunchtime, sleep it off in the afternoon and then gain a battling draw in the evening, a result which was sufficient to take Forest into the next round and another step towards winning the trophy. On the night before the 1979 League Cup final against Southampton, Clough ordered a dozen bottles of champagne and kept the players up until one o'clock in the morning. Come the match, it took them 45 minutes to shake off the hangover but after being a goal down, Forest fought back to win 3-2. Forest retained the European Cup in 1980 despite, or maybe because of, spending a week in Majorca in the run-up to the final. One player said: 'No-one who saw us stumbling around the streets in the early hours would ever have dreamed we were about to play the most important match in our lives . . .'

Clough always demanded good behaviour from the Forest fans. He launched a campaign to stop supporters swearing, and when Forest fans ran onto the pitch to celebrate after a Littlewoods Cup victory against Queens Park Rangers, Clough hit the headlines for clipping two lads around the ear and dragging them physically off the pitch. Later, he publicly made up with the pair and persuaded them to give him a kiss. The kissing of fellow managers and press men in public became another Clough idiosyncrasy.

Always an impressionist's dream, he seemed to develop into almost a caricature of himself in the years leading up to his retirement in 1993. The green sweatshirt became as ever-present as Dr Roose's undershirt, and the cries of 'young man' with which he seemed to address people of all ages became yet more frequent. He was never a slave to fashion. He once attended tennis at Wimbledon (where everyone dresses up to the nines) in his tracksuit, and used to arrive for Sunday lunch at a smart Derbyshire hotel wearing a rugby shirt and wellington boots. Among the items of furniture in the front room of his house is his mother's old mangle. On top of the mangle is a scroll declaring him to be a Freeman of the City of Nottingham. He says the mangle is there to remind him of his roots: 'When I was a kid, I used to mangle the sheets for my mam. It's a symbol to remind me where I came from to where I arrived.'

In all respects, it was an incredible journey.

The Poetry-Reciting Fans

The supporters of Pegasus, the successful amateur team of the 1950s drawn from Oxford and Cambridge undergraduates, used to wear mortar boards and gowns. And instead of the usual terrace chants, they preferred to recite poetry on the touchline.

The Name Game

In 1996, there can have been few stranger sounds on a football field than the touchline instructions being relayed to Aloeric School's under-12 team. For every member of the team was called Chris – and so was the substitute. And whilst this made life easy for the supporters, whose cries of 'Come on, Chris' covered a multitude of players, it created endless headaches for the coach of the 405-pupil school at Melksham, Wiltshire.

That honour fell to headmaster Peter Mowday. During one game against their local rivals, he shouted 'Chris, you take the corner' – and watched as five Aloeric players rushed over to fetch the ball. To add to the confusion, one set of opponents, Forest and Sandridge, had five boys named Chris in their team. The Aloeric goalkeeper, ten-year-old Chris Miles, said: 'I shouted, "Chris" really loud once and about six people stopped and turned round.' Perhaps not surprisingly, the game ended goalless.

Similarly, in 1994 a national five-a-side tournament was held in Kettering in which all 200 players were named Patel. One of their number, Ken Patel, admitted: 'We used a lot of first names.'

The Manager Who Hid in the Loo

The uncle of the Northants and England cricketer David Steele, manager Freddie Steele, guided Third Division Port Vale to the semi-finals of the FA Cup in 1954. But he was an extremely nervous spectator from the dug-out, and if a game was tight, he had to hide in the toilet for the last few minutes.

The Crowd-Pleaser

Between 1934 and 1956, Sam Bartram played 583 League games in goal for Charlton Athletic. With his wavy red hair, he cut a flamboyant figure on the pitch, often charging out of goal to head the ball clear and generally using any excuse to embark on a sortie upfield. Like most goalkeepers, he rated himself as an outfield player.

The Charlton fans loved his antics. They roared with anticipation during a match in February 1946 when, with Charlton leading Birmingham City 1-0, Bartram stepped up to take an 86th-minute penalty. Alas, his shot clipped the bar and went for a goal-kick, leaving Bartram with a mad dash back the length of the pitch to protect his goal. The crowd hooted with laughter.

He was not always as popular with opposing fans. Playing at Portsmouth in 1938, he was hit by a house-brick and his goal nets were set on fire. He got his revenge on the Pompey fans while he was guesting there in a wartime game for West Ham. He was beaten by a penalty but the ball went through a large hole in the net and finished up in the crowd behind the goal. To the anger of the home supporters, he retrieved the ball, calmly put it down for a goal-kick and proceeded with the game, leaving the referee in the dark.

Bartram did not take kindly to players who made a fool out of him. During another wartime game at Barnsley, when Bartram was guesting for York City, Barnsley's Beaumont Asquith coolly sent him the wrong way with a penalty. Bartram responded by angrily kicking the ball over the grandstand and into the street, necessitating a long search. It was a good job it was little more than a friendly . . .

A natural showman who enjoyed making routine saves look spectacular, Bartram enjoyed a particularly incident-packed 1937. In September of that year, he got married on a Saturday morning, helped Charlton to a 1-0 victory over Middlesbrough in the afternoon (he had run onto the pitch to the band playing The Wedding March), and half an hour after the final whistle he was back at the reception. Then three months later, on Christmas Day, a rescue party had to be sent out onto the Stamford Bridge pitch to locate Bartram, who was blissfully unaware that the game against Chelsea had been abandoned due to fog five minutes earlier.

Sam Bartram died in 1981 at the age of sixty-seven. As with many 'personality' players, he did not receive the recognition he deserved at international level and is still referred to today as England's greatest uncapped keeper.

Much Capped

Russian international goalkeeper Lev Yashin (1929-90), the man in black who played seventy-eight times for his country, always took two caps to a match. He wore one and put the other behind him in the net for luck.

Love Tangle

A goalkeeper took the laws of the game into her own hands by punching an opposition player who had tripped her centre-forward boyfriend. Sixteen-year-old Louise Nicholls was playing for Topyard A in the final of the 1996 Peterborough Youth Clubs Five-a-Side Championship when her boyfriend, seventeen-year-old Alun Evans, was brought down by a defender. An incensed Louise ran the length of the pitch and punched the culprit in the head. A brawl broke out before order was finally restored.

Mini Leap

The speciality act of spring-heeled former Nottingham Forest, Leeds and Everton forward Duncan McKenzie was jumping over Mini cars. It may have amused his team-mates but, fearing an injury to an expensive player, his managers were understandably less keen on this display of showmanship.

Mrs Malaprop Goes to Blackpool

Fortunately for supporters of Blackpool, Joe Smith, who managed the club from 1935 to 1958, had a better command of soccer tactics than he did of the English language. He was famous for his malapropisms. Attempting to describe the tremendous club spirit at Bloomfield

Road, he declared: 'We've got perfect harmonium in the dressing-room.'

Smith was never one for complicated tactics or team talks, so when, before a vital relegation match at Cardiff, he ordered all the trainers and reserves out of the dressing-room so that he could address the eleven players, everyone thought it was really serious. Smith stood there solemnly and began: 'I can't stress how important it is that when this game is over, you get in and out of the bath as quick as possible.' The players wondered whether crowd trouble was anticipated, but then Smith added: 'We don't want to miss the 5.15 train back to Blackpool.' With that, he marched out of the dressing-room, leaving the players dumbfounded. Blackpool went on to win 3-0 – and they caught the train.

Kept Goal in a Coat

In 1893-94, the mighty Preston North End trounced Reading 18-0. The Preston keeper that day was Welsh international Jimmy Trainor, and when it started to rain heavily in the second half, he wore a mackintosh, which he only took off on the two occasions when he was briefly called into action.

Similar tactics were adopted by the Arbroath goalkeeper Milne during his team's record 36-0 drubbing of Bon Accord in a Scottish Cup tie in 1885. Contemporary reports stated that he did not have to touch the ball during the entire ninety minutes, and spent the majority of the game smoking his pipe while sheltering from the rain under an umbrella.

In a League of Their Own

Concerned that teams in a local boys' league were becoming demoralized by heavy defeats, league officials appealed to players not to score so many goals! The plea came in 1993 from Wycombe and South Bucks Star League secretary Paul Kimbrey, who said: 'It is to my despair that team managers seem unable to recognize the damage they could cause by defeating opponents by scores in excess of twenty goals. If this trend continues, we may have to abandon competitive football in younger age groups.'

As a result of the campaign, big wins were listed in the local paper without a scoreline. The league's results secretary went a step further and suggested that teams put their top scorers in goal if a game became too one-sided. Alan Shearer was not available for comment.

A Formidable Foe

The Hon. Arthur Kinnaird (1847-1923) of Wanderers, Old Etonians and Scotland was one of the key figures in the game's formative years. He appeared in a record nine FA Cup finals, picking up five winners' medals, before becoming president of the Football Association from 1890 right up until his death. Famous for his flowing red beard and long white trousers, Kinnaird was not averse to letting his hair down in moments of triumph. After Old Etonians' victory over Blackburn Rovers in the 1882 final, Kinnaird celebrated by standing on his head in front of the Oval pavilion.

Kinnaird was very much the prototype for hard men like Norman Hunter, 'Chopper' Harris and Vinnie Jones. It was said of him: 'He neither spared himself nor the enemy, and on one occasion, when his wife expressed to a friend the fear that he might come home some day with a broken leg, the friend, who knew his Kinnaird, reassured her with the dry rejoinder that if he did, it would not be his own.'

Larking About

Fulham's Tony Macedo was another in the line of goalkeepers whose confidence in their own ability knew no bounds. He thought nothing of barging his own full-back off the ball in order to clear it upfield.

The son of Spanish parents, Macedo was athletic to the extent of being theatrical. So when the famous Harlem Globetrotters basketball team came to London in the early 1960s, Macedo was eager to study their wizardry at close quarters. Unfortunately, he decided to try and imitate their antics in Fulham's next match, against Spurs at Craven Cottage. Collecting the ball, he bounced it with either hand as he ran round the penalty area, those being the days before the four-step rule for goalkeepers. For an encore, he mimicked the clowning style of Meadowlark Lemon, pretending that he was going to throw the ball to an opponent. But just as Macedo switched his aim to team-mate Johnny Haynes, the ball slipped from his grasp straight to the feet of the unmarked Jimmy Greaves. Macedo was left to reflect on his folly as he picked the ball out of the net.

The Grannies

It's one thing following a club called the Lions, the Gunners or the Rams, but somehow the Grannies doesn't sound quite as intimidating. Yet that is the nickname of the Argyll Bombers ladies' football team from Teesside, and with good justification since the players' average age is eighty-two!

The Bombers were born when elderly residents of Argyll Court, Stockton-on-Tees, were asked to raise money for charity. Encouraged by seventy-nine-year-old Middlesbrough fan Charlotte Watson, they decided to start up a five-a-side team. With their white hair and Middlesbrough strip, they look like a group of Ravanelli clones, although they admit: 'We don't know the first thing about football.' And the oldest Bomber, eighty-eight-year-old Mary Maugham, confesses: 'When we began, I didn't know what a striker was. Somebody said to me, "What position do you play, Mary?" I said any position where the ball is.'

As their fame has spread, they have been invited to take part in competitions in France. But it is unlikely to turn their heads, especially as one of their players sums up the appeal of the game thus: 'It makes a nice change from knitting.'

The Exorcist

Struggling at the foot of the Beazer Homes League in March 1994, Dorchester Town called in the club vicar, Rev David Fayle, to bless the pitch and remove a curse which had apparently been put on it by a disgruntled supporter, David Green. After the vicar performed the exorcism, Green, a part-time druid, agreed to lift his spell by chanting in the middle of the pitch. The following day, Dorchester won their first game for months.

The Scorpion Save

In September 1995, Colombian Rene Higuita showed himself to be in the finest tradition of madcap South American goalkeepers when he pulled off his amazing 'scorpion' save during the friendly international against England at Wembley. As Jamie Redknapp shot for goal, Higuita did a handstand, arched his back and knocked the ball off the goal-line with the studs of his upturned boots.

The save from Higuita – who in 1993 was freed without charge having spent four months in jail on suspicion of being involved in a kidnapping case – caused raised eyebrows amongst Britain's goalkeeping fraternity. Southampton's Dave Beasant said it 'made a mockery of goalkeeping. Had the ball gone in off his studs, he would have been slaughtered. If I tried it, my back would go and I would end up being carted off the pitch on a stretcher.' Former Scotland and Arsenal keeper Bob Wilson added: 'It was unbelievable, outrageous. The only thing I've seen at Wembley that comes near it was an extraordinary elbow punch by the Russian Lev Yashin playing for FIFA against the Rest of the World in the 1960s.'

Send for Skinner

Barnsley's most famous supporter, Michael Parkinson, recalls Saturday afternoons on the terraces at Oakwell watching one of the club's great post-war legends, hard man Skinner Normanton, a player with such a fearsome reputation that the mere mention of his name was sufficient to discipline wayward children. Mothers would tell their offspring: 'If you don't be good, we'll send for Skinner!'

Stories of Skinner's exploits have been handed down through the generations. When Barnsley were awarded a vital penalty in one match, the kicker was preparing himself, unaware that Skinner was running at full steam from the halfway line. Without breaking stride, Skinner lashed the ball into the net, in the process forcing his team-mate to step aside.

Towards the end of his career, Skinner played for Barnsley reserves in the Midland League. These were often extremely physical encounters, which Skinner relished. In one particularly dirty game, he suddenly stood on the ball and beckoned someone to challenge him. Three opponents took up the offer and were promptly laid out. The referee ran across, pulling his notebook out of his pocket, at which Skinner simply held up his hand and said: 'Tha needn't bother ref, I'm going.' And with that, he walked off.

Padded Out

Middlesbrough goalkeeper Tim Williamson, who won seven England caps between 1905 and 1913, came up with a cunning ruse to make himself look more imposing to forwards. He used to wear several jerseys under the official one, so that by the time he took to the field, he was nearing 'Fatty' Foulke proportions.

An Optimistic Offer

Peter De Sisto, chairman of Jewson Wessex Leaguers Petersfield Town, wrote in 1994 to Diego Maradona's agent offering the Argentine star the opportunity to play for the little Hampshire club. 'This is no joke,' said De Sisto. 'We are prepared to put up an attractive financial offer.' Obviously the package was not attractive enough, since Maradona has yet to reply.

Psycho Babble

Enjoying pride of place in the living room of Peterborough civil servant Diana Anderson is a full-size cardboard cut-out of the Nottingham Forest and England defender Stuart 'Psycho' Pearce. In addition to overseeing numerous family meals, 'Pearce' is decorated at Christmas with a festive piece of tinsel along with a red and white hat.

Diana acquired the cut-out five years ago at a book signing session which Pearce was doing. She told *Total Football* magazine: 'I hold regular team-talks with him when things aren't going too well, and I like to rub a little Tiger Balm into any of his injured areas. I put a plaster on his forehead when he collided with France's Basile Boli in Euro '92. It seemed to do the trick.'

She is well aware that this is strange behaviour for a middle-aged woman. 'Many people think I am daft, and I would be the first to agree with them.'

A Sense of Priority

With the Cobbold family at the helm, Ipswich Town used to be run like a gentlemen's club. The late chairman, John Cobbold, was one of the old school, a man of breeding and integrity, known to all as 'Mister John'. And his equally charming brother Patrick once defined a crisis at Ipswich as being when the boardroom has run out of white wine. On another occasion he commented: 'We need to qualify for Europe again next year so we can stock up on duty free.' Such sentiments flowed in the family. At the 1978 FA Cup final (where Ipswich played Arsenal), the club president Lady Blanche Cobbold was waiting in the Royal retiring room when she was asked whether she would like to meet the guest of honour, Conservative leader Margaret Thatcher. Lady Cobbold replied: 'Frankly, I'd much rather a gin and tonic.'

The Player Who Had his Fingers Burned

Top Subbuteo player Tom Taylor's burning desire to polish his team's performance brought the fire brigade dashing to his home. Mr Taylor, himself a firefighter, was heating a can of shoe polish on a gas cooker to use on the inch-high football figures when it burst into flames.

The forty-four-year-old from Lichfield, Staffordshire, number eight in the Subbuteo England rankings, explained: 'I was trying to create a polish which the Dutch use to improve the slide of their players. I bought this polishing rag in Germany which you rub on the base of the figures to make them slide thirty-six inches. If you don't use it, the figures only go twenty-four inches.'

A fire blanket failed to stifle the flames, so Mr Taylor told his wife Sue – England's number one Subbuteo player – to phone his colleagues at the fire station. By the time they arrived, the blaze was under control. 'But it took longer for them to stop laughing,' admitted Mr Taylor.

A Header From the Linesman

A Cornish cub scouts match between St Erth and Hayle was delayed when one of the linesmen threw down his flag, marched onto the pitch and head-butted the referee. Michael May, a thirty-one-year-old farm labourer, was incensed when his son, who was playing in the under-10s game, was laid low by a blow to the groin. It had apparently been caused by the ball, but May thought his son had been punched and stormed on to remonstrate with referee Martin Rolfe. When Mr Rolfe asked him not to swear in front of the children, May butted him, leaving him with a broken nose.

In January 1997, Penzance magistrates put May, who admitted assault, on a year's probation. He also had to pay Mr Rolfe £150 compensation.

Afterwards, Mr Rolfe said: 'The attack has completely spoiled it for me. I have not picked up a whistle since, and I never will again. When you are refereeing children, the kids will accept almost any decision you make. The most you'll get back is a little bit of a moan. But the people on the touchlines – the parents – go berserk.'

The Sergeant Major

With his waxed moustache and harsh training regime, Bill Norman, who managed Blackpool and Hartlepools in the 1920s, was nicknamed the 'Sergeant Major'. He had no time for softies, as was illustrated on a bitterly cold day when his players were reluctant to strip off their warm everyday clothes for training. Seeing this, Norman promptly removed all of his own clothes and rolled naked in the snow.

The Expeditions of Albert Iremonger

Albert Iremonger – the very name conjures up images of bygone days when most teams had at least one outstanding personality in their side. For Notts County it was undoubtedly 6ft 5½in tall goalkeeper Albert, who between 1905 and 1926 played 564 games for the club.

Iremonger loved to venture out of goal. He used to take throw-ins, much to the consternation of his team-mates who preferred to see him back between the posts where he belonged. After one of Iremonger's sorties to the halfway line to argue with the referee, his captain gave him ten seconds to get back in goal. His antics were frowned upon at an ever higher level. The Notts County minute-book entry for 9 November 1908 reads: 'Iremonger appeared and was spoken to with regard to his gallery play at Trent Bridge and Bury.'

The dressing-down had little effect: Iremonger continued to play the only way he knew. His most spectacular expedition came in a match against Blackburn when he volunteered to take a penalty. As fate would have it, his forceful kick struck the bar and rebounded back into play, over his head and towards the vacant Notts County goal. Iremonger turned on his heels and hared back in pursuit of the ball. It developed into a frantic race back between him and the speedy Blackburn winger, and it looked as if Albert had saved the day when, with a desperate lunge, he booted the ball away from the forward. Alas, he merely succeeded in slicing the ball into his own net.

On account of his build and wanderlust, Iremonger was a frequent target for opposing supporters. At Villa Park he was once pelted with oranges, which he calmly collected and placed in the back of his net. When a helpful policeman tried to remove them, Iremonger said: 'You leave them there – they're mine.'

County fans still fondly remember Albert and have a constant reminder because the thoroughfare alongside their Meadow Lane ground is called Iremonger Road. It is a fitting tribute to a great character.

A Crazy Superstition

Southend United midfielder Phil Gridelet is a superstitious soul and always insists on being the last player to come out onto the pitch at the start of each half. Usually this presents no problem, but it was really put to the test when United met Ipswich in a First Division game on 1 February 1997. For when team-mate Andy Rammell had trouble with his contact lenses at half-time, Gridelet adamantly remained with him in the dressing-room, forcing Southend to kick off the second half with only nine men. Manager Ronnie Whelan labelled Gridelet's decision 'crazy'.

3 Horse Racing

The Curious Case of Dorothy Paget

Hon. Dorothy Paget (1906-60) owned horses on the flat and over jumps for thirty years, the most famous being the great Golden Miller who won the Cheltenham Gold Cup five years in succession between 1932 and 1936. In spite of her success, she was a formidable woman who shunned much of the human race and led one of the most peculiar lifestyles of the twentieth century.

The daughter of Lord Queensborough, Dorothy Paget inherited her wealth from her maternal grandfather and entered racing around 1930. In such a glamorous world, Paget stood out . . . on account of her dowdiness. Over a period of twenty years, she nearly always wore the same outfit at the races – a blue felt hat which owed little to fashion, and a shapeless grey ankle-length coat with blue specks and a plain, dark-blue collar. From time to time, wear and tear necessitated the purchase of a new coat, but its replacement was always identical to its predecessor.

She disliked human company, especially men, whose proximity was said to make her vomit. She thus surrounded herself with female aides which gave rise to rumours regarding her sexuality. When she planted a kiss on the nose of Golden Miller after one notable triumph, a racegoer remarked that it was probably the first time she had kissed a member of the opposite sex.

She certainly had a lot in common with horses – not least because she ate like one. Indeed, she was an obsessive eater whose weight ballooned to over twenty stone. Perhaps this was why she chose to ride side-saddle in point-to-points. Nobody could ever accuse her of being a slave to conformity, since her daily routine worked in reverse to almost everyone else on the planet. She had dinner at seven o'clock in the morning, slept through the day (unless she was due at the races) and then got up for breakfast at 8.30pm. She then spent the night devouring huge meals – a night cook was employed to prepare her favourite fish and chips – and telephoning her long-suffering trainers. Consequently, she rarely got to see her horses in training, instead relying on photographs sent to her by her patient trainers and stud managers.

It was definitely no picnic training a Paget horse; gratitude was very much at a premium. At Folkestone on 29 September 1948, Fulke Walwyn trained for her the first five winners on a six-race card, the sixth, Loyal Monarch, being narrowly beaten. Afterwards, her only comment to the press was: 'I'm disappointed at getting beaten in the last.'

Apart from food, her great excess was driving fast cars. However, she was not mechanically gifted and her cars often broke down on the way to the races. A lesser mortal might have panicked or requested help, but Paget merely flagged down the next passers-by, commandeered their car and drove it to the meeting! After this had happened once too often, she arranged for her second chauffeur to follow her to the races in a spare car, in case of breakdown.

She always took a bundle of nine sharpened lead pencils to race meetings. When her secretary presented her with a gold one for Christmas, bringing the total to ten, Paget gave it back to her after losing £20,000 in a day's betting. That was another thing about Dorothy Paget – she bet staggering amounts on her horses.

For the last years of her life, she existed as a virtual recluse at Chalfont St Giles in Buckinghamshire, shunning all human contact apart from her own small, devoted, exclusively-female entourage. She was not even keen on meeting men who had come to save her life. Once when her house caught fire while she was in bed, she declared: 'I have no intention of getting up until the flames are licking my pyjama legs.' She was as good as her word, and it was only when smoke began to seep through the bricks at the back of her bedroom fireplace that she slowly got dressed and went down to her car. As she drove off, she told her staff: 'Now you can send for the fire brigade.'

Mad Jack Mytton

Shropshire squire Jack Mytton (1796-1834) was an inveterate racehorse gambler and the life and soul of many a party. Even as a youth, the infamous squire of Halston regularly drank eight bottles of wine a day – small wonder that he was expelled from Eton, Westminster and Harrow. He later graduated to similar quantities of port or brandy, and if supplies ran out, he would turn to lavender water or eau-de-cologne, which he claimed was good protection against the cold. He was said to have been drunk every day of his life from the age of fifteen.

Not surprisingly, such a high level of alcohol consumption frequently resulted in outrageous behaviour. He would go duck-hunting stark naked and was said to have fought dogs and bears with his teeth. He even rode a bear into his dining-room to shock his guests, although the bear exacted some revenge for the humiliation by savaging Mytton's leg. A horse dealer who visited the house and naturally ended up drunk was put to bed with the bear and two bulldogs. The effect on his hangover when he woke up the following morning to find such unlikely bedfellows can only be speculated upon.

Mytton's pride and joy was a one-eyed horse called Baronet, and during inclement weather Mytton would knock on the door of a neighbouring cottage and ask whether Baronet could dry off by the fire. An unusual request it may have been, but since the cottage in question invariably belonged to the squire, he was seldom refused. He gave another of his horses, Sportsman, a bottle of port on cold days. Doubtless Mytton thought the effects would be beneficial, and he was apparently genuinely startled when the horse dropped dead shortly afterwards.

When out hunting, he would sometimes be joined by his pet monkey, mounted on horseback. Mytton is said to have owned 150 pairs of riding breeches, 700 pairs of boots, 1,000 hats and over 3,000 shirts. Yet when shooting in winter, he would often venture out in nothing sturdier than a thin shirt and a pair of dancing shoes. And although he couldn't swim, he often threw himself in deep water, just for the thrill of cheating death. He expected others to do the same. When one passenger in his gig foolishly mentioned that he had never been in a carriage which had overturned, Mytton immediately steered one wheel up a bank so that both he and his passenger were sent flying.

Deeply in debt, Mytton fled to France to escape his creditors. One night he suffered a bout of hiccups. Remembering that a sudden shock was supposed to be an effective cure, he decided to set fire to his own nightshirt. His friends arrived in time to save his life, but he suffered serious burns. There was a consolation, however – his hiccups had gone.

Pining for the hunting fields of England, he returned home, but having gambled away the family estate, he died in a debtors' prison at the age of thirty-eight. Mad Jack Mytton's friends had not forgotten him, though – and over 3,000 attended his funeral.

The Equine Love Match

When the Chevalier Odorado Ginistrelli (1833-1920) first came to England from Italy in the 1880s, he was not taken seriously by the Newmarket racing fraternity. But the little man's unusual training methods eventually made everyone sit up and notice.

In 1889, Ginistrelli won the Middle Park Stakes with Signorina. The horse was then retired to stud but remained barren for her first ten seasons. Then, after producing the Derby third Signorino, she was to have been covered in 1904 by a fine stallion called Cyllene. However, the deal fell through and to the astonishment of the racing world, Ginistrelli instead sent the mare to the vastly inferior Chaleureux. The reasoning behind this surprising selection owed nothing to the form book but everything to Cupid's arrow, for Ginistrelli was convinced that the two horses were in love! He arrived at this conclusion because, he maintained, whenever Chaleureux was led past

Signorina's paddock, he whinnied and she answered.

This unscientific union was soon blessed with a foal, Signorinetta, who showed very little form as a two-year-old. In spite of this, Ginistrelli, with his unshakeable faith in equine nature, was convinced that she would win the Derby the following year. Sure enough, unfancied by all except her aged trainer, she won the 1908 Derby at 100-1 and was led into the unsaddling enclosure to a stunned silence. Furthermore, two days later she completed a remarkable double by winning the Oaks too. The romantic fairytale was complete.

One person who was less than enamoured with Ginistrelli was jockey Billy Bullock, who rode the horse to both her Classic triumphs. Expecting the traditional gift by way of thanks, he received instead just the statutory £10 fee for each victory, plus a glass of sherry. But then again, the Chevalier Ginistrelli always did move in mysterious ways.

Rough and Ready

Dennis Ready, a nineteenth-century American steeplechase jockey, was notorious for being drunk whenever he climbed into the saddle. On 7 June 1865, in what is believed to have been the first steeplechase in America, Ready rode his own horse, Zig Zag, over fences at Paterson, New Jersey. But shortly before the run-in, horse and jockey got into a terrible mess and ended up taking the wrong course. Knowing Ready's history, most observers thought he was drunk again, although some suggested he had been deliberately pulling the horse – a common practice in those days – and so on this occasion was more dishonest than inebriated.

When Zig Zag raced again in November, Ready's condition left no room for speculation. He was simply too drunk to get on the horse. He died not long after, in 1867. His obituary said: 'He was very often three sheets in the wind when about to ride a hurdle race or steeplechase, and then he would insist upon a stirrup cup.'

Gambler Synonymous

Back in the eighteenth century, the name of racehorse owner Lord March, the Duke of Queensbury, was synonymous with gambling. He would place bets on all manner of races – between horses, footmen, even geese.

The man who later became known as serial womanizer 'Old Q' was a sly fellow. He once won a bet that he could send a letter fifty miles in an hour by obtaining the services of twenty-four fine cricketers, standing them in a large circle and inserting the letter inside a ball. The cricketers were able to throw the ball from hand to hand at such speed that it travelled the fifty miles well within the stipulated hour. On another occasion, when his jockey Richard Goodisson said he had been offered a sizeable bribe to lose a race, March told him to accept the money. With the jockey apparently squared, the bets piled on. Then, just as Goodisson was about to mount, March suddenly peeled off his cloak to reveal himself in a duplicate set of his racing livery. As the backers looked on aghast, March himself climbed on the horse and proceeded to win easily, thereby foiling the coup.

But in September 1751, Lord March's chicanery almost proved his undoing. His horse Bajazet was due to run in a match against Black and All Black at the Curragh, a contest which attracted heavy betting. Bajazet lost, even though in the course of the race his jockey had succeeded in disposing of the weights. To cover up the subterfuge, these were picked up and quietly handed back to the jockey before he weighed in. However, Black and All Black's owner Sir Ralph Gore got wind of the deception and angrily challenged Lord March to a duel.

Gore was not a man to be trifled with. He was a renowned crackshot and possessed a fiery temper – he had once thrown a waiter through the window of a Newmarket restaurant. The combatants met at five o'clock the following morning. A contemporary account tells of the shock which was awaiting March: 'Great was his lordship's surprise to see his opponent appear on the ground with a polished oak coffin which, sans ceremonie, he deposited on the ground, end up, with its lid facing Lord March and his party! Surprise, however, gave place to terror when his lordship read the inscription plate engraved with his own name and title, and the date and year of his demise, which was the actual day, as yet scarcely warm!' Nor was March able to derive much comfort from Gore's words. 'My dear fellow,' began Gore coldly, 'you are, of course, aware that I never miss my man, and as I feel myself in excellent form this morning, I have not a shadow of doubt in my mind but that this oaken box will shortly be better calculated for you than your present dress.'

Faced with the sight of his own coffin and fearing that it would soon be his final resting place, March decided to swallow his pride and apologize profusely. Fortunately for him, Gore was in a magnanimous mood.

Lord March was subsequently elected as one of the founder members of the Jockey Club. One of his first tasks was to write a long paper on the importance of jockeys carrying the correct weights . . .

Turning a Deaf Ear

Among the most colourful – and imaginative – of Britain's modern trainers is Rod Simpson. He used to have a horse that would only run well if it had cotton wool in its ears. One day there was no cotton wool available, so Simpson sent someone to the Red Cross room at the course to fetch two tampons. The horse duly ran with a tampon in either ear.

Stag-Drawn Carriage

Lord Orford was the seventeenth-century owner of Houghton Hall in Norfolk, where he entertained leading members of Newmarket racing society for the last meeting of the season. As a result, it became known as the Houghton Meeting. Orford liked to have his carriage drawn by stags instead of horses, but this arrangement nearly ended in disaster on one trip to Newmarket when hounds from a hunt picked up the scent of the stags. The terrified coachman managed to reach a nearby inn just in time for the courtyard doors to be slammed shut on the baying pack of hounds.

A Catalogue of Disasters

The most eccentric horse-race starter in history was surely Mr MacGeorge, who started the Derby in the 1860s. Urged on by an impatient crowd, he started the 1861 Epsom Classic even though four runners were languishing thirty yards behind the line and facing the wrong way. The following year, he dropped the flag long after most of the field had already crossed the starting line. The authorities took a dim view of his conduct, and he was severely reprimanded and threatened with dismissal if there was a repeat performance. So for the 1863 Derby, he was ultra-cautious. In torrential rain, and with jockeys and horses soaked to the skin, he started the race no fewer than thirty-five times before he was finally satisfied.

Weighing-Room Superstitions

Most jockeys have their pet superstitions, but jump jockey Graham Thorner had more than most. Quite simply, he hated using anything new. He would always get someone else to break in a new saddle or a new pair of breeches for him, and rather than wear a new set of colours, he would often jump up and down on them before putting them on for the first time, just to create that 'used' look. To complete the picture, he always insisted on wearing his 'lucky' underpants, the pair which he had worn when partnering Well To Do to victory in the 1972 Grand National.

Thorner also had an aversion to green saddle-pads and would never ride with one. Then one day at Newton Abbot, after he had fallen in the first race but still had five more rides, he was left with no option, because valet Tom Buckingham only had a green one left to give him. Thorner promptly went out and rode the winner of the next race – and from then on, he insisted on having a green saddle-pad for every race.

Red-Faced Jockey

Yorkshireman James Snowden (1844-89) could have been one of the top jockeys in the land but for the fact that he drank too much – often immediately before a race. Indeed, it was rumoured that he sometimes took a swig on the way round.

He once arrived at Chester to ride for the Duke of Westminster, only to find that the meeting had taken place the previous week. Needless to say, he never rode for the Duke again.

Another bout of drinking cost him the ride on Doncaster when the horse won the 1873 Derby. He did manage to get in the saddle to partner Bendigo in the Cambridgeshire but was so drunk that he threw the race away.

Once when decidedly the worse for wear, he went out to ride a horse which was wearing blinkers. He immediately ordered them to be removed, pointing out: 'A blind horse and a blind jockey will never do.'

The Squire of All England

Standing barely five-foot tall and with a muscular physique, George Osbaldeston was the ideal build for a jockey. But he was more than just a fine horseman – he also excelled at boxing, cricket, billiards, running, shooting, rowing and fishing. In short, he was a splendid all-round sportsman. And what he lacked in inches, he more than made up for in eccentricity.

Osbaldeston was born on Boxing Day 1787. His education, such as it was, began at Eton where he forged letters to enable him to go hunting and fishing. He moved on to Oxford but was still more interested in fox hunting than taking a degree. Having already inherited a sizeable fortune, he did not intend spending precious hours studying, and resolved instead to devote his life to leisure pursuits, particularly those of a sporting nature. While an undergraduate, he bought his first pack of hounds – from the Earl of Jersey – and went on to become Master of the Pytchley Hunt, one of the most famous in Northamptonshire. He was a dedicated huntsman and stated that any week in the hunting season which did not include six full days in the saddle was a waste of time. Such was his energy in the saddle that his hounds struggled to keep up with him, so he replaced them with mastiffs, hoping that they would last the pace better. They, too, fell by the wayside.

Soon his riding skills became known throughout the land and he was christened 'The Squire of All England'. Eager to defend his reputation against all-comers, he never shirked a challenge, even one as seemingly impossible as the one which he undertook in 1831. Although by then he was forty-four and suffered from a badly-crippled leg, sustained some years earlier in a hunting accident, Osbaldeston bet an old gambling associate, Colonel Charrite, the sum of 1,000 guineas that he could ride a horse 200 miles in ten hours. This meant travelling almost as fast as George Stephenson's wonderful new Rocket locomotive, which was capable of achieving a mind-blowing 24 mph. Surely the feat would be beyond even such a man as George Osbaldeston.

The wager became the talk of the nation, with Osbaldeston confidently backing himself to win thousands of pounds. He trained hard for the event, riding eighty miles a day in all weathers. His plan was simple. Rather than ride on public roads, he decided to cover the 200 miles by completing fifty circuits of the four-mile racecourse at Newmarket. He would change horses after each circuit and proposed using some twenty-eight animals in total, the fresher ones being employed three or more times over.

Then, a few days before the grand challenge was due to take place, noted racehorse-owner John Gully put a yet more tempting proposition to Osbaldeston. Gully knew that the squire could complete the distance in ten hours, but could he do it in nine? Assured that he could get even better odds if he took up the new challenge, Osbaldeston was unable to resist, despite the fact that it would mean him travelling at an average speed of just over 22 mph.

The day of the race dawned wet and miserable, but Osbaldeston was there at the crack of dawn in his purple silk jacket, white breeches and black velvet cap. To the cheers of intrigued spectators, he set off in pursuit of his goal. He rode like a demon and, pausing only for a lunch of partridge washed down by brandy and a struggle with one recalcitrant horse, he never looked in danger of failure. As he climbed wearily from the saddle at the end of the fifty laps, he learned that his time was an astonishing 8 hours 42 minutes. At this, he jumped onto another horse and galloped off to the Rutland Arms at Newmarket where, after a hot bath, he declared that he was so hungry he could 'eat an old woman'. Happily for the elderly ladies of the district, this was one challenge which George Osbaldeston did not attempt.

But he had clearly developed a taste for outlandish wagers and was soon offering to ride 200 miles in just eight hours. With everyone mindful of the fate of Colonel Charrite, there were no takers.

Osbaldeston's obsessive determination ensured that he accomplished many other remarkable sporting feats. He once played billiards for fifty hours without a wink of sleep (he had also been known to lose £3,000 a week in gambling on billiards); he won boxing matches despite conceding four stone to some opponents; he had been known to bring down 100 pheasants with 100 shots (once he even continued after being shot in the eye, and merely told the perpetrator of the accident: 'I said you would hit something eventually!'); he defeated the French tennis champion using his hand instead of a racquet; and as an aggressive bowler and hard-hitting batsman (notably with Sussex), he once saved a match despite bowling while hopelessly drunk and suffering from a broken shoulder.

For many years, Osbaldeston lived on his estate in Yorkshire, but gambling debts eventually forced him to sell up and move to London, where he spent the remaining years of his life married to his housekeeper. By then, he had fallen foul of the racing world after allegations that he had rigged a race. He died in 1866, but not before he had indulged in one last challenge. Confined to his bathchair by gout, he won a sovereign by betting that he could sit for twenty-four hours without moving. Within a few weeks, he would have been able to extend that time limit *ad infinitum*.

The Yellow Earl

Hugh Cecil Lowther, the Fifth Earl of Lonsdale (1857-1944), was a flamboyant character who loved to make a grand entrance at race meetings. He inherited the family estates in Cumberland and Westmorland in 1882 and owned coalfields and iron mines throughout the area, including the whole town of Whitehaven. He entertained the Kaiser and other European royalty, had his own personal orchestra and also financed private battalions to fight in both the Boer War and the First World War.

He didn't race on a large scale but owned some good horses, including Royal Lancer who won the 1920 St Leger. From 1926, he served as a senior steward with the Jockey Club and was a familiar figure at major meetings such as Ascot and Goodwood. Dressed in colourful clothes, adorned with an ever-fresh gardenia, and smoking a huge cigar, he always arrived at racecourses in a convoy of yellow Daimler carriages, earning him the nickname of 'the Yellow Earl'. He was immensely popular with the crowds – indeed, as he drove down the course at Ascot behind the King, he often received heartier cheers than the monarch himself.

Barking Mad

Flat-race jockey Greville Starkey usually had a face almost as stony as that of Lester Piggott, but the dour countenance hid a mischievous sense of humour and an uncanny talent for canine impersonations.

At the most unexpected moments, Starkey would suddenly start barking like a dog. English racegoers came to accept this behaviour, but those in Argentina found it a little difficult to comprehend. Starkey was riding for the International All-Stars against a team of South American jockeys at the San Isidro track in Buenos Aires when he began barking at spectators. At first, they were simply puzzled, but soon they began to enter into the spirit of the occasion and, for the rest of the afternoon, whenever Starkey rode past they started barking at him!

He excelled himself again at a 1973 dinner in London following a big race win at Deauville, France. His barking caused considerable disruption until he was eventually led out on all fours, still barking, by trainer Henry Cecil on a lead made from a paper napkin. After that, it was suggested that his next appearance should be at Cruft's rather than Newbury.

A Blantant Act of Bribery

Few people have been more desperate to win the Grand National than Captain D'Arcy, who rode his own horse, The Knight of Gwynne, in the 1849 race. D'Arcy had backed himself heavily to win and stood to miss out on a huge cash bonanza if he was not first past the post. So imagine his discomfort as, entering the home straight, he found himself trailing T Cunningham on Peter Simple by several lengths and showing no signs of closing the gap. Desperate situations call for desperate measures, and thus the not-so-gallant Captain decided to resort to appealing to the basest of human instincts – greed. All the way to the line, in a bid to secure his bet, D'Arcy shouted out bribes to Cunningham, urging the man in front to 'take a pull'. The offer started at £1,000, but as the winning post drew ever nearer, D'Arcy had increased it to £4,000. Unhappily for the Captain, but not for the good name of racing, Cunningham was an honourable man and stoutly ignored the pleas. He and Peter Simple went on to win by three lengths, leaving D'Arcy with wounded pride and considerable prejudice towards Cunningham.

A Veritable Dandy

Jem Mason was one of the first great jump-race jockeys, a superb stylist in every sense. His elegant clothes were made by a Savile Row tailor free of charge, he always wore white kid-gloves when racing and his magnificent riding boots represented the combined efforts of the two finest bootmakers in London. He enjoyed the distinction of riding the first Grand National winner, Lottery, in 1839, yet strangely enough, the horse was the one creature that could not stand the sight of the exquisitely-attired Mason. Lottery hated him so much that, in order to avoid being dumped unceremoniously on his backside, Mason had to disguise the true nature of his intentions by wearing his coat over his racing colours until he was safely in the saddle.

Training by Moonlight

A trainer in the north of England during the latter part of the nineteenth century, Irishman James 'Paddy' Drislane waged a constant battle against touts. Knowing that if word of impressive home-work reached the racing grapevine then the price of the horse would come tumbling down, he did his utmost to keep the schooling performances of all his horses a secret from the eagle-eyed watchers.

To this end, he once staged a steeplechase trial by moonlight. On another occasion, he smeared diluted cow-dung on the quarters and thighs of a fancied horse, to make it appear that the horse was scouring. Drislane then produced the horse before the touts, but at nothing more strenuous than walking pace. Seeing what appeared to be a sick animal, the touts spread the news that the horse had been stopped in its work. The layers reacted accordingly and the runner's price for its next engagement, the Chester Cup, began to drift. Drislane tried the horse in secret, got his price and saw the animal romp to victory in the big race.

Drislane's deceptions were not always as successful. He had one particularly miserable meeting at Newcastle, suffering a chain of misfortune of the kind which used to be the prerogative of Inspector Clouseau. Drislane entered a horse which was not supposed to win. To make sure that it didn't, he put up an inexperienced boy jockey from his yard, with the instruction that the horse should be allowed to run wide at the turn so that it would appear out of control. The youngster was then meant to pull the horse up. The outcome, Drislane calculated, would be a much better price the next time the horse ran. Unfortunately, the horse took such a strong hold that the boy was unable to pull it up as it powered its way through the rest of the field to win. On dismounting, the boy, confronted with a furious Drislane, burst into tears. 'Laugh, ye little devil, laugh, can't ye?' growled Drislane. 'Now is the time for ye to look pleased. Ye'll cry hard enough when I get ye alone tonight!'

But Drislane's nightmare was by no means over. In the next race, the Northumberland Plate, Drislane had backed his mare to win £1,000 but a sudden downpour seemed to have wrecked her chances, since she was not usually happy on soft ground. Given the underfoot conditions, Drislane hedged every penny of his bet. The horse won at a canter . . .

Just when it appeared that things could not get any worse, they did. Outside a jeweller's on his way to the station the next day, Drislane realized that his pocket had been picked. At that same moment, an organ grinder's monkey landed on his shoulder and the shock caused Drislane to fall backwards through the shop window. Angrily, he hurled the monkey back at the grinder and proceeded to attack the man with a walking stick. When the police arrived to investigate the commotion, Drislane was arrested and charged with damage and assault. It really hadn't been his meeting.

The Duelling Jockey

Ludovic, Duc de Gramont Caderousse, had the reputation of being the richest nobleman in France. A personal friend of the Prince of Wales, he was considered to be the leading light amongst the French gentlemen riders of the 1860s. But it would seem that this elevated position owed more to his social standing than his ability in the saddle, for the Duc was also regarded as an indifferent jockey.

He did not take criticism kindly and reacted angrily to comments made by an English journalist named Dillon, who worked as a racing reporter on the Paris newspaper *Le Sport*, after a race at Baden-Baden, Germany, in 1862. The Duc challenged Dillon to a duel with epees, and Dillon paid with his life for not knowing that the Frenchman was a better swordsman than horseman.

The Duc was no stranger to duels. He had survived two the previous year, along with a scandal following a very public racecourse row between two of his lady friends, a duchess and an ambassadress. His intricate love life became the talk of Paris; and in his defence, he did have a certain style. An actress whom he admired once emerged from the stage door of the theatre where she was appearing to discover a huge Easter egg waiting for her. When opened, the egg was found to contain a carriage and a pair of horses, together with attendants, ready to take her to the Duc's residence. He clearly did not believe in half measures.

A Winner at Any Price

Wealthy Scottish amateur jockey George Baird would go to any lengths to ride a winner, even to the extent of paying jockeys to stand down from a fancied mount and then reimbursing the trainer personally. He thought nothing of hiring a whole train to transport him from Newmarket to a small northern course just so that he could ride the favourite in a humble selling-plate.

Unfortunately for Baird's finances, his judgement was sometimes clouded by the demon drink. In November 1889, in a bid to secure the winning ride on Hungarian at Manchester, he gave jockey Fred Webb the sum of £200 and promised to put Lambourn trainer Charlie Humphreys on the odds for the same amount. But Baird forgot to place the bet and ended up paying £1,000. Two years earlier at Kempton Park, Baird, detesting the prospect of a walk-over which would have deprived him of the thrill of a proper race, had paid Berkshire trainer Tom Stevens junior £100 to race Country Boy against his own mount, Grand Composer. But the plan went adrift when Country Boy, ridden by Tom Cannon, trotted up. Afterwards, a furious Baird could be heard swearing at both trainer and jockey.

Another cause of Baird's eventual downfall was the dubious company he kept. A friend of Lily Langtry, he also used to mix with a gang of boxers who blackmailed him out of his inheritance (the family fortune had been in iron) by convincing him that he had once killed a man in a drunken rage and that they had been obliged to spend vast amounts of money to suppress the evidence. Baird willingly paid up, even though it seems unlikely that there was any murder. The trouble was, so much of his life had been spent in an alcoholic haze that he couldn't be sure! When he died from malaria in 1893, aged just thirty-two, his obituary stated bluntly that he had frittered away his fortune on 'horse racing, prize-fighting and harlotry' . . . though not necessarily in that order.

A Strange Host

The Derby was named after Edward Smith Stanley, Twelfth Earl of Derby (1752-1834), who planned that race and its sister Classic during a party at his house, The Oaks, near Epsom. The Earl was rather fond of parties and was known as a generous, if somewhat unconventional host.

Night after night, he would sit up with his guests well into the small hours, a habit which did not always go down well with his staff. When his chef complained that all these late suppers were killing him, the Earl told him to include on his bill a fixed sum 'for wear and tear of life'.

Apart from horse racing, Lord Derby's great passion was cock-fighting, which, much to the annoyance of his wife, he used to stage in the drawing-room after dinner.

The Answers Were in the Stars

William Hall Walker, Lord Wavertree (1856-1933), was obsessed with astrology from an early age. So it was somehow inevitable that when he became involved in racing as an owner and breeder, he based all of his major decisions on what the stars appeared to foretell.

He owned the Tully Stud on the Curragh and whenever a foal was born, he would meticulously record the date and hour of birth. From that information, he compiled an annual book of equine horoscopes, complete with an astrological chart of his horses and details of how, according to their stars, they should be trained and, more importantly, when they would win.

He consulted a female astrologer but, sadly, she had a few off days.

The prediction for Lindisfarne was that he would have 'a fine constitution, good staying power and speed' and would become 'a sought-after sire, with offspring very strong and sturdy'. It transpired that he was gelded and never ran a race. For Carrickfergus, the advice to the trainer in 1914 was: 'You might as well take his shoes off and let him run loose in his paddock all year.' Yet that summer, he won the St James's Palace Stakes at Royal Ascot at the rewarding odds of 100-6. The stars also advised Lord Wavertree to sell Prince Palatine, who went on to win the 1911 St Leger and two Ascot Gold Cups.

In spite of these minor hiccups, his lordship was convinced that the stars were always right and he would not hear a word against them. Not altogether surprisingly, this led to frequent clashes with his trainers, who preferred a more scientific approach. Indeed, trainers were summarily sacked if his horses failed to fulfil the destinies prescribed by their horoscopes. The unreliability of the stars, combined with the cantankerous nature of Lord Wavertree, ensured that he parted company with trainers and jockeys on an alarmingly regular basis. But it probably came as no surprise to him – he had seen it all in the stars.

The Meanest Jockey

Stories of miserly jockeys are commonplace, but few can compare with William Arnull who rode three Derby winners in the early nineteenth century.

Descended from a line of leading jockeys (both his father John and uncle Sam won the Derby), Arnull was so careful about money that his friends used to say he would go without food for a week if he thought it would earn him a sovereign. He was also extremely bad-tempered (his irritability was partly caused by the chronic gout from which he eventually died in 1835, aged fifty) and this trait, combined with his legendary meanness, made him the butt of many practical jokes. His Newmarket colleagues would derive much merriment from telling the town's poor folk that Arnull was a genuine philanthropist and then eavesdropping while he gave short shrift to their pleas for money. The most elaborate jape was set up by owner Edward Petre.

Arnull had been boasting that he was expecting to receive a hamper of wine from a grateful owner, and on returning from riding work one morning, he duly discovered a hamper waiting for him. Opening it eagerly, he was horrified when out jumped a dwarf called 'Little Peter'. In a blind rage at having been duped, Arnull chased the dwarf across town until the little fellow was able to seek refuge in a hostelry.

The Formidable Duchess of Montrose

Racehorse owner Caroline, Duchess of Montrose (1818-94), was definitely not a woman to cross. Dressed in masculine clothes, topped by a Homburg hat, she presented a formidable figure and became the scourge of jockeys, trainers and even vicars.

It was one late summer in the 1880s that she attended a service at St Agnes Church, Newmarket, and heard the Rev Colville Wallis pray for fine weather in which the local farmers could gather their harvest. It seemed an innocuous enough comment, but the Duchess immediately stormed out of church and afterwards informed Rev Wallis in no uncertain terms that he had better start looking for another job, as he should have known that her St Leger hopeful could only act on soft ground!

She frequently infuriated her jockeys. She once remonstrated with Harry Huxtable, who rode her lightweights: 'Why on earth did you not come when I told you to?'

'Beg your pardon, your Grace,' answered Huxtable, 'but I should have had to come without the horse.'

She detested handicappers and labelled one, Reginald Mainwaring, 'the man who murdered his mother', partly on account of his unfortunate physical resemblance to a stage villain.

She raced her horses under the alias of 'Mr Manton' (her long-suffering trainer being Alec Taylor at Manton) and saw off two husbands. In 1888, at the age of seventy and five years after she had been widowed for the second time, she created a society stir by marrying twenty-four-year-old Henry Milner. But then the Duchess of Montrose was never too worried about offending people.

——————

Prepared for all Eventualities

William Henry Cavendish Bentinck-Scott, Fourth Duke of Portland (1768-1854), was one of the leading lights in horse racing. A member of the Jockey Club for over fifty years, he was an enthusiastic owner who liked to make sure that his horses were able to cope with the noise and razzmatazz of the racecourse. His methods for making his horses shock-proof were revolutionary.

He exploded squibs in the stables to get the horses used to sudden bangs, and regularly staged his very own carnival on his estate at Welbeck, Nottinghamshire. He would hire a drum and fife band, recruit estate workers to shout and wave flags, and then order his horses to be ridden past them over and over again until the animals stopped flinching at the cacophony. After that, he reasoned that they would be able to handle any royal procession or racecourse fair . . . provided events at home hadn't frightened them to death by then.

To give support to the theory of hereditary eccentricity, his son, the Fifth Duke of Portland, was even odder. It was he who built a vast complex of underground rooms and tunnels at Welbeck because he was petrified of daylight and of meeting people. Only his valet was allowed near him, so that in the event of illness, the doctor had to wait outside while the valet took the Duke's pulse. Communication took place via double letter-boxes fitted in each room of the house.

The Grand Old Duke of Albuquerque

On various occasions between 1952 and 1978, the Grand National was enlivened considerably by the presence of that gallant Spanish amateur rider, the Duc of Albuquerque, who seemed to spend almost as much time in Liverpool Royal Infirmary as he did in the saddle.

After a succession of mishaps (in 1952 he fell at the sixth fence and almost broke his neck), bookmakers were offering odds of 66-1 against his finishing the 1963 race. He didn't let them down, parting company with his mount at the fourth. Two years later his horse collapsed beneath him, and in 1973 his stirrup broke. The ageing Spanish nobleman clung on for dear life before being deposited on the ground at the eighth.

In 1974 he fell off during training, thus arriving in casualty before the race had even started. Undeterred, he set off to ride in the National with a broken collar-bone and a leg in plaster, finishing a creditable eighth on Nereo. 'I sat like sack of potatoes and gave horse no help,' he explained to reporters. He had managed to complete the course for the first time in his less than illustrious career.

In 1977, the Jockey Club ruled that he was medically unfit to take part, and he finally gave up his quest to ride a National winner the following year, by which time he was fifty-nine. All the years of falling off had taken their toll.

The Father of the Turf

Hailed by scribes of the time as being 'as great an oddity as perhaps ever was heard of', Dorset squire William Tregonwell Frampton (1641-1727) made his name as the first 'Mr Racing'. In 1695, King William III appointed him Keeper of the Running Horses, paying him the princely sum of £1,000 per annum 'for the maintenance of ten boys, their lodgings etc, and for provisions of hay, oats, bread and all other necessities for ten racehorses'. Frampton's job was the equivalent of that of today's racing manager.

In total, he served four monarchs and became just about the most important man in racing, earning the label of 'Father of the Turf'. Many considered that he had usurped his position and he was accused of being crude and over-familiar when dealing with the sovereign. Indeed, for one who had risen to such heights, he was remarkably lacking in social graces. He was an uncouth misogynist (all the more surprising since Queen Anne was one of his employers) and, with no desire to impress the ladies of the land, never attempted to keep abreast of fashion. Thus, over a period of eighty years during which styles changed enormously, Frampton always dressed the same. It was noted that he was 'remarkable for a peculiar uniformity in his dress, the fashion of which he never changed'.

Frampton was a compulsive gambler who would go to any lengths to win a wager. It was even rumoured that he had castrated the famous sire Dragon in order to qualify him to run in a match as a gelding. In 1709, Frampton entered into a match with Yorkshire baronet Sir William Strickland's horse Old Merlin. Thousands of pounds were taken in betting and with so much money at stake, Frampton suggested that it might be an idea for the two horses to run a trial over course and distance before the match itself, as a form guide. Strickland agreed and Old Merlin won the trial by a length. But the devious Frampton had saddled his horse with 7lb overweight and was thus supremely confident of reversing the result. So he piled on the money, blissfully unaware that Strickland, knowing of Frampton's unscrupulous nature, had also put up 7lb extra on Old Merlin! Thus the match exactly mirrored the trial, with Old Merlin coming home the winner and Frampton going home a big loser.

A Most Unusual Jockey

A nineteenth-century amateur jockey by the name of Mr Canney was considerably handicapped by the fact that he was deaf and dumb. Without doubt, this cost him victory in the prestigious Grand National Hunt Steeplechase run at Melton Mowbray in 1864. For Canney's mount, Lord George, was well clear when the rider mistook the turning flag at the top of the course and overshot it by 300 yards before finally turning round. Spectators had shouted to Canney to tell him that he was going the wrong way, but of course he hadn't heard a word. By the time he had returned to the proper course, the race was lost. The unfortunate Mr Canney was killed two years later riding Whipper in the Foxhunter Stakes.

The Practical Joker

One of the leading owners in French racing, Lord Henry Seymour (1805-59) was a renowned prankster. He never married, which was probably just as well considering that he enjoyed nothing more than giving his friends powerful purges and exploding cigars. The son of the Second Marquis of Hertford, he was exceedingly rich but left much of his money to his horses. His will included sizeable bequests to his four favourite steeds, none of which were ever to be ridden again. It is no wonder that one author wrote: 'Seymour was thought odd, even for an Englishman.'

Drunk in Charge

When sober, Bill Scott was just about the finest jockey around; but when drunk, he was a liability. The brother of trainer John Scott, Bill won the Derby four times between 1832 and 1843 and also won nine St Legers and three Oaks. But in the latter part of his career, he developed an unhealthy thirst which frequently rendered him unfit to ride.

Nowhere was this better demonstrated than at the 1846 Derby, in which Scott was riding his own horse Sir Tatton Sykes. The combination had already lifted the 2,000 Guineas earlier in the year and they were strongly fancied to complete a Classic double. Unfortunately Scott decided to indulge in a hard drinking session on the morning of the Epsom race. Although he somehow managed to clamber into the saddle and sit facing the front end of the horse, Scott was clearly not at his most fluent. He became angry with the starter and continued to argue with him even after the others were running. Such was the quality of Sir Tatton Sykes that he managed to make up the lost ground, only for Scott to throw it all away again. He was too drunk to steer the horse in anything remotely resembling a straight line, yet as Sir Tatton Sykes weaved his way towards the finish, a remarkable victory was still within his grasp. But close to home, one final spectacular swerve cost him the race and he went down by a neck to Pyrrhus The First.

When the St Leger came around that autumn, Scott's friends took the precaution of keeping a close watch on him during the days leading up to the race to prevent any repeat of the scenes at Epsom. Their vigilance paid dividends as Sir Tatton Sykes gained some compensation for the Derby defeat. But nobody could monitor Scott twenty-four hours a day for the rest of his life. Two years later, his heavy drinking led to his death.

Planning for the Future

The eighteenth-century French nobleman, the Prince de Conde, built the luxurious Grands Ecuries at Chantilly for his racehorses. The reason he made the stables so palatial was that he believed in reincarnation and was convinced that one day he would return to earth as a thoroughbred.

The Red-Shirted Maestro

Jack Berry is acknowledged as being one of the best trainers of two-year-olds in England. But he is probably even more famous for his vast array of red shirts, one of which he wears whenever he goes racing.

Berry was an aspiring jockey in his early twenties when he bought his first red shirt, prior to a meeting at Ayr. The next day, he wore the shirt and rode a winner. After that, whenever he rode a fancied horse, he put on the red shirt to bring him good luck. It usually seemed to do the trick so, naturally enough, when he turned to training he continued the superstition, always wearing a red shirt if he had a fancied runner.

As people began to take notice of Berry's attire, they started sending him red shirts. Soon he built up quite a collection, and he is now obliged to wear one at the races. He admits: 'The owners would be upset if I didn't have one on!' He has donated red shirts to be sold off at charity auctions, where they are much sought-after. One fetched £70, the only problem being that Berry was wearing it at the time! He had no alternative but to take it off and hand it over there and then.

Berry's other lucky charm is the number eight. His stationery features a horse and jockey, the horse's saddlecloth bearing the lucky number. His horse boxes are also numbered eight. On one occasion, his head lad went to collect a box that had been repainted and saw to his horror that the number six had been painted on. The lad would not bring the box back to Berry until the number had been changed.

Idled His Life Away

Handsome, elegant and charming, George Stanhope, the Sixth Earl of Chesterfield, was a successful owner, winning the Oaks twice (in 1838 and 1849) and the St Leger once (also in 1838). He inherited his title at the age of ten but went on to fritter it all away – not because, like so many of his kind, he was an obsessive gambler, but because he was such an extravagant spender of money.

By middle age, he had spent himself to a standstill. Once blessed with enormous energy, he became slow and ponderous. Some days, the mere effort of getting up proved too much for him. When he did rouse himself, he would spend his London days just sitting quietly in his club, while up at Bretby, his Derbyshire estate, he would spend hours gazing into space through a telescope operated by his butler. He maintained this semi-conscious existence right up until his death in 1866 at the age of sixty-one.

The Longest Exercise

Shepherd-turned-jockey William Clift was an uncompromising Yorkshireman who stood no nonsense from man or beast. Described as a 'rough, uncultivated Indian', he could be hard on the horses he rode and unbearably rude to his employers, regardless of their status. But owners still used him in spite of his coarseness, for he was an able jockey who rode five Derby winners between 1793 and 1819. Even when he had long retired from the saddle, Clift believed in keeping himself at the peak of physical fitness and when he was nearly eighty, walked most days from Newmarket to Bury St Edmunds and back again (a round trip of thirty miles) 'just to give my legs a stretch'.

A Horse With No Name

Among his many eccentricities, breeder/owner James Carr-Boyle, Fifth Earl of Glasgow (1792-1869), had an aversion to naming his racehorses. Not surprisingly, this caused considerable confusion and might well explain why he proved spectacularly unsuccessful despite owning one of the largest strings in the country.

There was absolutely no method in his stud management. As one writer put it: 'He was obstinately loyal to certain blood-lines of proved uselessness.' Yet he could always find someone else to blame, sacking trainers and jockeys at an alarming rate only to change his mind and re-hire them again shortly afterwards. He acted very much on the spur of the moment. One day, he was being taken on a tour of the stables of trainer James Godding, with whom he had a number of horses. 'That's old Volunteer,' said Godding. 'He's won seventeen races and yet his owner has never seen him.' With the Earl looking puzzled as to why any owner should neglect to watch such a successful racehorse, Godding added the punchline: 'You see, the owner is blind.' The Earl was so outraged by what he perceived as a tasteless remark that he immediately arranged for all of his horses to be taken away from Godding's yard.

Such sensitivity was wholly uncharacteristic. A man with the shortest of fuses, the Earl was even harder on his horses than he was on humans. If a horse failed to come up to expectations (which was frequently), he would have it shot on the spot. Some mornings, following a trial, he would order as many as six horses to be executed. Of course, since he refused to name any of them, it can only be a matter of speculation as to whether he ever got rid of the right ones.

He was equally dangerous when out hunting and was likely to select his own huntsmen as the quarry. He was also an erratic shot, thus placing all around him in constant danger. Wildly unpredictable, he could inspire great loyalty but it is doubtful whether the steward at the Doncaster Club would have put the Earl at the top of his Christmas card list. Having been out one evening, the Earl returned to the club in the small hours demanding a whisky. To his intense indignation, there was no service because the steward had gone to bed. After careful consideration, the Earl thought of a solution to the problem: he marched upstairs and set fire to the steward's bed! It is not recorded whether he ever got his whisky.

A Few Trees Short of a Forest

Augustus Henry Fitzroy, Third Duke of Grafton (1735-1811), loved going to the races. An owner and breeder who won the Derby three times and the Oaks twice, he was a regular visitor to Newmarket despite the fact that he found the bumpy carriage journey distinctly uncomfortable. So he hit upon the idea of creating a smoother passage on grass, and accordingly ordered a tree-lined avenue to be planted from his park at Euston, Norfolk, to Newmarket eighteen miles away. Alas, this splendid avenue had to stop six miles short of its destination because the Duke, in his enthusiasm, had overlooked the minor fact that it would have to pass over somebody else's land.

For one with such an incisive mind, it was inevitable that he would make Prime Minister, a position he held with absolutely no distinction whatsoever between 1766 and 1770. He was notoriously idle and scandalized society by showing off his mistress, Nancy Parsons, in such public places as the races and the theatre. In 1768, when Grafton was at the height of his power, former Prime Minister George Grenville wrote scathingly: 'The account of the Cabinet Council being put off, first for a match at Newmarket and secondly because the Duke of Grafton had company in his house, exhibits a lively picture of the present administration.' In his later years, Grafton also developed chronic hypochondria and religious fanaticism.

4 Tennis

Big Bill Tilden

Bill Tilden was one of the giants of tennis in the 1920s. The United States number one for the whole decade, during which time he won the Wimbledon men's singles three times and the US singles on no fewer than seven occasions, Tilden was a big man with a big game and a big personality. Some have said that the biggest thing of all was his ego.

In some respects, Tilden was a prototype for today's outspoken players. He instilled fear into court officials and battled with authority throughout his career. He told American Davis Cup officials which team to pick, and woe betide them if they made the wrong choice. In 1922, Tilden's regular doubles partner was Vincent Richards, who saw himself as heir to Tilden's throne. But the king wasn't ready to abdicate yet and Tilden took umbrage when, after losing to Richards in a couple of minor matches, he heard the youngster boasting that he had the measure of Tilden. So in the final of the national doubles, Tilden decided to put his partner firmly in his place. He completely upstaged Richards – at one point, when putting away an easy overhead, virtually shooing him off the court. Richards reacted angrily to being embarrassed in public, and threatened to hit Tilden if he ever tried anything like that again.

Given the bad blood between the two, it was probably not a wise move to team them together for the Davis Cup challenge-round tie against Australia. Their uneasy alliance resulted in a crushing 4-6, 0-6, 3-6 defeat to Gerald Patterson and Pat O'Hara amid accusations that Tilden had deliberately engineered the defeat in order to humiliate Richards on his Davis Cup debut. Certainly, the statistics make interesting reading. In the course of the match, Tilden made twenty-five errors and won just seven points. Yet he was hardly out of form, since he won both his singles matches to help the US to a 4-1 victory. If sabotage was Tilden's intention, it worked. The selection of Richards was widely criticized and Tilden's rival did not play doubles again for the United States for another three years.

Tilden enjoyed toying with his opponents – it was often thought that he deliberately prolonged matches purely to entertain the public. But on one occasion it backfired dramatically. In the semi-finals of the 1927 Wimbledon singles, he was leading Frenchman Henry Cochet 6-2, 6-4, 5-1, and the result seemed a formality. Certainly Tilden thought so, for it is said that he deliberately lost the next game in order that he could win the match while serving from the end of the court nearest to the Royal Box. Such vanity received its come-uppance as Cochet went on to take the next seventeen points and the set 7-5. Suddenly Tilden appeared human and, moreover, tired, allowing Cochet to take the final two sets 6-4, 6-3, and complete a remarkable recovery.

Tilden made no attempt to disguise his feelings of superiority. When crossing the Atlantic with the Davis Cup team, he demanded a cabin to himself and the best hotel accommodation. If anyone in the crowd had the effrontery to criticize him, he was swift to rebuke them. But for all his faults, he was a tremendously brave player when he was in the right frame of mind. Two Davis Cup games illustrate the point while at the same time underlining his tendency towards the bizarre.

In September 1921, he was playing Japan's Zenzo Shimizu in the challenge round at Forest Hills. It was a day of intense heat and Tilden, trailing by two sets to one, was almost on his knees by the time the players took a short rest period. He staggered up the stairs of the clubhouse, kicked off his shoes and walked into a cold shower, fully dressed. Team manager Sam Hardy asked whether there was anything he could do to help and received the command: 'Undress me!' So Hardy, still in his suit, jumped into the shower and pulled off Tilden's clothes. Tilden emerged suitably refreshed and went on to win the last two sets, dropping only three games in the process.

Four years later, he was involved in another exhausting challenge-round battle, this time against Frenchman Rene Lacoste who had won the first two sets. Staring defeat in the face at the start of the third set, Tilden asked Sam Hardy to fetch him some aromatic ammonia. Hardy obliged, but instead of merely inhaling, Tilden drank a quarter of the bottle before Hardy could stop him. The sensation had a similar effect to that of spinach on Popeye. Tilden felt a surge of energy, discarded his shoes and, playing in just his socks, swept through the last three sets to clinch a dramatic victory for himself and his country. He was quite a character, Bill Tilden.

... It is Now

Danish Davis Cup player Torben Ulrich was not the most reliable of individuals. In 1954, he turned up late for a doubles match at Wimbledon, earning him disqualification from the tournament plus a suspension from his own club in Copenhagen. But he surpassed himself twelve years later, forfeiting his national title by walking off the court to go and watch the 1966 World Cup Final!

The Superstitious Champion

To an outsider, Swedish tennis ace Bjorn Borg is the least likely eccentric imaginable. The five-times Wimbledon winner was known as 'The Ice Man' for his steely-eyed, emotionless displays on court, yet that cool exterior could only be achieved by adhering to a rigorous pre-match ritual of superstitions.

Four days before a championship, Borg would stop shaving. Then before each match he would pack his bag with the utmost care and precision, arranging all ten racquets in a pile in descending order of tension. To establish the order of tension, he had to test each racket, something which often took up to an hour. Borg was always driven to Wimbledon by his coach Lennart Bergelin, the route taking them via Hammersmith Bridge, never Putney Bridge. And the car had to possess a radio, even if nobody listened to it. After car radio-assisted triumphs in 1976, 1977 and 1978, Borg and Bergelin were horrified to discover that their 1979 vehicle was a sound-free zone. Convinced that the lack of a radio would bring them bad luck, Bergelin wasted no time in exchanging the car for one with a full stereo system.

Borg's superstitions spread to the whole family. Every year, his parents alternated between watching their son at Wimbledon and at the French Open in Paris. They never attended both championships in the same year, for fear of bringing his winning run to an end. Up in the stands, Borg's mother Margarethe left nothing to chance, making sure that she always sucked a sweet during the final set. She faced a dilemma at Wimbledon in 1979 when after Borg had reached three match points, his opponent Roscoe Tanner rallied to deuce. She decided to spit the sweet on the floor but instantly realized the folly of her actions, picked it up and slipped it back in her mouth. The sweet may have lost a little flavour in its brief encounter with the dust and dirt of SW19, but for Borg and his mum there was soon the delicious taste of another victory.

A Nervous Wreck

Most top sportsmen feel butterflies before a major championship – it is all part of the adrenaline rush – but Herbie Flam's behaviour before America's 1957 Davis Cup inter-zone final against Belgium in Brisbane went beyond the realms of nervousness and into sheer eccentricity.

His first problem was one of sleep. He thought it might be something to do with his hotel room, so he asked whether he could be moved to another room . . . and another . . . and another . . . and another. Even after five rooms he was still restless, so he asked his captain Bill Talbert for permission to stay in a girlfriend's home. Talbert agreed, hoping that now the matter of accommodation was settled, Flam would finally be able to relax.

He was wrong. A few days later, Flam was as edgy as ever. He began fretting about his racquets and so a phone-call was made to California for a new batch to be flown out. Nothing changed. As the day of the match approached, Flam grew more and more tense. At one point, he gripped a glass of beer so tightly that it shattered in his hands.

The Americans knew that the only way they could get him through the match was to put him on tranquillizers. Thus it was in a complete daze that Flam took to the court for his encounter with Belgium's Jackie Brichant. The American fell over twice and groped around the court for his spectacles. So tenuous was his grip on reality, let alone the racquet, that he once went to change ends before the game was over. But Talbert succeeded in steadying him down with salt pills and, playing on automatic pilot, Flam not only got through the match but managed to win it 6-3, 3-6, 1-6, 6-3, 6-3. Nevertheless, it came as no great surprise when he was replaced for the next match.

Normal Service Will Be Resumed . . .

The most eccentric serve in the history of tennis belonged to Britain's Ellen Stawell-Brown, the great-grandmother of Tim Henman and the first woman to serve overarm at Wimbledon. Henman says: 'She used to throw the ball really high, spin round once and then hit it as it came down.' This curiosity obviously did her no harm because she was considered one of the leading lady players around the turn of the century.

Tea Break

Jack Crawford, Australia's leading player of the 1930s, always had a cup of tea during a long match. He would ask for, and receive, a pot of tea on a tray, along with hot water, milk and sugar. During change-overs, he would sit down and pour himself a cup. Cucumber sandwiches were extra . . .

Gone Fishing

The finest disappearing act at Wimbledon of recent years was that of twenty-six-year-old American Murphy Jensen, who skipped a mixed doubles match at the 1995 championships and was found fishing in Scotland.

Just ninety minutes before their second-round match was due to begin, Jensen had been happily practising with his Dutch partner Brenda Schultz-McCarthy. According to his mother Patricia, he then left the practice courts at lunchtime to collect something from the house in Wimbledon where the Jensen family (older brother Luke is also a player) were staying during the tournament. She claimed that on the way back, he got stuck in heavy traffic, missed the start of the match and heard on the radio that he had been defaulted. Fearing reprisals, he fled north and went missing for eighteen hours before finally telephoning his sisters in the United States to say that he was alive and well.

Meanwhile, a puzzled Schultz-McCarthy had been left twiddling her thumbs on number three court and, after the statutory fifteen-minute extension had expired, their American opponents Kelly Jones and Katrina Adams received a bye into the third round.

A Change-Over Cocktail

Down the years, tennis players have taken all manner of potions during change-overs in a bid to recharge their batteries for the struggle ahead. Barley water is the most popular, although, as we have seen, the odd individualist likes to take a pot of tea. Perhaps the days of a three-course meal are not too distant. But whatever is taken, the essential requirement is that it provides a fillip, and that is where British tennis player Randolph Lycett went wrong. For his chosen brew was so heady that it had the opposite effect and left him decidedly drowsy.

The year was 1921 and Lycett had worked his way through to the quarter-finals of the Wimbledon men's singles and a meeting with Zenzo Shimizu of Japan. Unusually for Wimbledon, it was a baking

126

hot day, but Lycett defied the elements to lead by two sets to one. A place in the semi-finals appeared within his grasp, but the heat and his advanced years (he was approaching thirty-five) began to take their toll and he started to wilt visibly. Desperately in need of a boost, he turned to the champagne and brandy which he had brought on court for just such an emergency. But the more he drank, the more his game suffered and he ended up losing in five sets.

The Yellow Sock Syndrome

British tennis ace Ann Jones had a thing about yellow socks. Apparently, she always thought it to be a lucky omen if the umpire for her match was wearing a pair. For the 1969 ladies' singles final at Wimbledon, she went so far as to persuade umpire Laurie McCallum to wear yellow socks and sure enough, the talisman worked: Jones went on to capture only Britain's second ladies' singles title since the war.

The Hand of God

Among the entrants for the 1879 All England men's singles championships at Wimbledon was John Thorneycroft Hartley, a thirty-three-year-old clergyman from North Yorkshire. Hartley fought his way through to the semi-finals, an achievement which presented him with something of a problem because, not having expected to reach that stage, he had not arranged for a substitute in the pulpit. The crucial match was due to take place on the Monday, but he was required up in Yorkshire on the Sunday to fulfil his duties.

Thus, straight after his quarter-final match on the Saturday evening, he set off on the 250-mile journey up to Yorkshire. Having swapped one type of service for another and completed his obligations on the Sabbath, he got up at the crack of dawn on the Monday morning to drive the ten miles by horse and carriage to Thirsk in order to catch the train for London. Time was tight and the train did not arrive at

King's Cross until around 2pm. This left him with a frantic race across town, but he managed to reach Wimbledon just in time for his semi-final against CF Parr.

Exhausted and hungry, Rev Hartley lost the first set but then, rather appropriately, the Gods intervened. A heavy shower necessitated the suspension of play, and during the enforced break Hartley was able to refresh himself with food and tea. When play resumed, he was like a man possessed, only dropping two more games en route to a 2-6, 6-0, 6-1, 6-1 victory. Buoyed by this success and with no more arduous journeys to disrupt his preparations, Rev Hartley went on to win the final.

The Man Who Played in a Tie

There were not many bigger names in Australian tennis than Norman Brookes, who served his country with distinction, first as a player and then as an administrator. In the early years of the century he had few peers, steering Australia to four successive victories in the Davis Cup from 1907 to 1911 (there was no contest in 1910).

Brookes was a conservative customer on and off court. Unemotional and reserved, he simply got on with the job in hand. His attitude was reflected in his playing attire. The shirts he wore on court were always buttoned to the throat as well as at the wrists, and the outfit was usually topped with a grey tweed peaked-cap. There was a distinct impression that he would have been happier playing in a three-piece suit – indeed, he had been known to take part in practice matches wearing a tie!

He did let his hair down in the 1914 men's singles final at Wimbledon against Otto Froitzheim of Germany. After winning the first two sets, Brookes dropped the next two and decided to fortify himself with champagne prior to the deciding set, which he went on to win 8-6.

As a result of his success in the Davis Cup, Brookes eventually came to view the trophy as his own property. He kept it on the sideboard in his dining-room, where his wife would often fill it with red peonies and use it as a high-class table decoration at dinner parties.

A Major Hitch

Joanne Russell had left herself plenty of time to get from her London hotel to Wimbledon, where she was due to play fellow American Pam Casale in a third round ladies' singles match. But that afternoon in 1982 was one she will never forget, as a series of catastrophes brought about the need for desperate, highly unconventional measures.

It all started when, for some unaccountable reason, the taxi which she had booked failed to arrive at her hotel. Glancing nervously at her watch every couple of minutes, she waited and waited until it became obvious that she had been forgotten about. As the first signs of panic set in, rather than risk another taxi, she decided to hitch a lift from a passing motorist. Soon a knight in shining armour came to her rescue, but just when everything seemed to be going smoothly, his car caught fire.

Clearly it was not the sort of problem which could be fixed in a few minutes so, thanking him for his trouble, she scuttled off in search of another car which might be heading in the general direction of Wimbledon. Vehicle after vehicle passed her by, so she reckoned that the only way to make one stop was to lie down in the middle of the road! Taking her life in her hands, she waited for a gap in the traffic and settled down on the tarmac, silently praying that the first car would stop. Fortunately it did and, sympathizing with her plight, the driver dropped her off at Wimbledon.

By the time she finally ran breathlessly through the gates, she was 1hr 40min late and dreading the worst – disqualification. But the fates had rewarded her spirit of endeavour, for when she sought out the match officials to relay her incredible story, they calmly told her that the start had been delayed anyway because of rain. She needn't have hurried . . .

When the match did take place, Russell won through to the next round. In view of her determination in the face of adversity, she deserved nothing less.

5 Golf

The Golfer Who Tried to Strangle his Putter

American golfer Ky Laffoon enjoyed a love-hate relationship with his clubs, especially his putter. If the putter behaved itself and holed a thirty-footer, Laffoon would caress its shaft lovingly; but if it let him down, he could be quite cruel and show little regard for its sensitivity.

After one missed putt, he was seen trying to strangle it. When that failed, he attempted to drown the poor implement – not by hurling it into a lake but by actually holding it down under water! Finally, he decided that a suitable punishment was to attach it with string to the bumper of his car and allow it to bruise itself on the tarmac as he drove to the next tournament.

On another occasion, he angrily broke his putter by smashing it against his foot. Unfortunately, the impact also broke his own toe.

To a certain extent, the exasperation experienced by Laffoon, who played in the 1935 Ryder Cup, was perfectly understandable. His putter did have a habit of making him look foolish. On the final green at a minor tournament in North Carolina, he was three feet from the hole with two putts for victory. His first effort hit the rim of the hole, leaving him a tap-in of no more than two inches. Before you could say 'Doug Sanders', he had somehow missed again. In frustration, he thumped the wretched putter down on top of the ball, propelling it two feet into the air and straight down into the hole. Sadly for Laffoon's career, the Royal and Ancient would undoubtedly have frowned upon any attempt to adopt such an unorthodox putting stroke.

Ky Laffoon was an unusual character all round. He started his career in golf by caddying for the legendary hustler Titanic Thompson, and was nicknamed 'The Chief' because it was thought that he was part Red Indian. In fact he had no Indian blood, but went along with the story because he considered it to be good publicity. He used to chew tobacco during a round, but if this was meant to calm his temper, it failed miserably: he was prone to all manner of impulsive behaviour. Apart from the confrontations with his putter, perhaps his finest hour was when he scratched from the Western Open because the car park was too far from the clubhouse.

Chi Chi's Cha-Cha

Born in Puerto Rico in 1935 and named after his childhood baseball idol Chi Chi Flores, the colourful Chi Chi Rodriguez had a style of play which delighted the crowds but sometimes infuriated his fellow professionals.

His fans, who were known as Chi Chi's Bandidos, worshipped his every move. They loved the way he chatted and joked with the gallery, how he whistled jauntily while walking between holes, and above all, the bizarre ritual he went through whenever he sank a long putt. He would flourish the putter like a rapier before sheathing it flamboyantly into his golf bag. If it was a birdie putt he would go several steps further, bowing elaborately to the crowd, placing his ever-present straw hat over the hole to prevent the ball from escaping and then dancing a cha-cha around it. The choreography was as good as the putt.

Little surprise then that in his younger days, Rodriguez was christened 'the clown prince of the US tour'. But some of his playing partners found his antics distracting and referred to him instead as 'the four-stroke penalty', the number of shots they reckoned he cost them on each round. Arnold Palmer and Jack Nicklaus advised him to tone down his on-course behaviour, which he did to a certain extent but not enough to pacify the notoriously volatile Dave Hill. Partnering

Rodriguez in the 1970 Kemper Open, Hill had to be restrained from hitting him at the end of the tournament. For a moment, there was a grave danger that Chi Chi's cha-cha would be slowed to a funeral march.

The Man Who Ate a Golf Ball

In his younger days, American golfer Andy Bean developed a taste for snacking on golf balls and wrestling alligators. He might have been better advised to swap things around.

The golf ball incident took place after he had seen his Florida University team lose to Wake Forest University. Bean was sitting at the wheel of his car, waiting to drive a team-mate to the airport, when he suddenly decided it would be a smart idea to sink his teeth into the cover of a golf ball. Biting off a large chunk, he handed it out of the window and told his friend: 'Here, take it. I've eaten my last golf ball. I'm going off the diet.'

If that brought about a puzzled reaction, it was nothing compared to Bean's next adventure. Playing in the pro qualifying school, he spotted a seven-foot alligator which had come out of a lake on the course to sun itself. Alligators posed no threat to Bean – he had been used to seeing them all his life – and so he strolled over to the reptile and grabbed its tail. The alligator instantly slid back into the water while Bean's horrified opponent beat a hasty retreat in the opposite direction. Thereafter, Bean was known as the alligator wrestler and by the time the story had reached the nineteenth hole, he was supposed to have swung the creature round his head three times and danced a tango with it. It's a shame to spoil a good yarn.

The Postman Who Played in the Open

Examination of the qualifying-round scores for the 1965 British Open shows one name firmly anchored to the bottom, way behind the rest of the competitors. The bare facts are that Walter Danecki (US) had rounds of 108 and 113 for a total of 221 – eighty-one over par. But behind these scores lies an extraordinary tale.

For forty-three-year-old Walter Danecki had never been a member of any golf club or even a driving range. His golfing experience consisted solely of seven years' playing on municipal courses in his native Milwaukee, for which he paid $1.50 a round. But what he lacked in ability, he tried to compensate for in self-belief. Despite never having had a golf lesson in his life, he was supremely confident that he could beat Arnold Palmer. In an attempt to fulfil his dream, he tried to join the US PGA tour and was genuinely aggrieved to be told that he would first have to serve a five-year apprenticeship.

However, he managed to get hold of an entry form for the British Open and when it came to the space where he had to indicate 'amateur' or 'professional', he took the plunge and wrote 'professional'. Then, taking part of his annual leave from his job at the Post Office, he secretly travelled to Britain for qualifying. None of his workmates had the faintest idea that he had even left the country, let alone that he was competing in the Open.

The fairytale ended the moment Danecki picked up a golf club in anger. After posting a first-round 108 over the par-70 course at Hillside, Southport, he fared even worse the following day, recording 113 at Southport and Ainsdale. He missed the qualifying mark by no fewer than seventy strokes.

As news of his feat emerged, Danecki discussed his rounds in time-honoured tradition with disbelieving reporters. Asked how he had enjoyed links golf, he replied straight-faced: 'Well, I guess your small British ball helped me some. If I'd had to play the big ball, I'd have been all over the place.'

Danecki, who thought he might have fared better but for a sore right hand, was also asked why he had lied on the entry form. 'Because I wanted that crock of gold. My conscience made me write down "professional". But, he was quick to add by way of explanation,

'I don't charge if I give a lesson . . .'

Defiant to the last, Danecki reiterated his vow to get on the PGA tour: 'What I'll do is win one of the big ones. Then they'll have to let me in.' Thirty-two years on, they're still waiting.

The Knight of the Links

On St George's Day, 23 April 1912, singer and actor Harry Dearth played nine holes of Bushey Hall Golf Club in Hertfordshire . . . wearing a full suit of armour. Dearth had worn the armour on stage when taking the role of St George in a production of *The Crown of India*, and now, for a wager, he lumbered onto the golf course in it. The only concession was that he didn't have to wear the visor. His opponent, a Graham Margetson, was dressed in more conventional golfing attire; but despite the heavy metal handicap, Dearth gave him a run for his money, only going down 2 and 1.

The Search for the Tin-can Safe

With 135 major tournament victories to his name, the great Sam Snead topped the world money-winning list on three occasions. But the more he earned, the more he wanted to keep, which led to the jibe that he was the first golfer to make a million – and save two.

The American harboured a deep mistrust of banks, and the rumour spread that he kept his cash in old tomato-soup tins buried in his front garden. Nobody knew whether or not to take the stories seriously but one night, a couple of his fellow professionals, who had been playing in a tournament not far from Snead's home, decided to find out for themselves. At the end of a heavy evening's drinking, they fetched a spade and set to work. Snead was woken from his slumbers by the barking of his dogs and when he peered out of the window, all he could see was two drunken figures digging up his lawn. Racing outside with a shotgun, he fired a couple of warning shots, causing the mystery intruders to flee before they could discover the truth about

Snead's underground vault. Years later, Snead was again asked about the tomato-soup can rumours. 'A damn lie,' he said, adding, 'I never used *tomato* cans.'

Snead's other pet obsession was his lack of hair, on account of which he always wore a straw hat on the golf course. At one time, he actually started walking on his hands in an effort to make his hair grow, because he had been told that it would make the blood rush to the scalp and stimulate the follicles. He was immensely proud of his fitness and at the annual dinner for previous winners, held on the eve of the US Masters at Augusta, he would make his entrance with a spectacular gymnastic back-flip so that he touched the top of the dining-room door with his foot. As a party-piece, it took some beating; but so did Sam Snead.

Golf On Ice

Golfers are known for their hardiness. It takes more than something as trivial as a hurricane, a monsoon or an earthquake to dissuade them from playing their beloved game. So missionary Dave Freeman had no qualms about setting up a course on the frozen waters of the Beaufort Sea in North Canada, a spot 400 miles inside the Arctic Circle where temperatures drop to below minus forty degrees Fahrenheit.

Freeman founded the nine-hole course in 1975. Each winter it has been staked out by Bill Josh, the base manager of the local airline at Victoria Island. The whole course is solid ice with the exception of the greens, which are layered with sand to prevent putts sliding off towards the North Pole. It is surely the only course in the world where polar bears constitute a natural hazard.

Old Thunder-Bolt

Playing with Tommy Bolt was always an experience never to be forgotten. For in addition to the usual bunkers and lakes, there was another hazard to beware of – flying golf clubs. Bolt, winner of the 1958 US Open and ten other tour events between 1953 and 1961, was blessed with a terrible temper and when things started to go wrong, he would hurl the offending club into the air in a fit of rage. Fellow American Jimmy Demaret reckoned that during one particularly fraught round, Bolt's putter had spent 'more time in the air than Lindberg'.

With Bolt, it wasn't a question of how many shots he would take, but how many clubs he would be left with. Approaching the eighteenth one day in Florida, he reputedly asked his caddie which club was required for a shot with a 220-yard carry over water. 'A six-iron,' replied the caddie wearily.

'A six-iron?' stormed Bolt. 'It's 240 yards to the flag. How can it be a six-iron?'

'Because that's all you have left in the bag.'

During the 1960 US Open at Cherry Hills in Denver, Colorado, Bolt hurled his driver into a lake. On another occasion, he had to pay a deep-sea diver $75 to retrieve the driver from the bottom of a canal. Yet despite his fiery temperament, he took time out to offer words of wisdom to youngsters who might be tempted to copy his behaviour. His advice was always to throw the clubs forward because it saves time having to retrace your steps . . .

Ironically, the PGA placed Bolt in charge of the tour's 'good conduct' committee. One of his first acts was to fine himself $100 for club-throwing.

Of course, Bolt didn't always toss his clubs around – sometimes he snapped them over his knee. A famous instance was after a heated Ryder Cup match in 1957 at Lindrick, Sheffield. In the singles, Bolt was drawn against the equally competitive Eric Brown. Sparks seemed sure to fly. As teeing-off time approached and there was no sign of the combatants, Jimmy Demaret remarked: 'They're out on the practice ground throwing clubs at each other at fifty paces.' It was meant as a joke . . . but only just. Brown won the match 4 and 3, a result which contributed to a historic British victory – the first for twenty-four years – and the two men exchanged angry words at the end of the contest. Back in the locker-room, Bolt took out his frustration on his wedge.

'Thunder-Bolt', as he was known, also landed in deep water after allegedly breaking wind loudly on the first tee of a tournament, apparently in protest at the introduction of a number of petty rules by the PGA. Reacting to the $25 fine he received, he complained: 'That was an air shot – I should only have lost one stroke.'

Golfing Superstitions

Jack Nicklaus always carries three pennies in his pocket and when he marks the ball, he always does it with the tails-side up. Tom Weiskopf adopts a similar tactic, always carrying around three dimes in his pocket. Naturally enough, Hubert Green always wears green in a tournament.

Severiano Ballesteros would not dream of playing in a competitive event with a ball marked number three, because he says it encourages him to three-putt. And when Gary Player opens a brand-new box of golf balls, he immediately removes all the odd-numbered balls and plays with only the even-numbered ones.

Mad Max

Max Faulkner was arguably Britain's most eccentric professional golfer. In the grey days of the 1950s, he lit up tournaments with his bright, even gaudy, outfits and fascinated experts with the curious contents of his golf bag.

His finest hour was winning the 1951 British Open at Portrush. He was certainly confident of winning, and it is said that after only the second round he was already signing autographs as the Open champion. For the final round, he wore canary yellow plus-twos with matching shoes and socks, and a blue-and-white striped shirt. He must have dazzled his rivals into submission.

Faulkner had a bag full of weird and wonderful clubs. He was particularly fond of putters and had a collection of around 300, many of which were home-made, including one which he had assembled using the shaft of a billiard cue. He liked to experiment with other clubs too, making subtle alterations here and there, the result being that he rarely played with what could be termed a conventional set.

He certainly created an impression wherever he played. The late Henry Cotton said of him: 'He always was mad. I once saw Max play the greatest nine holes you've ever seen. He then decided to entertain the crowd by walking the fifty yards to the next tee on his hands. He never hit another shot – he'd pulled all his shoulder muscles.'

A Golf Addict

Jake Engel, a sixty-four-year-old retired store manager from Oklahoma, loves playing golf. In 1996 he broke the world record for the number of holes played in a year, and this year he is aiming to do even better.

Engel played 10,076 holes in 1996, beating the previous record set by Ollie Bowers in South Carolina twenty-seven years earlier by just one hole. What made the achievement all the more remarkable was that Engel only began his bid in March – hence his confidence that there is more to come.

He said: 'I normally play about 400 rounds a year but when I heard about the world record, I decided to go for it and I really started rather late. I didn't realize how hard it would be – but I refused to give up.'

Most of his rounds were played on the same public course near his home. His effort included one marathon performance during which he played three rounds in one day and was halfway through a fourth when forced to call a halt by an inconsiderate thunderstorm. During the record attempt, he wore out five pairs of shoes and two bags, and his handicap soared from eight to seventeen because his scores varied between 72 and 103.

He admits: 'There are times when I ask myself why I am doing this. But I just get on and do it.'

Perhaps the least surprising thing about Jake Engel is that he is divorced.

Breaking and Entering

Victory in the 1936 British Open at Hoylake went to the host nation's Alf Padgham, but only after he had endured a nightmare start to the final day's play.

For reasons best known to himself, Padgham had left his clubs in the professional's shop overnight but had seemingly failed to ascertain whether anyone would be around to open up the shop in the morning. Thirty-six holes were to be played on that final day, necessitating an early start, but when Padgham arrived ready to tee-off, he discovered to his horror that his clubs were still locked away – and nobody had a key. Worried that a late start would result in disqualification, he chose to take the law into his own hands. He picked up a brick, smashed the window and retrieved his clubs.

The story had a happy ending, for Padgham recorded two rounds of 71 to take the title by one stroke. It is not known whether he was ever sent a bill for the broken window.

Things Go Better With Coke

Canadian golfer Moe Norman liked to make the game interesting. He enjoyed nothing more than a challenge,which probably explains why he once drove off in the Los Angeles Open using a Coca-Cola bottle. In another event, he landed on the eighteenth green and had three putts to win. It was all too easy, too boring, so he deliberately putted into a bunker and got down from there in two more strokes to secure the victory!

No mean golfer (he won the Canadian PGA in 1966 and 1974), Norman specialized in collecting course records and at one time held around thirty in the United States and Canada. He delighted in the unconventional. As a leading amateur in Canada, he caused raised eyebrows by insisting on carrying his own bag, instead of using a caddie. And when playing in tournaments away from his Toronto home, he would often prefer to sleep in the back of his car rather than in a hotel. The back of the car probably reminded him of home, for he lived like a hermit in one room without a telephone.

Usually he didn't take things seriously enough – during tournaments, he would often make side bets with spectators as to the outcome of a particular shot – but once he went to the other extreme. He was right up among the leaders in the US Masters when he received a tip from Byron Nelson. So convinced was Norman that the tip would improve his game that he went straight out on the practice range after play and hit hundreds of shots. Alas, he overdid it and the following morning woke up too stiff and swollen to swing a club, which forced him to retire from the tournament.

An Unusual Lie

During the first round of the 1974 English Amateur Championship at Moortown, Leeds, Nigel Denham achieved the curious feat of playing from the nineteenth hole to the eighteenth. It happened when Denham, hitting his second shot to the eighteenth, hooked it towards the clubhouse situated at the back of the green. The ball bounced on the concrete path which ran between the clubhouse and the green, up the steps, hit the framework of the open French windows and came to rest on the carpet in the middle of the bar, where two dozen members were enjoying a leisurely lunchtime drink.

At that time, the Moortown clubhouse was not ruled out of bounds and Denham, a Yorkshire county player, knew that if he declared the ball to be unplayable, he would incur a one-stroke penalty. So he weighed up the options to see whether he could play it from the carpet.

First, he was obliged to remove his golf shoes – no spikes were allowed in the bar – and his caddie had to wait outside on the steps, since caddies with clubs were also barred from entering. A gallery of drinkers formed around the ball, which was nestling on the freshly-cleaned carpet some thirty yards from the flag. 'It's an Axminster lie,' said one, 'just perfect for a pitch shot.'

After much deliberation, Denham asked for the clubhouse window to be opened so that he could play a wedge through a 4ft-by-2ft gap, down the slope and, hopefully, onto the green. Those sitting by the window were asked to move and other drinkers were requested to clear a path to the pin. The sober ones thought he had taken leave of his senses.

Hush descended on the bar as Denham took a few practice swings and then chipped the ball neatly through the open window and onto the green. To roars of approval from the crowd, it finished twelve feet from the hole. Perhaps overcome with the excitement of it all, Denham missed the putt and ended up with a round of 74.

The incident prompted the Moortown committee, perhaps fearful of further Dunlop 65s in their gin and tonics, to rule the clubhouse out of bounds in future. And the Royal and Ancient put a dampener on things by decreeing that Denham should not have been allowed to open the bar window. They said that by doing so, he had improved his line of play and should have been penalized two strokes.

Soldiering On

In 1914, one JN Farrar accepted a bet that he could complete eighteen holes at Royston Golf Club, Hertfordshire, in under 100. Nothing unusual in that – except that Mr Farrar was required to play carrying full infantry marching equipment including rifle, haversack, field kit and water bottle. He managed to overcome the unwieldy load and shoot 94 to win the wager.

The Crane Driver from Barrow

The exploits of Walter Danecki in trying to qualify for the British Open inspired rabbit golfers everywhere. Suddenly the humblest Sunday morning player entertained grandiose visions of rubbing shoulders with the likes of Palmer, Nicklaus and Player. In 1976, it was the turn of a forty-six-year-old crane driver from Barrow-in-Furness to hit the headlines as he took the Open by storm.

Maurice Flitcroft had never previously played a full eighteen holes of golf. He was not a member of any club and had only taken up the game eighteen months previously. Even then his practice was confined to the beach, which should at least have enabled him to master the art of bunker shots. Scarcely able to tame a crazy-golf course let alone the windswept links of Formby, Flitcroft returned a score of 121 in the first qualifying round of the Open. The championship committee were so appalled that he had been allowed to slip through the net that they refunded the £30 entry fees to the two unfortunates drawn to play with him.

Flitcroft went out in 61 and came back in 60, a score which included a traumatic 11 at the tenth. Although a mite disappointed at his performance, he saw definite grounds for optimism: 'I've made a lot of progress in the last few months and I'm sorry I did not do better. I was trying too hard at the beginning but began to put things together at the end of the round.'

The indomitable Flitcroft tried again in 1983, this time masquerading as a Swiss professional by the name of Gerald Hoppy. Playing in the qualifying round for the Open at Pleasington, he got as far as the ninth hole, by which time he had already taken sixty-three strokes. At that point, R and A officials, smelling a rat, caught up with him and suggested that Herr Hoppy might care to retire. Flitcroft lamented: 'Everything was going well and according to plan until I five-putted the second.'

The Monkey Tournament

The Atlanta Women's Golf Association organized a most peculiar contest in February 1927 – one where the clubs were selected by drawing lots rather than by personal choice. Whenever a shot was about to be played, the competitor would reach into a hat and pick out a piece of paper nominating the club to be used. This resulted in some strange sights. Players were seen trying to hole putts with a driver while, conversely, one woman had the misfortune to be forced to drive off at three holes with a putter.

The nine-hole event, called the Monkey Tournament, had other unique rules which were not exactly in keeping with the spirit of golf. Played between two teams, it permitted the participants to distract their opponents at the vital moment by crashing tin cans together, sounding loud blasts on police whistles or simply jumping up and down screaming – in short, the sort of behaviour which would earn a life ban from St Andrews. Players were also allowed to take practice shots right next to the game itself, just as their opponents put club to ball. In fact, the only activity to be frowned upon was touching either an opponent or an opponent's ball.

For the record, the match was between teams captained by Mrs Clarence Bradley and Mrs TT Williams. The former won by 76 strokes to 90.

Barnes-Stormer

The son-in-law of Max Faulkner, British Ryder Cup player Brian Barnes seemed to do his best to attain the same heights of eccentricity. Some of Barnes's actions were a result of his drink problem. A self-confessed former alcoholic, he used to have three or four brandies with his morning coffee before play. Then, on the course, he would carry around a litre bottle with a mixture of two-thirds vodka and one-third orange juice. When winning the 1981 Scottish Professional Championship at Dalmahoy, he actually marked his ball on the eighteenth green with a beer can.

Despite the continual presence of a soothing pipe (at the US Masters he once played bunker shots with his pipe still gripped between his teeth), Barnes could be a temperamental fellow. Nowhere was this better illustrated than at the 1968 French Open at St Cloud, where he twelve-putted at one hole from barely three feet! Playing the second round, he had taken three shots to the eighth and was left with a putt of less than a yard. But when he missed the putt, he began angrily stabbing at the ball while it was still moving . . . over and over again. While the ball stubbornly refused to drop into the hole, he also incurred a penalty for standing astride the line of a putt. The result was that a further twelve shots were added to his total, making a disastrous fifteen for the hole.

In hot weather, Barnes would stand out from the rest of the field by sometimes playing tournaments in shorts. He strongly opposed slow play and once took a folding chair to a tournament so that he could sit down and rest between shots. As one scribe noted: 'If he had taken a table, a silver service and a buffet lunch with him, nobody would have been surprised.'

The Golfer Who Went Round in One Shot

Eighteen-handicapper Neville Rowlandson claimed to have completed a round in just one stroke after his wayward tee shot at the first dropped into the eighteenth hole.

Playing in a monthly competition at Felixstowe Ferry Golf Club, Suffolk, in March 1996, Mr Rowlandson, a fifty-six-year-old lorry driver from nearby Trimley St Martin, saw his drive at the 428-yard par-four opening hole hit a yellow wooden marker sign ten yards in front of the tee, ricochet away at an angle, bounce twenty-five yards before striking the flag on the adjacent eighteenth green, and then drop neatly into the hole.

Mr Rowlandson and his two playing partners burst out laughing as he claimed that since the course has a par of 72, he had gone round in 71 under par. 'I wanted to draw the ball down the right-hand side of the fairway with my new driver,' he explained later. 'I was a bit upset when it hit the marker.'

While Mr Rowlandson bought drinks all round at the clubhouse – the traditional way of celebrating a hole-in-one – the *Guinness Book of Records* expressed doubts as to the validity of the claim for the world's lowest golf score. A spokesman said: 'This man is welcome to apply to us, but I do not think our editors will accept it – unless he can prove that his ball also went into the other seventeen holes.'

A Stone's Throw From the Hole

Along with her friend Emmeline Pankhurst, Dame Ethel Smyth was a fervent activist for women's rights in the early years of the century. Dame Ethel was also a keen golfer who played regularly at Woking GC in Surrey, so when the suffragettes were orchestrating a window-smashing campaign in 1910, where better for her and Mrs Pankhurst to practise than on the thirteenth fairway at Woking? By the time they left the course, so perfect was their aim that shortly afterwards they both ended up in Holloway Prison for breaking Government windows.

Dame Ethel also believed in golfers' rights and was quite prepared to waive the rules if it suited her needs. Once when she lost her ball in dense heather at Woking, she sent for the greenkeeper to bring out a scythe and cut down the vegetation in order that she might continue with her round.

The One-Hole Tournament

Unique in the golfing calendar is the Elfego Baca tournament, staged in New Mexico – for it consists of just one hole. The tee is set on the top of Socorro Peak, 7243ft above sea level. The hole, a patch of dirt 60ft in diameter, is two and a half miles away and 2500ft below. The competition was first staged in 1969 and the course record stands at eleven, held by Mike Stanley.

Not Toogood

A letter in the *Daily Mail* sparked an unusual golfing challenge in 1912. The correspondent expressed the view that, contrary to most experts who said it was essential for players to keep their eyes on the ball, the single most important factor in striking the ball successfully was to keep one's head still. The letter went so far as to state that provided the stance and swing were correct, it wouldn't matter whether the player was blindfolded.

The temptation to put this principle to the test was too great to resist and so Alf Toogood, professional at the Chelsea Golf School, donned a handkerchief blindfold to take on amateur Mr A Tindal Atkinson at Sunningdale. It quickly became apparent that there was precious little substance to the theory. The professional, deprived of his vision, struggled miserably. He nearly decapitated a photographer on the first and four-putted on the second. Indeed, it was Toogood's putting which was especially erratic, the ball frequently straying yards off line. It was a merciful relief when the match finished, the amateur running out the comfortable victor by 8 and 7.

The Golfer Who played in a Coat

The pride and joy of Joe Ezar, a professional of Armenian-American extraction, was a luxurious camel-hair coat. Ezar valued the garment so highly that he refused to leave it in the locker-room during tournaments, lest it be stolen. Instead, he used to wear it on the course, draped over his shoulders. On particularly cold days, he would play the entire round wearing the coat; on warmer occasions, he would hand it to his caddie before each shot.

Taking a break during the 1936 Italian Open at Sestriere, high in the mountains above Turin, Ezar bet the president of the Fiat motor company that he would shoot a course-record 64 the next day. Since the course record at the time stood at 68, this represented a sufficiently awesome task to persuade the businessman to offer Ezar the sum of 40,000 lire should he be successful. To add yet more spice to the proceedings, Ezar wrote down the score which he proposed to take on each hole. As Ezar adjourned to the bar, Henry Cotton, who was also competing in the tournament, told him that he was mad.

The next morning, Ezar, feeling somewhat delicate from the excesses of the night before, announced his intention to play the record-breaking round in his coat; but his caddie, who stood to lose money if the bid failed, urged him to compromise and only wear it between shots. Sense prevailed and Ezar set about burning up the course. He holed impossible putts, chipped in from hopeless situations and, just as he had predicted, went round in 64. Furthermore, all of his score forecasts were correct except for two holes. A poor tee-shot caused him to take four instead of three on the ninth, but the loss was rectified immediately when he conjured up an improbable birdie three at the tenth. Cotton, a witness to the amazing chain of events, said: 'You could call that round the biggest fluke of all time. He had all the luck in the world, but the fact is that he did it.'

Lucky Dip

After winning the Danny Thomas Classic in June 1981, American Jerry Pate celebrated by diving fully-clothed into the water hazard next to the eighteenth green.

Golf By Moonlight

In 1876, David Strath won a bet by completing eighteen holes of St Andrews at night in less than 100. Guided only by moonlight, he went round in 95 . . . without losing a ball.

Another nocturnal creature was Rufus Stewart, the professional at Kooyonga, Adelaide. In 1931, he played his home course at night and, using nothing more than a torch shone by a friend, went round in 77 strokes in just an hour and three-quarters. He too needed just the one ball.

Up A Gumtree

A number of golfers have odd traits on the course, but few were as consistent as Arnold Palmer's habit of constantly hitching up his trousers. During one tournament, a specially-hired trouser-watcher counted no fewer than 345 hitches.

Palmer explained: 'When I was young, my hips were always sort of narrow and my pants had a tendency to slide down. My mother was always on at me, saying: "Arnold, tuck your shirt-tail in!" So in order to please her, I started pulling 'em up all the time. I've done it so long now that I'm totally unconscious of even doing it.'

He had to be particularly careful that his trousers weren't at half-mast during the 1964 Wills Masters at Melbourne. For that was the occasion when his second shot on the Victoria Golf Club's ninth hole came to rest 25ft above ground in the fork of a red gumtree. Rather than incur a penalty stroke, Palmer climbed the tree with the help of a policeman and played a reverse shot with a one-iron while balanced precariously on a branch. To the cheers of the gallery, he managed to hit the ball 10ft-clear of the tree.

What Did You Do in the War, Harry?

American professional Harry Gonder decided that achieving a hole-in-one was merely a matter of perseverance. So one day in 1940, armed with two witnesses and a supply of caddies to tee up and retrieve balls, he embarked on an endurance test to see how long it would take him to get an ace on a 160-yard hole. He reasoned that for a golfer of his calibre, it should take a couple of hours at the most. He was a mite optimistic.

Ball after ball he hit towards the flag. His eighty-sixth attempt finished just fifteen inches short, but generally he was having difficulty finding his range. As the hours ticked by, Gonder started to feel hungry and after 941 balls he stopped for refreshment in the hope that it would improve his fortunes. The ploy nearly worked, for his 996th shot hit the pin and bounced three inches away. At 8.10pm, his 1162nd stopped six inches short and, beginning by now to get into his stride, he missed with his 1184th by just three inches.

It was a false dawn. As the church bells struck midnight, Gonder struck his 1600th ball. Like most of its predecessors, it finished nowhere near the target. By now, fatigue was beginning to set in and a nasty blister had appeared on his hand. Still he battled on, and was nearly rewarded twice in the space of a few minutes. His 1750th shot hit the pin, as did the 1756th which ended up no more than an inch from the hole. That seemed to convince Gonder that it was simply not his day – or night. So at 2.40am, 16 hours and 25 minutes after he first teed off, Gonder's 1817th shot finished ten feet from the flag – and he gave up.

The Waggling Count

Count John de Bendern had a style all of his own on the golf course. The 1932 British Amateur champion suffered, in the words of Bernard Darwin, 'from the waggling disease in its most exaggerated form'.

Aside from the extraordinary body-gyrations which made his swing a spectacle to behold, the Count had very much his own way of dealing with an awkward lie. Playing the thirteenth in the US Masters at Augusta, he saw his ball come to rest on the sloping bank of a brook. Realizing that his stance would necessitate putting one foot in the brook itself, he took off his right shoe and sock and rolled up his trousers. After practising his swing a couple of times on the top of the bank, he settled into his stance and promptly placed his bare right foot on the grassy slope – and his left foot, which was still in its shoe, in the water!

The Even-tempered Golfer

Sam Snead described American Clayton Heafner as 'the most even-tempered golfer I ever saw. He was mad all the time.'

Heafner, a former army sergeant from North Carolina who played in the 1949 and 1951 Ryder Cups, was a formidable adversary, weighing in at around fifteen stone. He would flare up at the slightest thing and walked out of tournaments on more than one occasion. Even the mispronunciation of his name by the starter was sufficient a crime for Heafner to storm off the first tee.

Another starter incurred his wrath by referring to a shot out of a tree which Heafner had been forced to play in the corresponding event the previous year. Heafner was furious about the reminder and decided that there was to be no risk of a repeat performance. So he marched off the tee, threw his clubs in his car and, before even hitting a ball in anger, drove out of the event in a cloud of dust.

A Peculiar Wardrobe

The most flamboyant player on the US tour today is Payne Stewart, who chooses to publicize the sport of American football by invariably wearing a cap, plus-fours and knee-length socks in the colours of one of the NFL teams. Stewart possesses a whole wardrobe of such outfits but in the final round of a tournament, he likes to wear the colours of the local team.

The Imposter at the US Open

Possibly a direct descendant of Walter Danecki and Maurice Flitcroft, seven-handicapper Barry Bremen made his mark by infiltrating the 1980 US Open at Baltusrol. Bremen managed to convince Open officials that he was Chuck Moran, a bona-fide competitor, and as such, took a courtesy car to the course, played on the practice range, chatted with his fellow 'professionals' and even had his photograph taken with Jack Nicklaus. Bremen did not join the action until the fourth hole, where he teamed up with Jim Thorpe and Bobby Nichols and succeeded in playing through to the end of the round before his ruse was uncovered.

How To Deal With Slow Play

American Dick Mayer was only too aware of the reputation for slow play of his fellow countryman Cary Middlecoff. So when the pair faced a head-to-head in the play-off for the 1957 US Open, Mayer was taking no chances. He took with him onto the course a camping stool, and proceeded to sit down on it in the middle of the fairway while his opponent agonized over every shot. Sometimes these preparations lasted so long that Mayer must have wished he had brought out a sleeping bag instead. The condemnation of his playing style seemed to unsettle Middlecoff, who finished up taking 79 to Mayer's 72.

Speed Test

In November 1971, Australian Ian Colston played a total of 401 holes in twenty-four hours at Bendigo Golf Club. Wearing a singlet and shorts, he boosted his tally by sprinting between holes and was assisted at night by friends who lit up the course with their car headlights.

Texan Tantrums

Texan golfer Lefty Stackhouse was so angry when he hooked his drive that he punished himself – by throwing himself into a thorn hedge. Although his hands were reduced to a bloody pulp, he refused all offers of help. Sometimes he decided that a wayward shot was not necessarily his fault and took out his frustration on his clubs instead. Once, he was seen thrashing a whole set of clubs into pieces against a tree stump!

Fairway to Heaven

In Scotland, where golf is almost a religion anyway, a new movement aims to bring players closer to God when they find themselves trapped in bunkers or waist-deep in heather. The Findhorn Foundation of Moray has launched a programme entitled 'Fairway to Heaven' which, for a week's tuition-fee of £550, claims to 'bring body, mind and spirit into harmony'. One of the movement's guiding lights, John Talbott, says he has been moved by the spiritual aspect of golf since the age of twelve. Among those who have been lecturing at the Foundation is David Icke. . .

Walter Hagen – The Showman Supreme

Walter Hagen was the first professional golfer to make a million, and he was determined to have the lifestyle to match. One of his favourite sayings was: 'I don't want to die a millionaire, just to live like one.' In the 1920s, when most golfers played in drab tweeds, Hagen took to the course in monogrammed silk shirts, flannel trousers and two-tone shoes. He was sartorially elegant to the point of vanity and did not think it at all unusual to change his entire outfit between two rounds on the same day. He was not only the first player to make a fortune from the game, he was also golf's first great showman.

With his hectic social life, Hagen often arrived on the first tee of a tournament straight from an all-night party. One New Year's Day, he was due to play in an exhibition match at Pasadena with tee-off at 10am. This was by no means an early start by golfing standards, but it was too early for Hagen after a night of New Year's revelry. To his credit, he turned up on time, albeit still wearing a dinner jacket and patent-leather pumps, having not had time to change after the party. Thus attired, he took his driver from the bag and prepared to tee off. With slippery-soled shoes, this was easier said than done and he began sliding in all directions, needing several attempts before even making contact with the ball. After his second shot, he wisely opted to change into spikes and more conventional clothes.

Hagen did everything in style, travelling to tournaments in a chauffeur-driven limousine. Rarely prone to bouts of humility, he was known to rebel against what he saw as petty officialdom, a trait exemplified by his behaviour on his first trip to England in 1920, to compete at the British Open at Deal. He was appalled to discover that, as a professional, he was not permitted to enter the clubhouse; so each day, he arranged for his hired limousine to be parked in front of the clubhouse and ordered champagne to be sent to him there. In a further attempt to undermine the Deal committee, at lunch his chauffeur would open a hamper in the boot for Hagen to tuck into a sumptuous repast.

Three years later, Hagen had another run-in with British officials, this time at the Open at Troon where professionals were not only barred from the clubhouse, they were not even allowed at the back door to collect their mail. Hagen's anger at the injustice led him to sabotage the prize-giving at the end of the tournament. Disregarding the cost, he took the unprecedented step of inviting the entire gallery back to the nearest public house for a drink. Nobody was going to turn down a free drink, least of all one bought for them by Walter Hagen, and so, to a man, they trooped off to the hostelry, leaving the committee with hardly a soul to witness their cherished ceremony.

Hagen continued to enjoy life to the full. His philosophy was: 'Never hurry, never worry, and don't forget to stop and smell the roses on the way.' He was at ease in any company, the more exalted the better. It is difficult to think of any other player who would have treated the Prince of Wales, the future king Edward VIII, with the same familiarity as Hagen did. Playing a round together, Hagen would ask him: 'Eddie – hold the flag, will you?'

Hagen's immense self-confidence did not endear him to everyone on the professional circuit. In the 1940 US PGA Championship at Hershey, Pennsylvania, Hagen was due to meet Vic Ghezzi in a second-round match (the competition was matchplay in those days), but at the appointed time there was no sign of the maestro. Ghezzi marched into the clubhouse, where his fury was intensified by the sight of Hagen sitting casually at the bar drinking scotch. Hagen dismissed Ghezzi with instructions to set off without him, adding that he would join in at the third. However, an official informed Hagen that the rules did not allow him to concede the first two holes just because he felt like it and that unless he began the match straight away, he would be disqualified. So Hagen downed his scotch and ambled over to the first tee. By now, Ghezzi's blood was boiling at Hagen's condescending attitude, which constituted a huge insult to a fellow professional, but despite winning the first two holes, Ghezzi lost 2 and 1. Hagen himself went out in the third round and never again played in the championships. It was not exactly his first brush with the event. In 1922, he had refused to defend his PGA title because of exhibition engagements.

Exhibition and trickshot events became an increasing part of Hagen's life, partly because they paid good money but also because they were fun. Among his regular partners was the Australian Joe Kirkwood, who won his native country's Open championship in his early twenties before moving to the United States at the end of the First World War. Kirkwood was a trickshot specialist. He could play with one arm or standing on one leg, but his most famous shot saw him tee-up two balls and, with a seven-iron, hit them simultaneously in such a way that one hooked and the other sliced, causing them to cross in mid-air! Kirkwood and Hagen regularly stayed at a New York hotel prior to exhibitions in the city. To relieve the boredom, they would hit golf balls out of the hotel window in the direction of people walking in Central Park below. When this pastime failed to provide the necessary stimulation, they would head out of the hotel and walk several blocks, each armed with a club and a ball. Then they would have a race to see who could play his way fastest back to the hotel, a course which took them through the hotel lobby, up the elevator, across their room and finally into their toilet bowl, which served as a hole. To Hagen's irritation, Kirkwood always won – because whilst Hagen was usually first into the room, he could never chip the ball into the toilet. For his part, Kirkwood never missed.

One of Hagen's great rivals from the 1920s was Leo Diegel, a golfer famed for an unorthodox putting style whereby his elbows protruded like wings. Diegel's death upset Hagen, and to prepare himself for the ordeal of the funeral, Hagen had a few too many drinks. The result was that he inadvertently led Kirkwood into the wrong church. The pair sat through most of the service before realizing they were at someone else's funeral. They finally caught up with the right party at the cemetery, where Hagen told the minister he would like a word with Diegel. Hagen knocked gently on the coffin. 'You in there, Leo?' he said tearfully. 'See you soon, old buddy.' Then a thought entered his head. 'How in hell did they get you in there anyway, with your arms stuck out?'

The High Court

The golfing encounter between the legal eagles of the Middle and Inner Temples was always a keenly-contested affair. But in September 1994, few were prepared for the sight of a fifty-seven-year-old Appeal Court judge clambering onto the Woking clubhouse roof to play his team's next shot.

The judge, Sir Simon Brown, was partnering Nigel Wilkinson, QC, when the latter's wayward shot landed on the clubhouse roof. Consulting the local rules, Sir Simon ascertained that the ball was still in bounds and so, with the aid of a ladder, he made his way up. Deciding that the tarmac lie called for a putter, he proceeded to play a clever shot to within a few feet of the pin. Given such heroics, the Middle Temple pair undoubtedly considered it a gross injustice that they eventually lost the match.

The Golfer Who Got The Bird

Putting on the seventeenth green at Bethesda Congressional Country Club, Maryland, in May 1979, Dr Sherman A Thomas, a sixty-six-year-old physician, was halfway through his backswing when a nearby Canadian goose honked loudly, as if to suggest that the ball would miss to the left. Suitably distracted, the doctor did miss the putt – but not the bird. In a fit of pique, he chased the goose and felled it with a blow to the head (although it is not recorded which club he selected for the task). Up before the local beak, Dr Thomas, a member at the club for thirty years, was fined $500 for killing a goose out of season, the federal magistrate giving short shrift to the medical man's rather limp claim that the goose had been wounded by his approach shot and that he was merely putting it out of its misery.

A Dickensian Character

W T Linskill was described by many who saw him as the perfect embodiment of Mr Pickwick. A portly man with a drooping moustache, he wore uncommonly high spats and used to drive from King's Cross to Wimbledon Common in a splendid four-in-hand coach, complete with guard and post-horn.

His twin fascinations were ghosts and golf, and as he was a ghost-story author of some note, it comes as no surprise to discover that he was convinced St Andrews was haunted. He claimed to have introduced golf to Cambridge in 1873 and also founded a club at Colden Common, Hampshire, but unfortunately forgot to take into account the nearby glue-works, the poisonous smell from which made the playing of the far holes on the course virtually impossible.

Possibly in the hope of spotting the odd ghost, Linskill was particularly fond of playing golf at night and used to indulge in moonlight matches at St Andrews with the likes of Young Tom Morris. The routine was to play two rounds on the ladies' putting course, with dinner taken in between and with candles placed in the holes. This fine character died in 1929, aged seventy-four.

Holed Out With An Umbrella

After missing two simple putts at the fourteenth at the Oakmont Country Club in 1919, American golfer Chick Evans was so angry with himself that he holed out with the handle of his umbrella. The US Open champion of 1916, Evans only carried seven irons and woods in his bag, but made up for this by carrying four putters because his work on the green tended to be somewhat erratic.

Bizarre Local Rules

Among the more unusual local rules at golf clubs throughout the world are the following: a drop without penalty should the ball come to rest adjacent to a rattlesnake (Arizona); a free drop if the ball lies in the immediate vicinity of a crocodile (Uganda); and a free drop should the ball finish up within six feet of a new-born lamb (Rakauroa Club, New Zealand). The Duke of Windsor once took advantage of a local rule at the Jinja Club in Uganda which permitted the ball to be lifted without penalty from a hippopotamus footprint.

The Man Who Destroyed a Bunker

Norman von Nida, a distinguished Australian professional of the post-war period, sometimes struggled to come to terms with the British climate. On very cold days, he was even known to play in an overcoat. Von Nida, whose custom was to wear a black beret on the course, once lost his temper in dramatic fashion during a tournament in England. Having taken a number of shots to get out of an awkward bunker, he vented his anger on the lump of turf which created the overhang. In fact, he decided to remove it and temporarily abandoned his round while he hacked away at the grassy mound with a variety of clubs. He was then seen furtively carrying the pieces off to nearby bushes and depositing them in a place where they could do no further harm. When later challenged about his destruction of the bunker, von Nida insisted that he was merely 'tidying it up'.

Haunted By Schoolboy Cheating

For twenty years, Brett Robbins was haunted by the memory of the day he cheated to help his American college team win a runners-up trophy. But in 1996, the thirty-five-year-old decided he could no longer live with the lie and wrote to the Idaho Schools Athletic Association to confess all.

His misdemeanour occurred in 1976 when, having taken a bogey four at a short hole, he put his score down as three, thereby helping Pocatello High School to finish second by one stroke. Eye-witnesses claimed he had taken a four, but Robbins steadfastly denied it . . . until last year, when his conscience finally got the better of him.

Since the sensational revelation which shocked the world of sport, Robbins has understandably gone to ground. But there was good news for him when tournament officials decided that he would not be penalized. Instead, it was decreed that the runners-up trophy be shared between Pocatello High and the school which originally finished third.

Bill Young, director of the schools association, said: 'There's no reason now to punish Brett's college after all this time. We teach kids to do the right thing. This sets a great example to stand up and be honest, no matter how long it takes.'

In the wake of the disclosure, expect further schoolboy confessions along the lines of: 'NIGEL MANSELL: THE DAY I FORGOT TO HAND IN MY DINNER-TICKET.'

Too Busy For Play-Off

As a gifted amateur, England's Roger Wethered did not play golf with the same intensity as his professional counterparts. Thus when he tied for the 1921 British Open with American Jock Hutchinson at St Andrews, he expressed grave doubts as to whether he would be able to stay for the thirty-six hole play-off because he had promised to turn out for his village cricket team in England!

In the end, he managed to combine both engagements, but the travelling took its toll as he lost the Open play-off by nine strokes.

That completed a fairly miserable tournament for Wethered. For a play-off would not have been necessary but for an unfortunate incident during the third round when Wethered, studying his shot to the fourteenth green, walked backwards and trod on his ball, thereby incurring a one-stroke penalty. As it turned out, that 'shot' deprived him of the Open title.

A Winter Wonderland

Every March, the Norwegian town of Hemsedal, 136 miles north of Oslo, stages its annual winter golf tournament on a course manufactured out of snow.

It takes 900 man-hours to convert the deep snowfields into a nine-hole course. To make the fairways and greens (or whites), the snow is first compacted by piste bashers, more usually to be seen preparing ski slopes. The flattened snow is then stamped down by human feet and skis, and a chemical compound, snow cement, is added to make the surface hard. A machine is borrowed from the local ice-rink to smooth the ice for the greens, but players are permitted to remove any loose lumps of snow from the putting areas. However, the 'rough' is left untreated and in parts the snow can be as much as two feet deep.

The tournament is played over two days with red or yellow golf balls. Naturally, some of the rules are slightly different from conventional golf. For example, teeing is allowed on the fairway, and ice and snow are not deemed casual water.

An Expensive Round

In May 1973, Rick Sorenson accepted a bet to play eighteen holes blindfolded at Meadowbrook Golf Club, Minneapolis. The rules of the engagement stipulated that he had to pay $10 for every hole he completed in a score over par and would receive $100 for every hole he did in par or better. He went round in 86, ending up $70 worse off.

A Costly Celebration

Diminutive Scottish golfer Bobby Cruickshank was overcome with relief when, competing in the 1934 Merion Open, he saw his ball hit a lakeside rock and bounce onto the green instead of plunging into the water hazard. In fact, he was so overjoyed that he hurled his club into the air in an act of spontaneous celebration. Alas, he forgot to remember the basic principle that what goes up must come down, and he was still rooted to the spot when his club descended from the skies onto his head. Despite being badly dazed, he managed to continue and finish joint third.

The Four-Legged Caddie

After a birdie and an eagle, a new creature has entered golfing vocabulary at Cherwell Edge Golf Club in Oxfordshire – a llama. Club professional Joe Kingston has discovered that Henry the llama makes an ideal caddie. Not only is Henry used to carrying heavy loads (so a bag of clubs is no inconvenience), his soft padded hooves do not damage the precious turf.

Once the round is over, Henry even pops into the clubhouse for a well-earned drink and some sugar. And there's no danger of him depositing natural hazards all over the greens. 'Henry's very well behaved,' says his owner Mary Pryse. 'We know if he wants to go to the loo – he starts humming. It's what llamas do if they are uncomfortable.'

The Two-Hour Hole

No chapter on golfing eccentrics would be complete without a mention of the admirable Maud McInnes who, playing in the qualifying round of the 1912 Shawnee Invitational for Ladies at Shawnee-on-Delaware, Pennsylvania, succeeded in taking 166 strokes for the 130-yard par-three sixteenth.

Her problems began when she drove her tee shot into the Binniekill River and the ball floated downstream. Not to be denied, she clambered into a boat and, with her husband manning the oars, set off in pursuit of her ball. Eventually, one and a half miles down the river, her spouse dutifully keeping score, she managed to beach the ball on terra firma. Unfortunately, the journey back to the sixteenth green from such an unusual approach necessitated playing through a dense wood. This did little for her score, and it was 165 shots and nearly two hours after driving off that she finally holed out. It is not known whether she qualified for the next stage of the tournament.

A similar fate befell Ray Ainsley in the 1938 US Open at Cherry Hills, although the end result was marginally less catastrophic. Playing the par-four sixteenth, he looked on aghast as his ball pitched in a shallow but fast-flowing creek near the green. He could see the ball, but getting it out onto dry land was more problematic, particularly as it was racing further and further downstream and away from the hole by the second. After a series of unsuccessful attempts at playing the submerged ball, his prayers were answered when it came to rest on a dry patch of ground, thereby enabling him to play out onto the fairway. He eventually holed out for a round-wrecking nineteen, only to discover that he could have saved himself a lot of trouble (and about fourteen shots) simply by taking a penalty stroke in the first place. When asked by puzzled officials why he hadn't done so, Ainsley said that he thought he had to play the ball where it lay.

A Drenching For The Mayor

For some weeks in the autumn of 1996, Mike Osley, the greenkeeper at a municipal course in Tallahassee, Florida, suspected that someone was sneaking onto the fairways before opening time to play a few practice shots. Although warnings were issued, the trespasser persisted; so one morning, Osley decided to teach him a lesson he would not forget in a hurry – he waited until the figure emerged from the gloom and then switched on all of the water sprinklers.

Unfortunately for Osley, the mystery golfer was the mayor of Tallahassee, Ron Weaver, who lived next to the course. Soaked to the skin, he was not amused and had the greenkeeper suspended for a week without pay. However, local residents were so angry at such an injustice that they held a collection to make up Osley's lost wages and the mayor was obliged to apologize.

Bringing The Catwalk to the Golf Course

'I think there is no more beautiful place in the world than a green golf course, and I want to dress for it.' These were the words of Texan golfer Jimmy Demaret, the Beau Brummel of the links, whose outfits used to grow more outrageous as the tournament progressed. For example, during the 1949 Ryder Cup in England he started off in a 'scarlet cap, salmon-pink sweater and cerise slacks' before changing into a 'chartreuse shirt, peach and purple suede shoes, violet and lemon argyles, green slacks and a Dutch baker-boy cap in raspberry and turquoise plaid.' At least there was no danger of losing him in the rough.

Demaret said that the clothes most golfers wore in tournaments 'made the place look like a funeral parlour', so he set about rectifying the situation by having his own shirts and slacks specially made from rolls of colourful, lightweight cloth which he had discovered in New York. Among his outfits was a 'golf tuxedo', made without armpit seams to allow for a free swing.

It has been said of Demaret that he practised less and had more fun than any other great player. He certainly enjoyed nothing more than partying all night, and in the 1930s, when he was sponsored by a bandleader and a Galveston nightclub owner, he used to tour the clubs singing for his sponsors in his spare time.

The Human Tee

Casual visitors to Esher Golf Club, Surrey, in November 1931 would have been alarmed by the sight of a player driving off at each hole from a human tee. For a challenge match with amateur Mr C Mansell, young professional George Ashdown persuaded nurse Ena Shaw to lie on the ground and have a large rubber tee strapped to her forehead with an elastic band. The ball was then placed on the tee and Miss Shaw said silent prayers as Ashdown brought the club down to within a few inches of her face.

Ashdown's superior status necessitated the concession of a stroke at each hole to Mr Mansell (who was using a conventional tee) but Ashdown still managed to win 7 and 5. Although Miss Shaw was said to have given a nerveless performance, doubtless she was quite relieved that the match did not go the full eighteen holes.

Self-Discipline

Bob Goalby was another of those Americans with a fiery temperament. On one memorable occasion, he was so disgusted with a shot that he threw himself, fully clothed, into a water hazard! At the 1968 Los Angeles Open it was the slow play of his partners that caused him to simmer with resentment. Hole after hole, he had to wait for them, until finally he could take no more. So he simply abandoned them mid-course and went off and finished the round alone.

6 Boxing

The Magnificant Screwball

Max Baer could never take himself, his opponent, or boxing in general seriously. Blessed with undoubted talent, he would surely have worn the world heavyweight crown for much longer than a year but for his tendency to skip training and clown around in the ring. Ultimately, he was a victim of his own eccentricity.

Baer is said to have taken up boxing after knocking a farm labourer through a shop door – the unsuspecting fellow had made disparaging remarks about Baer's girlfriend. Realizing that he could harness his punching power in a more profitable way, Baer took his first steps on the road to glory. He loved the fame which went with being a professional boxer, and with that recognition came scores of female fans. He couldn't resist any of them, and spent a fortune while getting engaged to a seemingly endless succession of chorus girls, actresses and beauty queens. He made Georgie Best look like a trappist monk.

Although of German Catholic extraction, Baer tried to cash in on the Jewish market by wearing the Star of David on his trunks. His trainer Ray Arcel eventually settled the dispute over Baer's ethnic background with the comment: 'I seen the guy in the shower, and believe me, he ain't Jewish!'

Baer became a true crowd-pleaser. Even at the height of a fight he would play to the audience, turning to the front row and grinning whenever he was hit by a hard punch. The press dubbed him 'The

163

Magnificent Screwball' and Baer himself candidly admitted: 'I've got a million-dollar body and a ten-cent brain.'

On 14 June 1934, he stepped into the ring in New York for a title fight with Italy's Primo Carnera, the 'Ambling Alp'. Baer wore the same dressing-gown that he had when starring as Steve Morgan in the 1933 movie *The Prizefighter and the Lady* – a film in which he was seen boxing Carnera. The gown still had 'STEVE MORGAN' in large letters on the back. To Baer, this fight was pure showbusiness.

It was also a farce. The ungainly Carnera had no answer to Baer, who began fooling around safe in the knowledge that, barring a disaster, the title would be his. At one point, as the pair fell to the canvas together, Baer grinned at the defending champion and said: 'Last one up is a rotten egg.' Baer even found time to pluck at the hairs on Carnera's chest, and at the start of round ten he walked over to the Italian's corner and shuffled his feet in his resin box, as Carnera looked on bewildered. By now, Carnera hardly had the strength to stand up and when Baer feinted to throw a punch, the Italian literally fell for it, going down without a blow being landed. Baer himself almost fell over laughing. Carnera was finally put out of his misery in the eleventh round when Baer floored him for the eleventh and last time. Max Baer was the new Heavyweight Champion of the World.

Having been able to joke his way through one title fight, Baer thought he could do it through them all. In 1935, he was set to defend his title against James J Braddock. Nobody outside of Braddock's camp gave the challenger a chance – indeed, it was subsequently claimed that an ambulance was standing by at the ringside ready to rush Braddock off to hospital. Baer certainly treated his opponent with disdain. He didn't train properly for the fight, preferring instead to dedicate his time to the unholy trinity, wine, women and song. Once in the ring, Baer soon started his clowning. He pretended to be hurt and acted punch-drunk. But Braddock hadn't read the script. He wasn't taken in by Baer, and as the champion's lack of preparation began to show and he tired visibly, Braddock took command to win on points. Baer's brief reign at the top was over.

Despite his fall from grace, Baer stayed in the limelight. It was the only lifestyle he knew. Even as a referee, he remained the consummate showman. In November 1959, after refereeing the fight between Zora Folley and Alonzo Johnson, he exited the ring by vaulting over the top rope. Maybe it was a stunt too far, because a few days later he suffered a fatal heart-attack at the Hollywood Roosevelt Hotel. When he collapsed, a bellboy asked if he wanted to see the house doctor. Unable to resist a crack, Baer gasped: 'I'd rather see a people doctor.' Those were his last words.

The Barefoot Title Fight

The 1954 world bantamweight title fight between the champion, Australian southpaw Jimmy Carruthers, and Chamrern Songkitrat of Thailand was staged in an outdoor stadium in Thailand. It was a night of torrential rain and the boxers kept slipping in the pools of water which had formed on the canvas. Just when it seemed that the bout would have to be abandoned, both men agreed to discard their boots and socks and fight on barefooted. Defying the elements, they continued to slug it out right up until the final bell, at which Carruthers was declared the winner on points. But he hardly emerged unscathed from the fiasco, suffering bad cuts over both eyes – injuries which forced him to retire from boxing just two weeks later.

An Unusual Sparring Partner

Cornishman Bob Fitzsimmons, who between 1891 and 1905 was world champion at three different weights (middleweight, heavyweight and light-heavyweight), kept a curious pet at his training camp – a fully-grown lion. By all accounts, boxer and lion got on famously until one day the lion escaped and caused havoc in the camp. As people fled for their lives, it is said that Fitzsimmons walked up to the lion and knocked the beast out cold with a single punch to the jaw. We are told that the lion bore no malice and that afterwards, the king of the jungle and the king of the ring returned to being the best of buddies.

Muhammad Ali – The Greatest

Considered by many experts to have been the greatest boxer of all time, Muhammad Ali was also one of the sport's most eccentric performers in and out of the ring, especially in his earlier incarnation as Cassius Clay.

He first captured the public's imagination by predicting in poetry how, and in which round, he would beat opponents. Before his 1962 contest with the veteran Archie Moore, Clay trilled:

> *'When you come to the fight*
> *Don't block the halls*
> *And don't block the door*
> *For y'all may go home*
> *After round four.'*

Clay was as good as his word – Moore did indeed fall in round four. His next fight was against Doug Jones, and once again, Clay attempted to forecast the outcome in rhyme:

> *'Jones likes to mix*
> *So I'll let it go to six.*
> *If he talks jive*
> *I'll cut it to five.*
> *And if he talks some more*
> *I'll cut it to four.'*

In this instance, Clay's prediction let him down. Jones was only outpointed at the end of the full ten rounds, but Clay was unrepentant. He told reporters: 'First I said six, then I said four. Six and four is ten, and the fight went ten, so I called it right again!'

February 1964 saw his world heavyweight title fight with the formidable Sonny Liston, whom Clay christened 'The Ugly Bear'. In the build-up to the fight, Clay talked about what he called the 'bear-hunting season' and taunted Liston with jibes like: 'You so ugly that when you cry, the tears run down the back of your head.' The scene at the weigh-in was sheer pandemonium. Clay danced around, screaming and yelling at his opponent, a performance which he later maintained was merely designed to upset Liston. But Alexander

Robbins, the Miami Boxing Commission doctor, was not so sure. As Clay had to be restrained and forced to sit down, Dr Robbins found his blood pressure to be so abnormal that he wanted to postpone the fight. 'Clay's acting like a man scared to death,' he said. 'He is emotionally unbalanced, liable to crack up before he enters the ring.' Subsequent events showed that Clay was in control of the situation, for when Liston failed to get off his stool at the start of the seventh round, Clay captured the heavyweight crown.

Changing his name to Muhammad Ali, the champion transferred his eccentric behaviour into the ring. At Houston in February 1967, he cruelly tormented Ernie Terrell for fifteen rounds, refusing to knock him out although there was plenty of opportunity to do so. Ali wanted to make Terrell suffer for refusing to call him by his new name, and every time Ali got him on the ropes he would scream at Terrell, 'What's my name? What's my name?' He dished out similar treatment to former champion Floyd Patterson.

But perhaps Ali's most bizarre fight was the famous 'Rumble in the Jungle' in Zaire in October 1974 against George Foreman. At the time, Foreman was considered invincible while Ali, who had been forced to relinquish his title for refusing to join the US Army, was thought to be way past his sell-by date. Ali spent most of the fight backing off and sliding along the ropes, not giving Foreman the room to land any effective blows. And when Foreman did connect, the supporting ropes helped take the impetus from his punches (Ali later referred to this as his 'rope-a-dope' technique). Eventually, Foreman flagged in the heat and the fresher Ali, who had scarcely thrown a punch in anger, was able to step up a gear. In the eighth round, it was all over. Foreman was knocked out and Ali regained his title.

Four years later, Ali was to recapture the world heavyweight title for a second time, the only man ever to have done so. His little ring-dance, the Ali shuffle, was a trifle more laboured than in his heyday but he remained the sport's most charismatic figure.

Dressed For The Wrong Sport

When Irishman John McConnell turned up to fight Charley Davis for the English middleweight title in London in 1873, he discovered that the bag containing his ring gear had vanished. A lengthy delay ensued while substitute garments were produced until, to the vast amusement of the crowd, McConnell entered the ring wearing an old pair of cricketing trousers that had been made for a man at least a foot shorter and about a foot wider. If this was not handicap enough, McConnell also had no ice in his corner. As he floundered around the ring trying to hitch his trousers up, all the while sweating buckets, it was little wonder that the verdict went to his opponent.

Boxing by Numbers

American middleweight Gene Fullmer had a novel way of outwitting opponents in the ring – he often fought by numbers, delivering the combinations called out to him by his manager from the ringside. Fullmer, who retired in 1964, two years after losing his world title to Dick Tiger, was also a practising Mormon and always gave ten per cent of his earnings to the church.

The Champion With One Eye

Boxers didn't come much dirtier than Harry Greb. The American's favourite ploy was the thumb in his opponent's eye, but it was a case of the biter bit in 1921 when Kid Norfolk got his retaliation in first, leaving Greb permanently blind in his right eye.

Most fighters would have called it a day, but incredibly Greb went on to have ninety-two bouts with just one eye and somehow rose to the dizzy heights of world middleweight champion.

A veritable ladies' man who wore a beautiful silk gown, had his hair parted immaculately down the middle and whose face was heavily powdered, Greb's training methods were far from conventional and the 'training' usually took place in bordellos and nightclubs. He was rumoured to have had sex in his dressing-room immediately before fights and once had to overcome the attempts of a gang of Ohio gamblers to chloroform him. They partly succeeded, but he managed to recover in the half-hour or so before the fight and went on to win the bout, thereby wrecking the syndicate's scheme. He feared nobody, and once threatened to throw referee Marvin Hart bodily out of the ring.

In 1923, the one-eyed Greb (only he knew of his impediment) challenged Johnny Wilson for the world middleweight title. During the build-up to the fight, Greb decided to lull Wilson into a false sense of security by feigning drunkenness. Every night after training, he visited New York speakeasies where he drank like the proverbial fish before staggering out hours later in what appeared to be an alcoholic daze. Word got back to Wilson that his opponent was drinking himself into oblivion and was so hopelessly unfit that victory for the champion would be little more than a formality. What Wilson didn't know was that Greb's performance was one big act and that his glass had always been filled with water, not gin.

Wilson swallowed the bait and lost the title on points. In round six, presumably in an effort to put Wilson on an equal footing with himself, Greb resorted to his usual tactic of thumbing his opponent in the eye. When the referee demanded to know what Greb thought he was doing, Greb snapped: 'Sticking my thumb in his eye. What does it look like?'

Greb surrendered his crown to Tiger Flowers in 1926. In that same year, he finally had his right eye removed and replaced with a glass substitute. However, not long afterwards, he was involved in a car accident which damaged his nose. Fearful of losing his good looks, he went into hospital to undergo minor plastic surgery, but in the course of the operation he suffered a fatal heart-attack. After everything Harry Greb had been through, it seemed such a tame way to die.

Singalong-a-Rinty

Win or lose, after every fight, Belfast flyweight Rinty Monaghan used to serenade the crowd over the ring microphone with a rendition of 'When Irish Eyes Are Smiling'. In fairness, he had more to sing about than most, retiring in 1950 as the undefeated world champion, having held the title for three years.

The Groom Wore Boxing Trunks

Irish-American middleweight Ken Overlin dedicated his life to boxing, so much so that he even got married in the ring. A career which saw him crowned world champion in 1940 began when he was seventeen years old, in 1927, and shortly afterwards he got engaged to one Madeline Smith. He decided to make the wedding one to remember and, under special licence, the ceremony was performed in the ring before Overlin's bout with Spike Webb in Virginia. The groom wore boxing shorts and ring shoes, and his opponent was best man! It was probably one of the few occasions when the groom and the best man were trading punches minutes after the wedding.

A Reformed Character

The champion bare-fist fighter of all England, William 'Bendigo' Thompson (1811-80) was so famous that he had a drink, a racehorse and a town in Australia named after him. An unruly ruffian both in and out of the ring, Thompson was the least likely person to find solace in the Lord, yet in his later years he became haunted by a mad preacher known as 'Undaunted Dick', whom he claimed pursued him everywhere like a Victorian Spiny Norman.

Thompson hailed from Nottinghamshire and was one of twenty-one children. His mother, a fearsome woman who possessed a ferocious right hook and smoked a pipe, nicknamed her triplets Shadrack, Meshack and Abednego. The latter was shortened to

'Bendigo' and a legend was born.

Backed by his supporters, a bunch of thugs who called themselves the 'Nottingham Lambs', Thompson became a formidable adversary. Never was the term 'a wolf in sheep's clothing' more appropriate. When he wasn't in jail for some act of violence, Thompson was taking on all-comers and in 1839 became English champion when the holder, James 'Deaf' Burke (who in one fight had been returned to consciousness by his seconds biting his ear), was disqualified for butting.

Having taken everything that any fighter could throw at him, Thompson contrived to injure his knee while performing somersaults to entertain children, and announced his retirement. But his domineering mother was having none of it and forced him to fight again. When he did eventually call it a day, he had suffered only one defeat, and that was on a foul. The surprise was not that he had been guilty of committing an illegal act in the ring but that any referee had been brave enough to disqualify him.

Thompson continued to divide his time equally in and out of prison, but it was during his twenty-eighth and final jail-sentence (for drunken brawling) that he suddenly saw the error of his ways. Moved by the sermons of the prison chaplain, on his release Thompson joined a religious sect, the Good Templars, where he became friendly with a hell, fire and brimstone preacher, Dick Weaver, more commonly known as 'Undaunted Dick'. Thompson began to feel haunted by the omnipresent Dick. He claimed Dick peered at him through the windows of public houses, and when Thompson gallantly saved a woman from drowning, he emerged from the water to find Dick watching him like a ghostly conscience.

The converted Thompson started to spread the word across the land, using first-hand experience to preach against the evils of drink. As he was illiterate, he was obliged to learn his speeches parrot-fashion. It is reassuring to learn that within the new man, there were still traces of the old Bendigo. At a meeting in Birmingham, he was halfway through his sermon when he was upset by a group of hecklers. Quietly asking for 'five minutes to himself', he descended the rostrum and promptly laid out four of the men who had dared to interrupt him . . .

Self-Inflicted Knockout

Before a fight, Daniel Caruso liked to psyche himself up by pounding his gloves into his own face. Preparing for his bout in the New York Golden Gloves championships in January 1992, he went into his usual routine prior to the introductions but overdid it somewhat and scored a direct hit with one punch, breaking and bloodying his own nose. Doctors examined him and ruled that he was unfit to box.

Sugar's Sweetheart

When the United States' Sugar Ray Leonard won the Olympic light-welterweight gold in 1976 at the expense of Cuba's Andres Aldama, he wore photographs of his girlfriend and their two-year-old son pinned to his socks.

The Monocled Mutineer

By no stretch of the imagination has Chris Eubank ever conformed to the stereotypical image of a boxer. Stressing his most valued asset as brain rather than brawn, Eubank eschews the usual T-shirt and jeans in favour of tailored tweed jackets and monocle. With his distinctive lisp, the air conjured up is that of an eccentric country squire.

The Brighton-based Eubank has courted controversy throughout his career. He has antagonized the boxing world with his arrogance and lack of respect towards opponents. Before his successful WBO middleweight title fight with Nigel Benn in November 1990, Eubank stated: 'What we have here is a competent, intellectual boxer against the shallow-minded puncher. I may just decide to stand back and play with him before I maul him.' After his victory, Eubank proposed to his girlfriend from the ring.

The gesture was typical of his showmanship. He used to make a grand entrance to the strains of Tina Turner's 'Simply the Best' and would vault into the ring over the top rope. Then he liked to indulge in a session of statuesque posturing and posing, strutting around the ring and showing off his muscles like a bodybuilder. It was all calculated to instil a feeling of inferiority into his opponent.

Eubank has made no bones about the fact that the only reason he fought was for the money. Indeed, he was quite happy to bite the hand that fed him, describing boxing as 'barbaric'. Popularity has never been high on his agenda. He once admitted: 'I don't have friends. I'm a natural psychologist. If a psychologist has friends, he can't be very good.' In years to come, whenever the name of Chris Eubank is mentioned, feelings will run high as to exactly how good he was or whether he was just a novelty act.

A No-Action Fight

Bare-fist fighters were renowned for punching each other to a standstill in a frenzy of non-stop action. But there is always an exception to the rule and it was provided by Jim Mace and Joe Coburn, who met in a bare-fist contest in Canada towards the end of the last century. Right from the start, neither fighter showed the remotest interest in hitting his opponent and both steadfastly refused to launch an attack. Instead, they just stood opposite one another for 1 hour 17 minutes until the fight was finally called off without either man having thrown a punch.

The Champion Who Was Knocked Out
by a Woman

John L Sullivan, the 'Boston Strong Boy', held the world heavyweight title from 1882 to 1892. During that time, he earned a reputation for being able to withstand the hardest of punches . . . which makes it all the more remarkable that when he was finally knocked out for the first time, it was by a woman!

By 1892, Sullivan was just about the most famous boxer in the world. Supplementing his title fights, he toured the theatres of the

United States in exhibition sparring-contests which proved extremely popular with the crowds. Among his advisers was one Charles Converse, who ran a boxing school in Worcester, Massachusetts. Converse was married to a woman by the name of Hessie Donahue, an imposing figure who, at her husband's suggestion, was brought in to spar with Sullivan to add a bit of fun to the roadshow.

Sullivan and Hessie Donahue came up with an act whereby the champion would insist that he could beat anybody in the audience and would offer money to anyone able to defeat him. He would then announce that he had been challenged by a woman, at which the ample form of Hessie would clamber into the ring in boxing gloves, blouse, flowing skirt, long stockings and bloomers.

The act went down well until one night, Sullivan made the mistake of not pulling his punches, with the result that he caught Hessie full in the face with one blow. Although her physical presence was such that her pride was hurt more than her cheekbone, she reacted angrily and, completely forgetting the script, lashed out with a right to the jaw, sending the world champion tumbling to the canvas where he remained stunned for the best part of a minute.

The knockdown became the talk of boxing and created such interest that Sullivan, realizing it was good for business, decided to keep it in the act. On 7 September 1892, he returned to the prizefighting ring for a serious fight, a title defence against James J Corbett, but in round twenty-one Sullivan was knocked out – for the first time by a man. Hessie Donahue had obviously softened him up . . .

The Fat Freak

American heavyweight Tony Galento didn't believe in conventional training methods – he preferred to train on beer and cigars in his New Jersey bar. This unusual diet caused more than a hint of obesity and earned him the less-than-complimentary nickname of the 'Fat Freak'. Remarkably, Galento scaled the heights of challenging for the world title; less surprisingly, it was a short-lived attempt, Joe Louis knocking him out in the fourth round of their fight in June 1939.

The Boxer Who Shot His Trainer

Born Stanislaus Kiecel in 1886, middleweight Stanley Ketchel went on to acquire the nickname of the 'Michigan Assassin'. He seemed determined to live up to the tag, and once shot his trainer in the leg for waking him in the middle of a nap.

Ketchel was no stranger to guns. As a teenager, he captured a murderer – and a $1,000 reward – by pretending to be dead after being shot at. A tough, hard-drinking womanizer, Ketchel had another brush with death when he fought Jack Johnson, who knocked him out with such force that two of Ketchel's front teeth were later found embedded in Johnson's glove. So severe were Ketchel's injuries thought to be that he was given the last rites by a priest before eventually regaining consciousness.

The respite was short. In 1910, when he was world champion, guns and women returned to haunt him and he was shot dead by a jealous love-rival.

Mother's day

Minna Wilson simply couldn't take any more as she watched her son Tony take a fearful third-round battering from Steve McCarthy during a light-heavyweight contest at Southampton in 1989. She decided that if her boy couldn't beat McCarthy, then she would.

So with Tony desperately trying to fend off further blows on the ropes, Mrs Wilson climbed into the ring, removed one of her high-heeled shoes and, to the delight of the crowd, began pummelling McCarthy around the head with it. The referee quickly intervened, but not before Mrs Wilson had inflicted considerably more damage than her son on the unfortunate McCarthy. Bleeding from a cut to the head, which he claimed was the result of Mrs Wilson's soft-shoe shuffle, McCarthy refused to box on, only to be disqualified for failing to continue with the fight. To the astonishment of the McCarthy camp, Wilson was declared the winner, but subsequently a re-match was ordered and this time Mrs Wilson was banned from attending.

An Unpredictable Fellow

Senegalese light-heavyweight Battling Siki led an existence which can only be described as colourful. As a fifteen-year-old in his native country, he was adopted by a prominent member of Paris society who brought him to the French capital as her toy boy and bestowed on him the name 'Louis Phal', in honour of what she considered to be his outstanding asset. He went on to win the *croix de guerre* for wiping out a machine-gun post single-handed.

Utilizing his fine physique, Siki turned to boxing but his reputation was merely that of a wild, crude brawler. Nevertheless, in 1922 he fought Frenchman Georges Carpentier for the world title. The outcome was supposed to have been pre-arranged, with Siki allowing himself to be knocked out in the fourth. But, deciding that Carpentier wasn't even putting up a good show, Siki changed his mind and instead felled the Frenchman in the sixth. All hell broke loose and Siki was mysteriously disqualified for tripping, only for further pandemonium to follow when the decision was reversed an hour later. Siki was the new champion.

As such, he demanded to be noticed. He took to parading through the streets of Paris with two lions on a leash, and if he felt he still wasn't receiving the attention which his status commanded, he would fire a pistol into the air, scattering passers-by. One authority which paid him a great deal of attention was the British Home Office. Perhaps not quite ready for lions being marched along Oxford Street, they branded him 'undesirable' and so he was forced to defend his title in Dublin where, on St Patrick's Day 1923, he was beaten by Mike McTigue. Two years later, Battling Siki's brief but turbulent life came to a sudden end when he was shot dead in New York.

7 Rugby

The New Zealand Cap

A shrewd tactician who developed into one of the pioneers of the fly-half position, Otago and New Zealand's Jimmy Duncan often played in a woollen cap, principally to conceal his rapidly-receding hairline. Inseparable as it was from Duncan's skull, the trademark headgear caused much merriment amongst players and spectators and became a prized trophy during a match. On the occasion when a New South Wales player succeeded in snatching the cap from Duncan's head, a huge cheer went up from the crowd.

Duncan, who won one international cap in 1903, was not averse to turning his hat to his advantage on the rugby field. Playing for Otago against Auckland in 1896, he sold a brilliant dummy by passing his cap to team-mate Fred Given. As the Auckland men converged on Given, Duncan ran through the gap with the ball to score the cheekiest of tries. He repeated the ruse in later years, but eventually opponents grew accustomed to his trickery.

His Country or His Wife

Many great sportsmen freely admit that they would not have achieved such a level of success without the support of their wives. French rugby union international Joe Anduran earned his moment of fame *despite* his wife.

Madame Anduran was never afraid to speak her mind, and made no exception when a delegation of French selectors pulled up in a taxi outside her husband's Paris art shop on 31 December 1909. They had just seen off the team to play Wales in Swansea the next day, but there were only fourteen players on board the train, the fifteenth having been detained in Bordeaux while completing military service. In desperation, the officials called on Anduran, a solid club player, and begged him to travel with them to Wales.

At first, Anduran thought it was some kind of a joke – it was his first hint of international recognition – but it was no laughing matter when he put the suggestion to his wife. Laying down the law, she stated quite categorically that there was no question of him going to Wales to play for his country – she had arranged for him to visit relatives the next day!

Sadly, there was not a fly on the wall to record the ensuing conversation but Anduran went to Swansea and won his first and last French cap in a 49-14 defeat. But if he thought the reception from the Welsh forwards was hostile, it was surely nothing compared to the one waiting for him when he got home.

Barefoot on the Park

Harry Garnett of Bradford and England (he won one cap in 1877) never wore boots when he played. A rugged forward who later became president of the Rugby Football Union, he preferred to tread carefully in bare feet.

Not altogether surprisingly, the trend failed to catch on, although Bob Scott, the Auckland full-back who won seventeen caps for New Zealand between 1946 and 1954, did entertain the crowds at charity matches by kicking goals with his bare feet. When Scott was younger, his family had not been able to afford to buy him a pair of boots, so in teenage rugby he was forced to play without any. He got it down to a fine art too, even managing to land barefoot goals from the halfway line.

The Camborne Colossus

They don't make them like Tommy Adams any more. The twenty-five-stone second-row forward for Cornish club Camborne is a throwback to a bygone age, to the days when the most important attributes for a rugby player were sheer physical size and drinking capacity.

Adams fits the bill on both counts. Although he denies that he is a dirty player, he can look after himself, a euphemism for behaviour which, from time to time, has landed him in hot water with referees. 'I was always picked on because of my size,' he protests, 'and every time it happened, I used to hit someone.'

Alas, he has not always been too selective in whom he has chosen to hit. Attempting to exact retribution, he once missed the opposition prop and broke the nose of his own hooker.

Adams does not believe in protective measures such as headbands, gumshields or painkillers. Nor is he a disciple of warming up, which he describes as 'prancing about before kick-off'. Instead, he opts for a match-day routine of hearty breakfast and massive lunch, preceded by a steady night's drinking: 'Just six or seven pints – just social, like.'

Given his girth, it comes as a surprise to learn that thirty-two-year-old Adams is a keen sevens player. However, it should be noted that the team he turns out for, Billie's Bulldozers, require their members to be over sixteen stone and to drink three pints between each round of matches. This presents no problem to Adams, who in the course of one tournament is rumoured to have downed thirty-eight pints of Guinness. This may, of course, be a slight exaggeration – but it would be wise not to contradict him.

High Drama

Widnes fan Alan Duffy wanted to leave his mark on Wembley when his team played there in the 1930 Rugby League Challenge Cup final against St Helens. So, shortly before kick-off, he made his way onto the pitch, scaled one of the uprights and planted his black-and-white cap at the very top of the post. His act of bravado certainly seemed to inspire Widnes, who ran out 10-3 winners.

Dress Optional

Franck Mesnel, the dashing French fly-half who made his international debut in 1986, used to encourage his team-mates at Racing Club to wear something unusual on the pitch. Several times they played in the French club final wearing bow-ties, whilst on other occasions the Racing Club backs took to the field in huge baggy pants and berets.

For Mesnel, there was method in his madness. He became synonymous with a pink bow-tie and when he started up his own range of sportswear, a bow-tie logo was stitched onto all of his garments.

The Hissing Mascot

Like most tourists, the Australian rugby union team which came to England in 1908 had their own mascot. But instead of a cuddly koala or a fluffy wallaby toy, they chose to bring with them a live carpet-snake by the name of Bertie. To get past customs, the serpent was smuggled into Britain wrapped around the body of one of the Australian players, but the enterprise turned out to be in vain because Bertie died before the first match of the tour against Devon.

It was later suggested that it was not the 12,000-mile voyage from Australia which led to Bertie's demise. Rather it was the fifteen minutes of being placed in such close proximity to eighteen stone of sweaty rugby flesh which probably proved too traumatic for him.

Never On a Sunday

South African flanker Paul Roos, the first Springbok captain, loved his rugby so much that he used to cycle a round trip of 140 miles each Saturday to get to Pretoria for a game. His dedication paid off in the shape of four international appearances between 1903 and 1906. Yet Roos, a schoolteacher by profession, flatly refused to have anything to do with rugby on a Sunday because he considered such an act to be sacrilege. In addition to not playing on the Sabbath, he would not even travel anywhere that day and repeatedly turned down the honour of being selected for any Western Province representative match where his journey would have to begin on a Sunday.

Stand-Offish

Twenty-six-year-old stand-off Jamie Kahakura was a popular newcomer with New Zealand rugby league club Whakaki. His team-mates liked him, although they did wonder why he always avoided leaping in the bath with them afterwards. Then, after playing in the Gisborne East Coast Competition in 1989, the true reason for Jamie's prudishness was revealed – and he was banned from playing because he was a woman.

Lost in the Translation

Officiating at the 1913 France-Scotland rugby union international in Paris, English referee John Baxter incurred the displeasure of a patriotic and volatile crowd with a string of incomprehensible decisions. Unfortunately, Mr Baxter's command of the French language was marginally worse than his command of the laws of rugby, with the result that he mistook the jeering which rang round the ground for applause. Acknowledging what he thought was his new-found popularity, he began smiling, waving and bowing to the crowd, actions which merely served to make the French spectators even more irate, since they were convinced that he was mocking them. In the circumstances, Mr Baxter could consider himself a shade fortunate to have escaped with his life.

One Trick Too Many

Scottish-born 'Barney' Armit played as a winger for Otago and New Zealand in the latter part of the last century. He was an elusive customer with a spectacular, crowd-pleasing trademark – that of hurdling prospective tacklers. As they crouched low to make the tackle, Armit would simply vault over them and hare off towards the line. The tactic brought him numerous tries, but eventually cost him his life.

The tragedy occurred on 26 August 1899. Playing for Otago against Taranaki, Armit attempted to hurdle Alf Bayly in his usual fashion. But as Armit sailed over the top, Bayly rose and caught his heel. Armit crashed to the ground and broke his neck, dying eleven weeks later in Dunedin Hospital. Bayly was so upset by the incident that he gave up the game shortly afterwards.

The Golden Oldies Festival

First held in Auckland in 1979, the Golden Oldies rugby festival proved a tremendous success, attracting in the region of 500 players, all over the age of thirty-five. By 1983, when the festival was staged in Sydney, more than 5,000 players from sixteen countries converged on the Australian city, consuming over 28,000 cans of beer on the first day alone. With a motto of 'Fun, Friendship and Fraternity', the festival is all about enjoyment. Indeed, the pace of the game is usually considerably slower than the socializing. Teams boast such evocative names as The Gangreens, The Toothless Wonders and The Horny Derelicts, and participants have been as old as ninety. To protect the most senior of citizens from flying tackles by youths of forty-five, each player wears a certain colour of shorts to denote his age. For example, any man in a gold pair is over eighty and must be handled with appropriate care.

Wife Invades Pitch

Following what is referred to in popular parlance as a domestic dispute, Mrs Christine Kenyon marched onto the pitch during the 1989 fixture between Aretians Thirds and Bristol Saracens to remonstrate bitterly with one of the players, her husband Mike. Receiving no satisfaction, she then deposited his kit bag and pet dog at his feet. While the other twenty-nine players looked on in wonderment, the referee decided to take firm action and ordered the two humans and one canine to the touchline. One spectator said of Mrs Kenyon's intervention: 'These days it's not often you get a woman invading the pitch with her clothes on.'

Slaves To fashion

Irish international Basil Maclear, who was capped eleven times between 1905 and 1907, liked to cut a dash on the field and frequently played in expensive white calfskin gloves. And against Wales, he once made a further fashion statement by donning military puttees.

A contemporary of Maclear's who also relished the opportunity to wear inappropriate attire on the rugby field was the New Zealand full-back Billy Wallace. On the 1905 tour to England, he scored a try against Cornwall while wearing a sun hat.

Busman's Holiday

Australian rugby league player Jack Raynor, a member of the party which visited England in 1948, was a policeman and whilst on tour set about collecting as many British truncheons as possible to take home as souvenirs.

A Journey To Remember

One Saturday lunchtime in 1930, England hooker Sam Tucker was tidying the desk at his Bristol office in readiness to go home when he received a telephone call from Sydney Cooper, secretary of the RFU. Front-row forward Henry Rew had apparently fallen off his motorbike and would therefore not be fit to play in that afternoon's international in Cardiff. Cooper wanted to know whether Tucker would be able to take Rew's place in the England line-up, and so began one of the most extraordinary journeys in the annals of rugby union.

Tucker was more than happy to try, but actually getting to Cardiff in time was easier said than done. The last train from Bristol had gone and, in the days before the Severn Bridge, the journey was too long by road. The only viable alternative was to fly from nearby Filton and so Tucker dashed to the airstrip. Arriving at 1.45pm, just seventy-five minutes before kick-off, he arranged for a small two-seater biplane to ferry him to Cardiff.

Tucker had never flown before, so the bumpy ride in an open cockpit was hardly the ideal preparation for a big match. To make matters worse, there was a thick layer of cloud and the pilot had to keep searching for a break so that he could find somewhere to land. Eventually, he managed to come down safely in a field. Not having the faintest idea where he was, Tucker jumped out of the plane and ran across the fields to the nearest road, where he hitched a lift to Cardiff on a coal truck.

He arrived at the ground at 2.30, but his problems weren't over yet. The sheer weight of the crowds made it impossible for him to get through, and it was only when he managed to convince a police inspector of the truth of his story that he was ushered in through a side entrance. Even then, he found himself on the wrong side of the pitch and was left with a frantic dash round the stands, finally reaching the England dressing-room with just five minutes to spare. The incredible journey was over.

In case Tucker hadn't made it in time, Norman Matthews of Bath had been drafted in as an emergency replacement. Tucker's arrival was Matthews' misfortune. England won 11-3 and by the end of the season, Tucker had been appointed captain. Matthews was never asked again to play for his country.

Playing on the Blind Side

DB Walkington, an Irish rugby player of the 1880s, was so short-sighted that he wore a monocle during matches. One scribe wrote of him: 'He is as good as he can be on a bright day, but in the dark his sight tells terribly against him.'

'Monkey' Gould

Arthur Gould, full-back and centre with Newport, was a stalwart of the Welsh team, winning twenty-seven caps from 1885 to 1897. He was an intrepid adventurer who earned the nickname of 'Monkey' for his remarkable agility at climbing trees and goalposts. Many a training session was marked by the sight of Gould perched on the crossbar, calling down to his team-mates. Gould was such a popular player that he was accorded the honour of a testimonial game which raised £400 for him, sufficient to buy a house. However, the payment caused him to be labelled a professional in some quarters and both Scotland and Ireland refused to play Wales in the 1896-97 season on account of it.

The Artful Dodger

A half-back with Batley in the 1880s, Herbert 'Dodger' Simms was one of rugby league's first real characters. His speciality was taking part in unusual challenges. In June 1889, he played and beat a team of nine brewery draymen single-handed, and shortly afterwards he accepted a bet to race a greyhound. Simms was given a twenty-yard start and made it to the finish line at exactly the same time as the dog.

The Codebreaker

Moss Keane was a giant of Irish rugby between 1974 and 1984, during which time he played in fifty-one internationals. He was a tireless forward, but he and his team-mates found themselves up against it when the mighty All Blacks came to Lansdowne Road in 1978. The Irish were consistently second-best in the lineouts and realized that their only chance of success was to baffle the New Zealanders with an indecipherable code of lineout calls. However, it has to be said that the visitors did receive help from an unexpected source when, following one complex lineout call from the Irish half-back, they heard Keane shout: 'Oh God, not to me again!'

A Night on the Tiles

In March 1994, Welsh rugby fan Steve Spiller sold the slates off the roof of his house in order to raise money for a ticket to the England-Wales game at Twickenham. He got £200 for the slates, covered his house in felt and set off for the match. His understanding wife Debbie said: 'He was determined to go, so I have to forgive him.' Whether Steve showed the same enthusiasm on the journey home is debatable: Wales lost 15-8.

Shotgun Wedding

The Irish rugby team of 1887 contained the Limerick forward John Macauley. He had been selected to play in the game against England but was dismayed to discover that he had used up all his annual leave from work. A quick glance at his conditions of employment revealed that the only circumstances in which he could be granted additional leave was for a honeymoon. So without a moment's hesitation, he proposed to his girlfriend and fixed the wedding date for the morning of the match. At the conclusion of the nuptials, Macauley and his new bride raced to the ground in time for him to take his place in the Irish line-up.

8 Athletics

The Olympic Quickstep

Having discovered that the sound of music enhanced his performance, Italian distance walker Ugo Frigerio set about ensuring that there was suitable accompaniment for the 3,000 metres walk at the 1920 Antwerp Olympics. Just before the start, he strode over to the middle of the stadium and handed the conductor of the band several pages of sheet music, with the request that it be played during the race. With the band calling the tune, Frigerio led throughout and eventually crossed the line twenty metres ahead of his nearest rival. The only lapse in his rhythm came in the closing stages when he paused momentarily to reprimand the band for not playing at the correct tempo.

The Runner Who Stopped Off For a Picnic

The 1912 Olympic marathon in Stockholm was run on a day of unbearably high temperatures. A number of competitors fell by the wayside, but none more bizarrely than Shinzo Kanaguri of Japan. As he struggled along in the intense heat, he spotted a family relaxing and enjoying a picnic in their roadside garden, a prospect which seemed considerably more appealing than that of running another ten miles. So he decided to gatecrash the picnic and was welcomed into the family gathering with open arms. Feeling refreshed, he concluded, however, that it was probably too late to rejoin the race and instead began the long journey back to his homeland. In doing so, he omitted to inform any Olympic officials and was thus considered a missing person until he arrived back safely in Japan.

A Handicap Start

The favourite for a 1980 marathon at Port Moresby, Papua New Guinea, was local runner Tau John Tokwepota, but his pre-race preparations received a setback when he woke on the morning of the race to find that his car had been stolen during the night. With the start about to take place from a point three miles away, most athletes would have stayed at home and read about the race in next day's papers, but the intrepid Tokwepota was not to be denied his place in the line-up. Running all the way to the start, he arrived 5min 18sec after the rest of the field had set off, yet somehow managed to make up the lost ground and win in a national record time of 2hr 39min 43sec.

The Man Who Never Spoke

A true Seneca Indian, Lewis Bennett was better known as the American distance runner Deerfoot. After some success in the United States, he came to England in 1861 where he achieved a great deal of publicity, chiefly for his unusual attire of wolfskin blanket, headband and eagle feather.

To add to the mystique, Deerfoot never uttered a word in public because his British promoter, George Martin, maintained that his client couldn't speak any English. It would seem that this was little more than a publicity stunt, because Deerfoot seemed to know enough to obtain a lucrative contract – unless, of course, Martin communicated with him via smoke signals.

A crowd of 4,000 flocked to see his first race in London, the *Sporting News* noting that 'his appearance caused a great rush to obtain a peek at him, as he stalked in stately manner, with his wolf skin wrapped around him, looking the very model of one of Fenimore Cooper's Mohicans or Pawnees.' Despite the interest in Deerfoot, some expressed reservations about the legality of his races and in 1863 he returned to the US under a cloud.

A Late Developer

At a time of life when most people are enjoying a gentle retirement, American Ruth Rothfarb took up marathon running. She was a mere seventy-two when she first took up athletics in 1973, but it was another eight years before she made her marathon debut at the ripe old age of eighty.

Yet she was a veritable youngster compared to the Greek runner Dimitris Iordanidis, who was ninety-eight when he ran from Marathon to Athens in the Popular marathon of 1976. His time was 7hr 33min.

The Hurdling Waiter

Guernsey-born Percy Hodge, who won Olympic gold in 1920 in the 3,000 metres steeplechase, possessed a most extraordinary hurdling style. Displaying perfect balance, he was able to hurdle in an upright position and often demonstrated this technique at sports meetings and exhibitions by hurdling while carrying a tray of glasses.

That Hodge reached the 1920 Olympics at all was due to a remarkable performance in the qualifying event, the AAA steeplechase. His chances seemed to have been wrecked on the second lap when he lost a shoe after being spiked. By the time he had stopped to put the shoe back on, the rest of the field were 100 yards ahead, but he eventually forged through to win by seventy yards.

The Barefoot Maestro

Ethiopia's Abebe Bikila took the athletics world by storm at the 1960 Rome Olympics by romping to victory in only his third ever marathon. Furthermore, he did it running barefoot.

He repeated the feat four years later in Tokyo, shattering the Olympic record by one and a half minutes just six weeks after undergoing an appendix operation. In fact, he wasn't even expected to run, let alone pose a threat, yet he had so much energy left at the finish that he was treating the crowd to a display of callisthenics as the second and third men entered the stadium four minutes behind him.

A Wasted Journey

One of the epic journeys in Olympic history was undertaken by Italian Carlo Airoldi in order to compete at the 1896 Games in Athens. Opting to compete as an individual, Airoldi set off on foot from his home in Milan on 28 February and reached Ragusa in Yugoslavia on 19 March, having covered the 695 miles at an average of thirty-three miles per day. Giving his feet a well-deserved rest, he boarded a boat on 23 March and sailed via Corfu to Patrasso, where he arrived four days later. Then it was back to pounding the rough roads until five days and 136 miles on, he finally made it to Athens. Proud of his achievement and with high expectations of a medal, Airoldi handed in his Olympic entry. . . only for it to be refused because he was thought to be a professional.

A Close Shave

Soviet javelin thrower Elvira Orzolina arrived at the 1964 Tokyo Olympics as the reigning champion and fully expected to collect another medal, preferably gold. So when she could only manage a final position of fifth, she was deeply upset – so upset that she went straight to the hairdresser at the Olympic village and demanded to have her head shaved as a form of punishment. The perplexed Japanese hairdresser was none too enthusiastic about the task, so Orzolina seized the clippers and began scything away chunks of her flowing tresses. Fearful that such a horrific haircut leaving the premises would be bad for trade, the hairdresser relented and finished off the job professionally, thereby enabling Orzolina to depart with the shiniest of domes.

The Wrong Preparation

Training is all part of a marathon runner's preparation but Canadian Gerard Cote overdid it somewhat in the build-up to the 1936 Boston marathon. Just two days before the race, he chose to run the full course in practice. Hardly surprisingly, when it came to the real thing he was forced to drop out halfway round through exhaustion. His training methods were somewhat unusual anyway because after races, he enjoyed nothing more than a cigar and a few beers – items not normally associated with a strict fitness regime.

The Dashing Lord

Lord David George Brownlow Cecil Burghley, the Marquess of Exeter, was one of the great British Olympians. Gold medallist in the 400 metres hurdles at the 1928 Amsterdam Games, he was elected to Parliament three years later and went on to become a distinguished athletics administrator. But it was for his eccentric challenges that he has gone down in the sport's folklore.

In 1927, during his final year at Cambridge, he sprinted around the Great Court at Trinity College in the time it took the Trinity Clock to toll twelve o'clock. The feat had been accomplished once before, in the 1890s, but in those days the clock took five seconds longer to complete its toll. Burghley created another odd record by racing around the upper promenade deck of the liner *Queen Mary* in fifty-seven seconds, dressed in his ordinary street clothes.

Ingenuity was Burghley's forte. Arriving for a meeting at Antwerp, he was refused admission at the main gate. Sizing up the situation, he took a few steps back, pulled his bowler hat tightly down onto his head and hurdled the 4ft perimeter fence before the security guards could stop him.

To perfect his hurdling technique, he used to place matchboxes on the hurdles and practise knocking over the boxes with his lead foot without touching the actual hurdle. Contrary to what was portrayed in the film *Chariots of Fire*, he did not also put glasses of champagne on hurdles. As his daughter, Lady Victoria Leatham, said: 'He was never one to waste champagne.'

Jumping For Joy

Italy's Valerio Arri was so thrilled at taking the bronze medal at the 1920 Olympics that, on breaking the tape, he stunned spectators by performing a series of cartwheels.

Daley Goes to the Dogs

To raise money for Britain's 1980 Olympic appeal, decathlete Daley Thompson raced greyhound Autumn Groves at Wimbledon dog track. Despite running 290 metres in twenty-nine seconds, Thompson had to be content with the runners-up spot. Afterwards, he said: 'One more leg and I would have beaten him.'

The Athlete Who Took a Short Cut

The least successful attempt to cheat at the Olympics was carried out by American Fred Lorz in the 1904 Games at St Louis.

As spectators in the stadium awaited the return of the marathon runners, the sprightly figure of Lorz bounded in looking remarkably fresh. The patriotic crowd erupted, little knowing that they were the victims of a hoax.

It was only when the real race leader, fellow countryman Thomas Hicks, arrived looking tired and dishevelled that officials began to query Lorz's physical state. They discovered that, after dropping out with cramp early in the race, Lorz had accepted a lift in a car for over half the distance. When the car also broke down about four miles from the stadium, Lorz had resumed running and decided to milk the applause.

He insisted that the whole thing was meant as a joke and that he would have owned up. At first, he was banned for life for his misdemeanour, but the authorities later relented and the ban was lifted.

Marathon Oddities

For confirmation that people do the strangest things in city marathons, one only has to look at the number of competitors prepared to run the twenty-six miles in gorilla costumes or suits of armour. Usually these are occasional athletes earning money for charity, but serious runners have also been known to indulge in strange gimmicks. At the 1982 London marathon, Switzerland's Roger Bourbon completed the course as a waiter carrying a tray and bottle. Yet his finishing time of 2hr 47 min 18sec was only seventeen minutes outside his personal best.

In the same year, Donald Davis ran backwards for the whole distance of the Honolulu marathon in a time of 4hr 20min 36sec.

The Man in the Iron Mask

A $100,000 bet struck at London's National Sporting Club in 1907 sent thirty-one-year-old playboy Harry Bensley off on an attempt to walk round the world without once showing his face.

The rules stipulated that Bensley had to complete his journey while pushing a pram and wearing an iron mask at all times. He was obliged to travel through a specified number of British towns plus 125 towns in eighteen other countries, in the course of which he somehow had to find himself a wife – an onerous task, since she too was not permitted to see his face! On setting off, Bensley's worldly goods were restricted to £1, a collection of postcards and a change of underwear. To finance his travels, he had to sell the postcards.

Bensley left Trafalgar Square on 1 January 1908, wearing a 4½lb iron helmet and pushing a 200lb pram. At Newmarket races, he met King Edward VII and managed to persuade the monarch to purchase a postcard, but shortly afterwards, Bensley was arrested by an over-zealous policeman in Bexleyheath, Kent, for selling postcards without a licence. The magistrate ordered Bensley to remove the mask in court, but when the situation was explained to him, the official relented and Bensley escaped with a 2s 6d fine and his mask intact.

Over the next six years, Bensley pushed his pram across twelve countries, passing through New York, Montreal and Sydney. He received no fewer than 200 offers of marriage but rejected them all. In August 1914, he arrived in Genoa with just six more countries to visit. However, the First World War had broken out and the patriotic Bensley wanted to do his bit for king and country. So the bet was cancelled and, for his trouble, Bensley was given a consolation prize of $4,000, which he generously donated to charity. He died in 1956 at Brighton.

The Resourceful Pole-Vaulter

Olympic pole vault champion Irving Baxter turned up for the 1901 AAA Championships without an essential item of equipment – his pole. When his fellow competitors flatly refused to allow him to borrow theirs, the American was faced with the prospect of not being able to compete – until he spotted a nearby flagpole. After testing its flexibility, he pulled it from the ground and decided to use it in the competition. What's more, he did well enough with his makeshift pole to share the title, with a vault of 9ft 10in.

A Glutton for Punishment

It would be something of an understatement to say that New York producer Mike Kasser was keen on marathons. After completing the 1983 London marathon in a time of 2hr 56min 30sec, he hopped onto Concorde and the following day finished the Boston marathon in 3hr 8min. Before going home to put his feet up for a well-deserved rest, he admitted: 'I just love running. In fact, I'd do another marathon tomorrow if I had the chance.'

The Forgotten Sport of Naked Racing

We are told that in nineteenth-century Lancashire, one of the most popular sports among the locals was that of naked racing! An onlooker at a contest in 1824 at the village of Whitworth, near Rochdale, wrote: 'The runners were six in number, stark naked, the distance being seven miles, or seven times round the moor. There were hundreds, perhaps thousands, of spectators, men and women, and it did not appear to shock them as being anything out of the ordinary course of things.' Presumably, the only reason this splendid sport has yet to acquire Olympic status is the pain which would be inflicted when competitors pinned on their numbers.

These Boots weren't Made for Running

Manuel Dias of Portugal made a fatal decision before the start of the 1936 Olympic marathon in Berlin – he chose to wear new running shoes for the race. At first, all went well and after ten miles he was lying second, but then the newness of the shoes began to tell. He managed to mince another mile or so before the state of his feet deteriorated to such an extent that he was compelled to toss aside the offending shoes.

Not relishing the idea of completing the course in bare feet, Dias sought out a spectator willing to lend him some footwear.

Unfortunately, the only person he could find was a boy from the Hitler youth movement, who lent him his heavy marching boots! Naturally, this did little for the medal hopes of Dias, but he goosestepped his way home to finish seventeenth.

A Sporting Gesture

For the great Finnish distance runner Paavo Nurmi, the 3,000 metres steeplechase presented a new and somewhat daunting challenge. Competing in the 1928 Amsterdam Olympics, Nurmi was simply not used to the obstacles and during his heat, he fell at the water jump. Luckily, a helping hand was nearby in the shape of French runner Lucien Duquesne, who stopped and helped the wet Finn to his feet. Touched by the gesture, Nurmi thanked the Frenchman and then shepherded him for the remainder of the race, even inviting him to break the tape first, an offer which Duquesne declined. By the time the final was run, Nurmi had perfected the art of hurdling and he went on to take the silver medal. But Duquesne, without whose assistance Nurmi would never have made the final, was sadly unplaced.

Reverse Gear

Arvind Pandya of India ran backwards across the United States from Los Angeles to New York in 107 days between August and December 1984. Six years later, he engaged reverse to cover the 940 miles between John O'Groats and Land's End in twenty-six days and seven hours.

But the leading light in the world of backwards walking was Plennie L Wingo of Abilene, Texas. On 24 October 1932, thirty-six-year-old Wingo arrived in Istanbul at the end of an 8,000 mile transcontinental reverse marathon, the starting point for which had been Santa Monica, California, on 15 April 1931.

A Flying Start

The most eccentric exhibition of hurdling at senior level was surely that given by South Africa's Tom Lavery at the 1950 Empire Games in Auckland. Like a coiled spring, he was crouched on the start-line for the 120 yards hurdles – but when the gun sounded, the first thing that rose from its blocks was the button on the front of his shorts. No sooner was he in motion than he could feel his shorts slipping inexorably down. As he cleared each hurdle, he hastily hitched up his shorts without breaking stride, and relied on the pumping action of his legs to prevent them from descending below thigh level and causing the biggest embarrassment in track history. But perhaps the most remarkable point about Lavery's run was that, in spite of his problems, he still managed to capture the bronze medal.

The Munich Imposter

Following in the footsteps of Fred Lorz sixty-eight years earlier, a German steward by the name of Norbert Sudhaus decided to make his mark on the 1972 Olympic marathon in Munich. With the crowd anticipating the arrival of the leader, Sudhaus suddenly appeared on the track and was heading for the tape and his moment of glory when he was led away by officials. Moments later, with the crowd still in a state of confusion, the eventual winner, the United States' Frank Shorter, entered the stadium to the sound of sporadic applause and fading laughter.

The Rain Man

Italian runner Emilio Lunghi, a silver medallist in the 800 metres at the 1908 London Olympics, once won a long-distance road race in Genoa while carrying an open umbrella because it was raining.

Postal Chaos

Fred Lorz may have captured the headlines at the 1904 Olympic marathon, but the real star of the race was the 5ft Cuban postman Felix Carvajal.

Forced to hitch-hike his way across the United States to St Louis after losing all his money in a game of craps, Carvajal arrived at the starting-line wearing his everyday clothes. One of the other runners kindly cut off Carvajal's trousers at the knee, leaving the little moustachioed Cuban to run in a beret, a long-sleeved white shirt, shorts of a fashion and boots. It was hardly the outfit of which Olympic champions are made.

Nevertheless, Carvajal would surely have finished among the medallists had he not stopped twice during the race, both times for the most peculiar of reasons. First, presumably still thinking he was on his postal round, he paused awhile to chat to some of the spectators who lined the route. Then he made a short detour to stop and pick some apples from an orchard. Sadly for Carvajal, they were unripe and left him with severe stomach pains. In agony, he staggered gamely on towards the finish, crossing the line in fourth place, very much a victim of his own folly.

9 Motor Sport

A Great British Hero

The 1920s was an era rich in wonderful motor-racing characters, and none was more colourful than the dashing Sir Henry Birkin, one of the famous 'Bentley Boys' and a hero of Le Mans.

Born in 1896 to a wealthy Nottingham lace-making family, young Henry was given the nickname of 'Tim' after the children's character Tiger Tim. By the age of fifteen, he had developed a passion for motor cars and in an attempt to exhaust the obsession, his uncle and two godfathers bet Tim £15 that he could not build a car capable of travelling the length of the driveway of the family home, Ruddington Grange, by his sixteenth birthday. The driveway was nearly a mile long and so the three men stationed themselves over a quarter of a mile apart. Tim emerged from the garage in a strange-looking mongrel of a car which he had built himself out of bits and pieces. But amazingly, it went, and as he drove past each man, Tim held his hand out for the fiver. He used the proceeds to buy better spare parts.

Together with his equally car-mad brother Archie, Birkin entered his first race at Brooklands in 1921 in an American Dodge Brothers car. But he preferred to drive British machines and soon bought two huge Bentleys, one for himself and one for his brother. However, Tim's new bride was none too keen on his racing and forced him to hang up his goggles. He may have been forced to turn his back on racing, but cars remained a major part of his life. He kept his hand in by making full use of the long, empty roads which ran between London and Norfolk. A regular challenge that he set himself was to race his Bentley from Piccadilly to his favourite public house in Norfolk. If he beat his set time, his reward was breakfast; if he didn't, the punishment was an empty stomach and an immediate return to the city.

Unable to resist the lure of the track any longer, he returned to racing in 1927 (at the cost of his marriage). In the wake of the death of brother Archie at the Isle of Man motorcycle TT races, Birkin accepted an invitation to join the Bentley team and, in typically gung-ho fashion, entered every race on the calendar. That year's Le Mans 24-hour race nearly ended in disaster for him when a tyre burst at 100 mph. To reduce weight, the Bentleys weren't carrying jacks and Birkin had to try and free the wheel with 'a jack-knife, a file, a hammer and some pliers' before running an astonishing three miles to fetch a jack! Nearly three hours behind the pacesetters, he proceeded to drive like a demon through the night with the result that he managed to finish a highly creditable fifth. Two years later, Birkin, driving in his familiar blue-and-white spotted scarf, teamed up with Woolf Barnato for a magnificent Bentley victory at Le Mans, a performance described by Birkin as 'a pleasant little triumph'.

As Bentley's supremacy was threatened by foreign manufacturers such as Alfa Romeo, Maserati and Mercedes Benz, Birkin, to his despair, was forced to drive a non-British vehicle and when he won again at Le Mans in 1931, it was at the wheel of an Alfa. In his usual fearless and determined fashion, Birkin drove a privately-entered Maserati into third place in the 1933 Tripoli Grand Prix. He might have fared considerably better but for the fact that he had to do all his own pitwork because Maserati had sent only one mechanic to cover three cars. Consequently, he had to enlist the services of a local garageman who 'turned out to be a hopeless drunk and spent the entire race dozing under a palm tree!'

It was to be his last race. Reaching out of the Maserati for a cigarette, he had burned his arm on the hot exhaust-pipe. The wound flared up and three weeks later, on 22 June, he died of blood poisoning – a curious end for such a daredevil racer.

The Opera-Singing Driver

Guiseppe Campari (1892-1933) always wanted to be an opera singer and fully intended to take it up when he retired from motor racing. However, he frequently managed to combine the two, bursting into an aria from Rigoletto or Gioconda while driving at breakneck speeds. The better the car was going, the happier he was and the louder he sang.

Weighing sixteen stone, the swarthy Italian was a larger-than-life figure in every respect. He adored food as much as music and once ate dozens of snails in a restaurant prior to a win at Monthlery in France. When he won the 1924 French Grand Prix at Lyons, he was presented with a giant sausage which he cooked wearing a convict's striped pyjama-suit.

Campari was in good voice while driving his Alfa from London to Liverpool en route for the 1929 Ulster TT race. Realizing he was in danger of being late for the boat to Ireland, he clocked up 106mph through a 20mph zone. The police spotted him – but were powerless to catch him.

He was generally a sunny character, although the Latin temper did flare up during the 1932 Mille Miglia endurance event. Having reached a prominent position, he took a much-needed break and handed over to his mechanic Sozzi, who promptly drove them into a wall and out of the race. A furious Campari seized a hammer from the tool kit and, waving it menacingly, chased the hapless Sozzi down the road.

Prior to the Italian Grand Prix of September 1933, Campari took on his compatriot Tazio Nuvolari in the Grand Challenge Bicycle Race at Monza, the idea being that the loser paid for dinner. While Nuvolari rode a modern racer, the ample figure of Campari was compressed onto an old-fashioned machine. Aided by the fact that Campari was unable to bend, Nuvolari triumphed in a sprint finish, leaving his rival to foot the dinner bill. A few days later, Campari was dead, killed in the Grand Prix. Ironically, he had announced beforehand that it would be his last race. He never did achieve his ambition of being an opera singer.

The Man With the Tin Leg

Few people on the Formula One circuit realized that Alan Stacey, the British driver killed in the 1960 Belgian Grand Prix, drove with an artificial leg. That was principally because Stacey himself went to great lengths to ensure that doctors in particular were unaware that his right leg was made of tin. At continental meetings where drivers had to undergo a pre-race medical examination, Stacey and his Lotus team-mates came up with an elaborate ruse to prevent the truth being uncovered. When reflex-testing was taking place, Stacey's pals would wait until his left leg had been done and then, with the doctor about to tap the tin knee with his hammer, they would create a diversion by knocking something over. As the doctor's gaze was averted, Stacey simply crossed his legs again and sat there waiting for the hammer blow with his left leg uppermost. Apparently, the manoeuvre never failed.

As a result of his disability, Stacey was unable to heel and toe with the brake and throttle while changing gear. Therefore a special twist-grip throttle – the sort used on motorcycles – was incorporated into the gear-lever of his cars, so that he could operate the throttle by hand when changing gear.

The tin leg became the focal point of many a practical joke. One of Stacey's favourite japes was to fiddle with a pencil and casually push it into one of the holes in his leg beneath his trousers. Those who had no idea about the false leg would look aghast at what they thought was a pencil boring into human flesh. He also liked to terrify hotel chambermaids by hanging the leg, complete with shoe and sock, over a chair in his room. An unintentional scare was caused on the day he lost the bolt out of his ankle. After hours of fruitless searching, he finally had to settle for a replacement . . . from the Lotus workshop.

The Frenchman with Two Hats

Nicknamed 'Phi Phi', Frenchman Philippe Etancelin was a popular racing driver in the period after the First World War. When racing, he always wore a cloth cap back to front. This was standard practice

among the majority of drivers in those days, but what made Etancelin
so different was that even when crash helmets became compulsory, he
still wore his cloth cap over his helmet!

Lipstick Repairs in the Mille Miglia

There was no more gruelling event in the motor racing calendar than
the Mille Miglia, run over 1,000 miles of rough Italian countryside
with a start and finish in Brescia. Only the most courageous, battle-
hardened drivers could expect to succeed, so imagine everyone's
surprise when an actress wearing an elegant red dress and a fur jacket
suddenly declared her intention to take part.

Attired as if attending a premiere, Mimi Aylmer arrived in Brescia
for the 1929 Mille Miglia in a Lancia Lambda with her chauffeur at
the wheel. Officials and spectators assumed that those would be the
driving arrangements; but at the last minute, Miss Aylmer took the
wheel and proceeded to drive the entire race.

Her progress was relatively sedate – though not without moments
of alarm – and seven hours after the leader, she arrived back on the
outskirts of Brescia. However, Miss Aylmer had no intention of facing
her public looking anything other than immaculate, and so, to the
amazement of onlookers, she pulled off the road for five minutes to
attend to her hair and put on fresh lipstick. She then rejoined the race
and crossed the finishing line to tumultuous applause. Stepping out of
the car, she looked truly radiant, as if she had been for nothing more
arduous than a drive round the block. By contrast, her chauffeur
looked haggard and ill, and thoroughly deserving of the special award
he received for 'most courageous man of the race'.

Tazio Nuvolari – A Man Who Knew No Fear

The son of an Italian farmer, Tazio Nuvolari (1892-1953) became a
motor racing legend for repeated shows of courage which bordered on
the reckless. He seemingly had no concept of fear and believed in

pushing himself and his car to the limit in every race. In particular, he liked winning against the odds. At just over 5ft tall, he relished nothing more than taking on the big boys, especially the Germans, and beating them.

Even as a boy, Nuvolari was utterly fearless. He once tried to jump off the roof of his house with a home-made parachute and was fortunate to escape without any broken bones. He later acquired a Bleriot aeroplane and careered into a haystack on take-off. The plane burst into flames, but again young Nuvolari emerged unscathed. Nevertheless, it was scarcely surprising that he was considered 'too dangerous' to drive ambulances for the Italian army during the First World War.

Between 1924 and 1946, his 'win or bust' approach brought him victory in fifty major races. Inevitably, he was involved in some spectacular crashes – but accidents which would have confined most drivers to the sidelines for months were brushed aside by Nuvolari. All he wanted to do was get back on the race track. No hospital could hold him.

On numerous occasions, he competed in races while heavily swathed in bandages. Driving an Alfa Romeo at a trial at Monza in 1925, he was hurled through a wire fence and suffered serious back injuries. He was told he would need at least a month's rest, but his only concern was the Grand Prix of the Nations motorcycle meeting at Monza in six days' time. Using all his powers of 'persuasion', he coerced the doctors into bandaging him in such a manner that he could sit on his 350cc Bianchi and be push-started. He went on to defy both his lack of mobility and the treacherously wet track to conjure up an incredible victory, after a fierce battle with Britain's Wal Handley.

In 1934, Nuvolari broke his leg when his Maserati crashed in the wet at Alessandria. Confined to hospital for four weeks, he became thoroughly restless. Itching to get back onto the track, he ignored the advice of the medics and entered to drive a Maserati at Avus, near Berlin. Since one foot was still in plaster, he ordered the pedals of the car to be modified so that all three could be operated by his functional foot. To the horror of his wife and doctor, he hobbled out on crutches to take part in practice. Although he had to be helped in and out of the cockpit and suffered badly from cramp during the race, he still managed to finish fifth.

There was no sign of Nuvolari letting up. In 1936, during practice for the Tripoli Grand Prix, his twelve-cylinder Alfa Romeo was travelling at over 125 mph when it hit a marker stone. Flung through the air, Nuvolari was found unconscious with severely bruised ribs. He came round in hospital, where he was put in plaster and told to rest for several days. 'But of course,' replied Nuvolari. 'After the race, I shall do so.' Sure enough, the following day, wearing a plaster 'corset' which virtually eliminated all movement, he drove a replacement Alfa into seventh place. For Nuvolari, that made the pain worthwhile.

During races, he liked to talk to his car and pat it, as if to encourage it to go even faster. His refusal to admit defeat was perfectly illustrated at the 1933 Monaco Grand Prix when, on the last lap, his car caught fire and blew up. Undaunted, Nuvolari jumped out and attempted to push the stricken vehicle to the finish line, hotly pursued by irate marshals waving fire extinguishers. In the end, the effort proved too much – he collapsed 200 yards from the finish and was disqualified. At the 1936 Ciano Cup race at Leghorn in western Italy, his Alfa had the misfortune to break down on the first lap. Whereas most other drivers would have accepted defeat and ambled back to the pits, Nuvolari immediately began screaming and shouting at pit chief Vittorio Jano to call in one of the other Alfas so that he could take the wheel. The innocent victim was his team-mate Pintacuda, who was called into the pits and physically yanked out of the car by Nuvolari. Rejoining the race over a minute behind the German Auto-Unions, Nuvolari drove magnificently and tore through the field for a famous victory.

He had more problems in the 1948 Mille Miglia where, although he was now fifty-six, his determination was as great as ever. A collision with a wall deprived him of the bonnet cover of his Ferrari and badly damaged the front left wing, which was pointing upwards at such an angle that it restricted his vision. Realizing that the situation called for desperate measures, and without stopping, Nuvolari shouted 'Hold tight!' to his mechanic Scapinelli (who travelled with him) and deliberately drove the car against the side of a bridge in order to knock the wing off completely. No sooner had they negotiated that minefield than Nuvolari's seat broke. Showing commendable initiative, he acquired a bag of oranges and lemons and used that as a rather lumpy cushion. No wonder his great rival Achille Varzi called him 'the boldest, most skilful madman of us all'.

Monte Carlo or Bust

Dudley Noble, a public relations man for Rootes, entered the 1932 Monte Carlo Rally driving a Hillman Wizard . . . and towing a caravan. Starting from Glasgow, he motored through Britain and France, demonstrating the car's suitability for family holidays. The enterprise was obviously not a serious attempt to win the rally, but it did attract plenty of headlines. Whether it did much for the sales of the Hillman Wizard is not recorded.

For the 1961 Monte Carlo Rally, BBC Television entered a London taxi driven by Tony Brooks and Willy Cave, with the meter running all the time. The word was that they might have finished up among the leaders had they not hung around at each checkpoint for half an hour waiting for a tip.

Hell Fire Harry

Although he failed to win a Grand Prix in his fourteen-year career, American driver Harry Schell was among the most popular figures on the Formula One scene. For Schell was a playboy who lived life to the full and with him around, there was rarely a dull moment.

Serving with the US army during the Second World War, he somehow rose to the rank of corporal despite once inadvertently marching a squad of German prisoners into a brick wall. Schell was in the middle of barking out orders when he became wrapped up in a conversation with a fellow officer, as a result of which he completely forgot about the troops and allowed them to march straight into the barracks wall.

His driving prowess was also called into question – he succeeded in turning over a tank – but nevertheless, when he left the army in 1946, one of the first things he did was acquire a Maserati. Being deeply patriotic, Schell arranged for the Stars and Stripes to be painted on the car next to the cockpit. Unfortunately, they were painted on upside down.

Throwing himself enthusiastically into Grand Prix racing, he also opened his own bar in Paris called 'L'Action Automobile'. The establishment lived up to its name, earning him the nickname of 'Hell Fire Harry'.

Schell met with mixed fortunes on the track, but astounded the motor racing world when piloting an exceedingly moderate Cooper to the front row of the grid following practice for the 1959 United States Grand Prix at Sebring. Nobody could believe his time, and rumours quickly spread that he had taken a short cut along the back stretch. The Ferrari team protested and Schell offered to stand down, but the timekeepers remained adamant that his time was legal. Thus, he started from the front of the grid, only to be forced to retire after just seven laps. Whenever the matter of his Sebring qualifying time was raised subsequently, Schell offered nothing in reply except for a conspiratorial smile.

Like many drivers, Schell was superstitious about the number 13. He had good reason to be. On Friday 13 May 1960, he was killed in practice at Silverstone, aged thirty-nine.

Whistle-Stop tour

A feature of the Mille Miglia were the millions of race fans, or *tifosi* as they were called, who used to line the route. As many as ten million – men, women, children and dogs – would turn out for the event, often standing in the road to get a better view of the approaching cars and only jumping to safety at the very last moment.

This caused enormous problems for most of the drivers, but not for the redoubtable Italian Conte Gastone Brilli Peri. The Conte, who won the 1925 Italian Grand Prix, regularly competed in the Mille Miglia right up until his death in 1930. He always made a point of wearing a silver whistle tied around his neck, and as he approached a corner, he would give a long blast on his whistle in the hope of frightening spectators into jumping onto the pavements.

Spoilsport

When plans were announced for the 1898 Paris-Amsterdam-Paris road race, Monsieur Bochet, the Paris police engineer, was determined that it would not take place. To this end, he unearthed an obscure by-law which demanded that all competing cars be issued with a certificate to prove that they were safe to be driven on public roads. In charge of issuing these certificates was Monsieur Bochet himself, and he had already refused the vast majority of the cars permission to race! To underline his stance, he stated that half a squadron of the 23rd Hussars and two cannons would be placed in the middle of the road, with instructions to shoot any transgressors. Ultimately, the threat of bloodshed on the streets of Paris was removed – by switching the start and finish of the race to a point outside Bochet's jurisdiction.

The Fawlty Belgian

Belgian motocross ace Joel Robert was one of the most gifted of riders, winning the world championship on six occasions between 1964 and 1973. He was also one of the most temperamental and was prone to throwing spectacular tantrums if things went wrong.

At one meeting, he became so angry after three false starts that he rode out from the start line for fifty yards, stopped, threw his bike down and sat beside it, refusing to move. He had also been known to hit any spectator who happened to upset him, and had even been seen assaulting his engine, Basil Fawlty-style, if it had the nerve to break down on him.

Family Misfortunes

The Zborowskis were an unlucky family. Count Eliot Zborowski was killed in 1903 competing in a hill climb, when his sleeve caught in the vehicle's hand-throttle. His son, Count Louis Zborowski, was killed driving a Mercedes in the 1924 Italian Grand Prix at Monza. Spookily, he was wearing the same cufflinks that had caused his father's death.

Count Louis was born into wealth in 1895. The family had homes in New York and England and the intention was to have him educated at Eton, but he left there after only a year when it was realized that academic works were not his strong subject. He was far happier with a car-maintenance manual, and in the years following the First World War, he built up a string of huge Mercedes cars which were affectionately known as Chitty-Chitty-Bang-Bangs because of the sound made by the exhausts. He began racing these monsters as a private entrant and turned up at Brooklands in Chitty I, a vehicle boasting a twenty-three-litre airship engine, identical to that used in Zeppelins. Accompanied by his crew, each dressed in identical black shirts and oversize check caps (the latter specially imported by him from Palm Beach), the Count would drive the huge car up from his estate near Canterbury, the living image of Mr Toad.

His expeditions to Brooklands did not all end happily. In 1922, a tyre blew on Chitty I and the car careered into a bridge, spun round in circles and slid backwards through a trackside timing box, removing a number of the timekeeper's fingers as he tried to jump out of the way. That was to be the last time the Count ever raced Chitty I at Brooklands, although he continued to drive Chitty II, a gleaming white Mercedes.

He and his wife also took Chitty II off on an epic tour of North Africa which led them 150 miles into the Sahara desert. Following on behind throughout the marathon journey was Chitty III, driven by the Count's loyal assistant Clive Gallop and bearing every item of the Zborowskis' luggage. What a curious sight this entourage must have been for the locals.

The Driver With Three Ears

Many sportsmen carry strange items in their pockets, usually to bring them good luck – but the needs of charismatic French racing driver Jean Behra (1921-59) were more practical. In 1955, his right ear was severed by the lens of his goggles in a crash during the Tourist Trophy race at Dundrod, Northern Ireland, and thereafter he had to wear a plastic ear. And naturally enough, lest history should repeat itself, Behra always kept a spare plastic right-ear in his pocket. As a party piece, he used to enjoy alarming the mademoiselles by removing his ear at an opportune moment – a chat-up line which must have been unique in the annals of civilization.

The Co-Driver From Hell

After eighty-eight of the 110 laps in the inaugural British Grand Prix at Brooklands in 1926, Frenchman Robert Benoist was leading the field in his Delage and looking set for victory. But then it was time to hand over, for the last part of the race, to his co-driver and fellow countryman Andre Dubonnet. Benoist must have feared the worst when Dubonnet climbed into the racing machine wearing a blue lounge-suit and a beret, but it also transpired that Dubonnet had never even driven on the track before. Not surprisingly, the lead which Benoist had so patiently built up was soon whittled away and Dubonnet eventually limped home a disappointing third. The only consolation was that at least he didn't stop to ask directions.

The Incredible Sulk

Giuseppe Farina (1906-66) was crowned the first motor racing world champion in 1950, yet the Italian doctor of engineering possessed none of the verve of his compatriot, Tazio Nuvolari. On the contrary, Farina was a dour individual with a tendency to sulk if he didn't get his own way.

When he was with Alfa Romeo, the team decided which of their drivers would be allowed to win and would often signal one of the Alfas to slow down and enable a team-mate to pass. At the 1946 Turin Grand Prix, Farina was handily-placed in third when he spun off at a corner. But instead of carrying on, he retired in a fit of pique because he was not going to be permitted to win. Three years later, at the Italian Grand Prix at Monza, he was at the wheel of a new Maserati which was unable to compete with the Ferraris for speed. Whereas Nuvolari would have relished such a challenge, Farina retired from third place in a huff, simply because he couldn't catch the two leading Ferraris. There wasn't even anything wrong with his car! In fact, one of the Ferraris was forced to drop out shortly afterwards, meaning that if Farina had kept going he would have finished second. But that was no use to Farina – he was too self-centred to settle for second best.

Half Car, Half Bed

Driving a Panhard in the 1902 Paris-Vienna race, Britain's Charles Jarrott was facing an early exit following the collapse of his car's wooden chassis-frame. Then, during an overnight stop, he had a brainwave and decided to repair the broken frame with wood taken from the bedstead in his hotel room. First he carefully dismantled the bed and then managed to smuggle sections out to his car by stuffing them down the legs of his trousers. Jarrott was never one for convention: in the course of the Circuit des Ardennes in Belgium, he once accepted and drank a bottle of champagne handed to him by a passer-by. What effect this had upon his steering can only be speculated upon.

A Boyhood Prank

The youngest competitors in any senior motor race must surely be the two unnamed brothers, one aged ten and the other twelve, who managed to infiltrate the 1955 Mille Miglia.

The boys lived on the race route in Verona and, aware that a large group of little 500cc Fiats would be passing through the town at night, they borrowed their mother's similar car, painted on false numbers and sneaked into the race. Enjoying the adventure of a lifetime, they drove at great speed for some miles; but in their excitement they had forgotten to check the fuel tank, with the inevitable result that they soon ran out of petrol.

With the boys in tears at the roadside beside the stricken car, angry race officials gave them a sound ticking-off and sent them back home. However, when Conte Aymo Maggi, the founder of the Mille Miglia, heard the story, he took pity upon the youngsters and arranged for them to attend the official luncheon in Brescia to honour that year's winners, Stirling Moss and Denis Jenkinson. As an added bonus, Maggi sat the boys between himself and the great Juan Manuel Fangio.

A Wee Problem

Competing in the 1954 Buenos Aires 1,000-kilometre race, Carroll Shelby and co-driver Dale Duncan finished tenth in an Allard. But the bare facts disguise the high drama which occurred during a pit-stop, when fire broke out in the carburettor. With no fire-fighting apparatus available, the situation looked critical until Duncan took matters into his own hands – and extinguished the fire by urinating on it.

Drove With One Leg

Tom Thornycroft drove the whole of the 1906 car TT race on the Isle of Man with one foot. His leg was so badly injured that it had to be strapped to the side of his car for the 120 miles. He had hurt the leg two days before the race, after falling off a wall while trying to get a glimpse of a Manx cat. . .

Segrave's Road-Safety Laws

Sir Henry O'Neal de Hane Segrave (1896-1930) was obsessed with speed. After a successful career in motor racing, he turned his attention to speed records and captured both the land and sea versions, for which he was knighted in 1929. Mercifully, his influence did not extend to the laws governing public roads, because his theory for safety at crossroads was revolutionary to say the least.

Basically, his idea was to roar over a crossroads at breakneck speed, disregarding all other traffic, because, he reasoned, that way there was less chance of a collision. He explained: 'Supposing you take the crossing at 60 mph, you are in the "zone of danger" for something less than a second; whereas if you cross at 20 mph, you are in the dangerous area for three times as long, and consequently the risk of meeting cross-traffic is three times as great.' It was only a pity that nobody was ever treated to his views on roundabouts. Surely, he would simply have advocated roaring across the middle.

Young Henry had been secretly driving his father's cars from the age of nine, aided and abetted by Mr Segrave's motor servant, who would let him go for surreptitious spins along the driveway of the family home. Apparently, his father did not learn of this deception until 1936, six years after Henry's death.

Given this early start in life, Segrave's graduation to car racing was perhaps inevitable. His cheerful disposition and never-say-die attitude won him a great many friends among the motor sport fraternity. He was always willing to offer a helping hand. Knowing of a friend's fondness for military antiques, Segrave despatched a mountain of armour and old weapons to the friend's house in a taxi. On the track, Segrave's spirit was unwavering. Practising in late afternoon for the 1922 Coppa Florio, a hazardous road-race run through the mountains of Sicily, he was caught first by a heavy downpour and then by nightfall. As a result, he and his mechanic were forced to spend the night in a barn, but they still recovered to finish second in the actual race.

His final race was the Essex six-hour sports car event at Brooklands in 1927, an occasion which he marked by suddenly disappearing unannounced halfway through the race and driving off with his wife down to Southampton in order to go boating. Such unreliability manifested itself again when he arrived twenty minutes late for his knighthood, claiming to have been delayed by three level-crossings. King George V mocked him about his tardiness, joking: 'There you are, you see: a speed king – held up by a mere railway train!'

Segrave enjoyed the joke, but the following year, speed was to prove his downfall when he perished while making an attempt on the world water-speed record at Lake Windermere.

Go Slow

Arguably the most unusual race to grace the streets of Paris was a 'Go Slow' competition held along Rue Lepie in October 1950. The winner was a Monsieur Durand, who, demonstrating admirable control, covered 722 yards in the agonizingly slow time of 10hr 40min 51sec, which worked out at an average of three minutes for each complete wheel-turn. Race officials kept a close watch on all of the cars to check that their wheels were turning continuously. Any vehicle which stopped even for a split second was liable to disqualification.

There have been reports of a similar event being staged in Britain – every evening on the M25 during rush-hour.

Fashion Gurus

American Ernie Triplett, who raced at Indianapolis in the 1920s, invariably drove in a black bow-tie and red pantaloons. The fashion obviously caught on, for thirty years later, Britain's Mike Hawthorn, motor racing world champion in 1958, was also famous for racing in a bow-tie.

A Dutch privateer of the early 1960s, Jonkheer Carel Pieter Anthonie Jan Hubertus Godin de Beaufort, had as much difficulty squeezing his ample frame into the tiny cockpit of his bright orange

Porsche as he did fitting all of his names onto the race entry forms. With space at a premium, he used to drive in his socks, claiming that the addition of shoes made it awkward for him to operate the pedals.

Self-Inflicted Pain

Davey Allison was not one to take defeat lightly. Blessed with a fiery nature, the young American responded to one setback by punching the transporter which was carrying his car, and consequently ended up injuring his hand. Son of the race driver Bobby Allison, Davey was a determined character. In July 1992, he suffered a broken back and concussion following an accident at the track at Pocono, Pennsylvania, but a week later he was back racing, his body encased in a special cast. He once said: 'If I get killed in a race car, I'm gonna die with a smile on my face.' He was killed in a helicopter crash in 1993, aged thirty-two.

The Mighty Otto

German driver Otto Merz (1889-1933) was known as the 'strong man' of motor racing. Said to be able to drive six-inch nails into a plank of wood with his fists, Merz demonstrated his sheer strength during the 1929 Ulster Tourist Trophy race at Ards. When he damaged the front wing of his Mercedes in a collision with a solid-iron water pump, Merz ripped off the wing with his bare hands, threw it in the back of the car and continued on his way. He later stopped to tie it back in place.

Merz had also excelled himself in the previous year's German Grand Prix, a race run in searing heat. He finished second, and as he stepped out of the Mercedes, the steering wheel of the car was found to be sticky with blood from his hands, which had been chafed raw by the tortuous drive.

It is not generally known that Merz played a small part in history.

As chauffeur to Archduke Franz Ferdinand of Austria, he had what amounted to a walk-on role in the Archduke's assassination at Sarajevo in 1914. For it was Merz who carried the dying Archduke into a nearby house – a noble, but ultimately futile gesture.

The Fake Lap

At the 1939 lightweight motorcycle TT on the Isle of Man, Ted Mellors was hot favourite on his Benelli. But nobody present could believe the amazingly fast lap-time he posted on the last morning of practice. And they had good reason to be sceptical, for Mellors had craftily taken a short cut.

Having run out of fuel part of the way round the course, Mellors had stopped off at the village garage at Ballacraine. When the official 'Roads Open' car had passed by to let ordinary traffic know that the roads were free of racing machines, Mellors made his way back leisurely towards Douglas. On reaching Union Mills, he took a quiet country road and arrived at Cronk-ny-Mona to find that the official car had not yet passed, thus making that section of the course still closed. Thinking that nobody had spotted his detour, he accelerated swiftly through the final part of the course to astound the timekeepers.

He might have got away with it had a reporter on the special TT newspaper not spotted him at the garage and revealed the truth. Confronted with the evidence, Mellors cheerfully admitted the deception and went on to win the race anyway.

Ascari's Dark Superstition

Alberto Ascari, motor racing world champion in 1952 and 1953 and son of the legendary Italian driver Antonio Ascari, was deeply superstitious. A man prone to dark moods, he suffered many premonitions, claimed he was haunted by the devil and believed in communication with the dead. Indeed, he only took up motor sport to avenge his father's death in the 1925 French Grand Prix.

Alberto was particularly fearful of the number 13 and he would also become hysterical at the sight of a black cat. If he was driving along a road, he would turn round and seek another route rather than risk passing a black cat sitting on the pavement. Fortunately, he was unlikely to come across one on a Grand Prix circuit, otherwise he would presumably have engaged reverse and shot back to the pits to hide.

In 1955, Ascari's car crashed into the harbour during the Monaco Grand Prix, but he managed to extricate himself from the cockpit, surface and swim to safety. While still convalescing, he asked to be allowed to try out a sports Maserati, but he lost control on a corner and met his death ominously close to the thirtieth anniversary of his father's demise. Perhaps he was right to be superstitious after all.

The Daredevil Depailler

French ace Patrick Depailler (1944-80) believed in living dangerously, much to the despair of the teams for whom he drove. Having joined the ranks of Formula One with Tyrrell in 1973, he contrived to break his leg ten days before a Grand Prix after falling off a motorbike. Tyrrell responded by inserting a clause into Depailler's contract that he had to 'keep away from dangerous toys'.

The warning fell on deaf ears. In 1978, he teamed up with Ligier, and midway through the following season was lying a promising third in the drivers' world championship. But then he decided to indulge in a spot of hang-gliding and suffered a serious injury, as a result of which he was out of action for the rest of the year.

By now, Depailler's reputation as a madman off the circuit was firmly established, and before races, he was a familiar sight in the pit lane riding a bicycle while sitting on the handlebars. Sadly, his antics came to an end when he was killed during practice for the German Grand Prix at Hockenheim.

Pit-Stop Picnic

The 1908 car TT on the Isle of Man was an incident-packed race for one AE George. He got off to a flying start and was leading the pack when he came into the pits for fuel on the seventh lap. The pit stop took six minutes (things were a little slower in those days), during which time George eased the waiting by devouring a dozen oysters. Happily, there was no adverse reaction to the seafood diet, but George's luck ran out on the final lap when, just twenty-five miles from the flag, his car caught fire. Although he managed to extinguish the blaze using a spectator's overcoat, the lost time relegated him to third place at the finish. Thus, he left the island with a disappointing result and a possible claim for compensation from one cold spectator.

A Carefree Approach

'I think the danger of motor racing is greatly overrated. It is not as dangerous as it seems.' These were the words of Woolf Barnato (1895-1948), one of the famous Bentley Boys and a wealthy extrovert who, despite the nature of his chosen sport, did not believe in life insurance.

It was not as if he couldn't afford it, because money was no object, a point illustrated by the fact that he often spent as much as £1,000 a week socially, mainly on lavish parties at his country house, - Ardenrun, near Lingfield in Surrey. Cynics might say that his place in the Bentley team was bought rather than earned, since he invested the substantial sum of £100,000 in the company – on condition that he was given a place in the team and had the pick of the cars for his own private use.

Nevertheless, he drove with considerable distinction, helping to put Bentley on the map with three successive victories in the Le Mans 24-hour race between 1928 and 1930. It was only fitting that at his funeral, one of the grand old cars was driven to his graveside.

A Nightmare Journey

The 1937 Mille Miglia turned into a nightmare for the Italian driver Casalis, who was at the wheel of a Fiat Siata in the 750cc sportscar class. It all began when he was involved in a nasty crash which resulted in his co-driver Marone being taken to hospital. But Casalis wasn't prepared to give up without a fight, and after working frantically on the car, he somehow managed to get it going again. However, he still needed a co-driver – and his prayers were answered when he spotted another car broken down nearby, with the crew still sitting inside. Coercing one of them into joining him, he was able to get the Fiat back into the race.

Everything seemed to be going relatively smoothly as Casalis and his new acquaintance covered several hundred miles together, but disaster struck again shortly after they had been checked through the Rimini control. For on leaving the city, the unfortunate Casalis took the wrong route and headed along the coast towards Ravenna, instead of veering inland for Bologna. More precious time was wasted as Casalis was forced to retrace his steps, but no sooner had he reached Bologna than his illicit co-driver was thrown out by officials and put on a bus back to Florence. Casalis went on to complete the course to Brescia alone, but on crossing the finishing line, he was severely reprimanded and ultimately disqualified. Basically he had gone to a lot of trouble for nothing.

Military Inspection

Britain's Gwenda Hawkes, one of the leading women drivers of the 1920s, was a stickler for discipline. Miss Hawkes, who specialized in breaking speed and endurance records, came from a military background and always insisted that the car be lined up on the track two hours before either the race or record attempt, so that she could inspect it from head to tail. Furthermore, she demanded that all of her mechanics had spotless white overalls and was liable to dismiss any crew member found with as much as a hint of grease about his person. Whilst this stipulation for cleanliness was rather at odds with their work, the mechanics learned to tolerate Miss Hawkes' eccentricity – particularly as she footed the laundry bills.

A Playboy Image

Born into a wealthy Milanese family, Eugenio Castellotti was able to indulge his love of fast cars and fast women. When he was old enough to drive, the tall, dark and handsome Castellotti was able to acquire a flashy sports car, followed shortly afterwards by a beautiful actress girlfriend. Proud and temperamental, he was determined to make it to the top in motor racing and took the first step on the ladder by driving a privately-entered Ferrari in the 1950 Mille Miglia. Two years later, he finished second in the sportscar Grand Prix at Monaco but had only himself to blame for not winning. For he was leading the race when he decided to make a pit stop . . . simply because he was thirsty! By the time he had guzzled the can of drink, he had lost the lead and was unable to regain it. Such actions were hardly guaranteed to advance his career and it was a further three years before he made the break into Formula One, being signed up by Lancia. But before anyone could really discover whether the unpredictable Castellotti was capable of following in the footsteps of the Italian greats of the past, he was killed at Modena in 1957 while practising in a Ferrari. Fast cars could be dangerous playthings.

The German Joker

Any racing driver who chooses 13 as his lucky number has got to be something of an oddball – and Bernd Rosemeyer was just that. Both he and his wife were confirmed fatalists, which meant that they approached everything in life with a carefree, reckless abandon. Their philosophy was simple: what will be, will be.

The young German originally made his name riding motorcycles, where his brash style brought him to the attention of Auto-Union. His first car Grand Prix victory came in 1935, a year in which he had a narrow squeak at Pescara when the brakes on the Auto-Union seized and he had to steer the car back onto the track between a telegraph pole and the wall of a house. When subsequently measured, the gap was found to be just six centimetres wider than the car. It had been a remarkable manoeuvre.

In 1936, Rosemeyer walked away with the European Championship, which at the time was the pinnacle of achievement for Grand Prix drivers. Yet he often caused his team manager, Willi Walb, sleepless nights, never more so than when he landed a place in the German four-man bobsleigh team at that year's Winter Olympics.

Rosemeyer's sense of fun made him a great favourite. He loved practical jokes and once plugged a firecracker into a toy car and let it off among unsuspecting bystanders. By 1937, the Nazis were at their most potent and the German Grand Prix, in which Germany's Rudolf Caracciola came first in a Mercedes with Rosemeyer back in third, was seen as a propaganda coup. At the victory ceremony, Caracciola was presented by Hitler's representative Adolf Huhnlein with a large bronze trophy depicting the Goddess of Speed. To the delight of the crowd, when Huhnlein's gaze was averted, Rosemeyer slipped a cigarette between the Goddess's lips. Hearing the laughter, Huhnlein turned round, by which time the cigarette was back in Rosemeyer's mouth.

Success had done nothing to blunt Rosemeyer's edge. During final practice at the 1937 Coppa Acerbo, he again showed his complete disregard for danger by climbing into the car minus a shirt and wearing only a linen helmet, goggles, gloves, shorts and a pair of sandals. He was dressed for a stroll on the beach, yet he broke the lap record by twelve seconds.

But the following year, shortly before his thirtieth birthday, the seemingly indestructible Rosemeyer was killed in a 250 mph crash during a record attempt on the Frankfurt-Darmstadt autobahn. It was a tragic waste of a great talent.

Raymond, Coeur De Lion

In many respects, Frenchman Raymond Sommer (1906-50) adopted the same philosophy to motor sport as Bernd Rosemeyer. Although not as dashing a competitor as Rosemeyer, the man they called 'Raymond, Coeur de Lion' ('Raymond the Lionheart')would go to any lengths to attain a place on the starting grid. If a car was capable of some form of forward motion, Sommer wanted to drive it. Sometimes he would still be working frantically on a broken car while the rest of the field were roaring around the track. He would finally start up to an hour late. It was hardly the ideal situation; but for Sommer, any kind of race was better than no race at all.

On one memorable occasion, the only way he could get his car moving off the starting grid was to siphon petrol from another car to his own by means of suction. In the course of this delicate operation, he succeeded in swallowing a considerable amount of fuel, but he pressed ahead regardless.

Knowing that he always gave of his best, no matter how adverse the conditions, Sommer was not necessarily one for adhering to team instructions. At the International Trophy meeting at Silverstone in August 1950, Sommer was driving an Aston-Martin but told team manager John Wyer not to trouble him with pit signals during the race – as far as Sommer was concerned, it would be quite sufficient if he just went fast. Sadly, this was to be one of his last races, for the following month he was killed driving a Cooper at Cadours in his home country. France had lost a true hero.

10 Extras

The Crazy World of Bill Veeck

Bill Veeck was a desperate man. The owner of the St Louis Browns baseball team, he had seen a steady decline in gates and was prepared to do just about anything to stop the rot.

Leaving no gimmick unturned, he introduced a wide range of new attractions for the 1951 season which he was convinced would lure the people of St Louis back to the stadium in their thousands. He bought 6,000 baseball bats from a bankrupt businessman and handed them out to fans. Then he tried other free gifts – orchids, cakes, Cadillacs, live lobsters, stepladders and five tons of nuts and bolts! He brought in an exploding scoreboard which, whenever the Browns scored, erupted in a dazzling display of fireworks to the strains of Handel's *Messiah*. Eager to feature the latest word in stadium catering, he appointed a team of midgets to sell midget hot-dogs. If there was a medal for tackiness, Bill Veeck would have struck gold.

But his masterstroke was to employ one of the aforementioned midgets as the team's secret weapon. Thus, the 3ft 7in Eddie Gaedel took the field for the Browns and instantly posed a whole new set of problems for the opposing pitcher. The rules of baseball stipulate that the ball must be pitched in the zone between the batter's knees and armpits, usually a space of around 2ft 6in. However, in Gaedel's case, the legal area amounted to an inch and a half, making it virtually impossible for the pitcher to hit the target. After four misplaced pitches, the batter is allowed to move to first base. Not surprisingly, Gaedel was quickly able to do this, whereupon Veeck had him replaced by a substitute.

It was clearly a gross infringement of the spirit of the game, and the following day Veeck was banned from any further involvement in baseball. Defiant to the last, he complained to reporters that the action was 'discrimination against little people'.

Life According to Frank

Denver-born Eddie Eagan was a great sporting all-rounder. In 1920, the future lawyer won gold in the Olympic light-heavyweight boxing, and twelve years later, he completed an amazing summer-winter Olympic double by helping the United States' four-man bobsleigh team to victory at Lake Placid.

Eagan was remarkable in one other respect – he modelled his lifestyle on that of Frank Merriwell, the fictional hero of dime novels. Eagan explained in 1932: 'To this day, I have never used tobacco, because Frank didn't. My first glass of wine, which I do not care for, was taken under social compulsion in Europe. Frank never drank.' It's as well for the rest of the bobsleigh team that Frank didn't exist solely on a diet of Brussels sprouts.

The Woolly Grand National

Spectators from as far afield as the United States flock to a corner of rural Shropshire to see what is believed to be the world's only jumping race for sheep.

The one-furlong steeplechase track with two turns and four fences, each about a foot high, is the brainchild of former amateur jockey Edward Dorrell and his wife Carolyn from Hoo Farm near Telford. The Dorrells keep all manner of creatures on their farm – deer, ostriches and llamas – and six years ago decided to introduce the sheep racing as a novelty. But its popularity has spread to the extent that it is now a firm fixture on Britain's sporting calendar.

Edward Dorrell says: 'We always noticed that sheep were very competitive when we were feeding them in the field. There would always be a mad rush to be the first one to get to us. So we decided to organize it into a proper race.'

There are eight or nine runners in each race and every sheep has a name, hat and number cloth – but no jockey. There is even betting of a sort, although wagers are usually restricted to a modest 50p. The highlight of the year is the Sheep Grand National, although the Dorrells also stage an Ascot evening where guests are wined and dined after the racing.

If only because they know that food is waiting for them at the end of the course, the sheep appear extremely enthusiastic about their racing, although Edward points out that they can be 'spooked' by the sight of an ostrich suddenly peering over the rails at them. This will quite likely cause them to stop in a heap or turn round and race the wrong way.

So if newsreels reveal an ostrich on the course at Aintree that afternoon in 1956, it could be that at last the mystery of Devon Loch has been solved.

Sailing Buff

In 1971, Nicolette Milnes-Walker, a twenty-eight-year-old research psychologist at the University of Wales, achieved the distinction of sailing the Atlantic single-handed . . . and in the nude. Having spent most of the forty-three-day voyage in a state of undress, Nicolette told captivated newshounds: 'Sometimes I wore a shirt and bikini pants, but much of the time I wore nothing at all. When I was on deck, it was a choice between putting on oilskins and becoming waterproof or taking everything off and being waterproof. I took everything off.'

The People's Champion

To many people, snooker player Alex 'Hurricane' Higgins was just another in the line of rowdy, unruly sportsmen, along with the likes of Connors, Nastase and McEnroe. Yet in his earlier years, Higgins's frequently outrageous behaviour was more endearing, particularly as he often ended up as the victim.

The sight of Higgins around the table – chain-smoking, nervy and twitchy, and looking as if he had suffered a major fall-out with his tailor – represented the exact opposite of the air of calm authority exuded by most world-class players. Yet somehow it worked for him. And contrary to appearances, he was rarely lacking in confidence – if anything, he could be too brash – but he had an unfortunate habit of picking on the wrong people. In 1973, after beating sixty-three-year-old Norman Squire in an exhibition match in Sydney, Higgins allegedly said of the Australian: 'He's nothing but an old has-been.' Higgins was immediately physically ejected from the club and made to sit in the gutter outside and write a fulsome apology on a piece of toilet paper before being allowed back in. On another occasion, he was none too gracious in defeat against Graham Miles in a tournament in Wales. Higgins's description of him as 'a jammy bald bugger' displeased Miles, who promptly sent the Irishman tumbling into the crowd. The fight continued in the dressing-room.

A former stable-lad, Higgins liked a flutter on the horses and regularly lost £7,000 a day at the races. At Wolverhampton in 1976, he lost £13,000 in an afternoon, but proudly relates how he won it all back the next day. Yet his most spectacular challenge was against hell-raising film star Oliver Reed, who invited Higgins to his house to take part in a weekend quadrathlon of snooker, armwrestling, table tennis and non-stop disco dancing. It is thought that neither man could remember who won.

Over the years, Higgins, who once played in the Mercantile Classic on television sporting a black eye following a fight, has had his fair share of scrapes. On his way to a match in Birmingham, the car giving him a lift broke down. He managed to hitch another ride but arrived an hour late and discovered, to his horror, that his favourite cue had fallen down the side of the seat and got trapped in the car door, and was now two and a half inches shorter. During the 1982 world championships at the Crucible Theatre, Sheffield, Higgins was playing Kirk Stevens in the practice room when he was caught short. 'It was midnight and there were only four people around,' says Higgins. 'It was a long way from the room to the loo, so when I spotted a rubber plant, I realized it was my only choice.' Unfortunately for Higgins, a security guard materialized to make a fifth person, and Higgins was reported and fined £1,500 by the sport's governing authority.

That year, Higgins won the world title for the second time and proclaimed himself to be the 'People's Champion'. Although his subsequent decline has been rapid, those who remember the time at Blackpool when he badly gashed his arm jumping over a wall on the way back from a pub and turned a 7-2 deficit against Tony Knowles into an epic 10-9 triumph with blood dripping on the table, would not argue with the accolade.

Special Branch

Thomas Birch, a keeper of books at the British Museum during the reign of Queen Victoria, was a keen angler. To improve his chances of a catch, he decided he needed to blend in with the surroundings, and so he set about disguising himself as a tree.

He devised a costume which concealed him inside an imitation tree-trunk, his arms protruding as branches. With his fishing rod covered by a spray of blossom, he would stand on the river bank for hours on end, looking to all intents and purposes like a perfectly ordinary member of a forest. He firmly believed that any movements he made would be mistaken by fish 'for the natural effect of a mild breeze'.

Learned to Ski in a Library

There was never any doubt as to which skier would finish last in the slalom at the 1960 Winter Olympics at Squaw Valley, California. Prior to arriving at the Games, Kyung Soon-yim of South Korea had never even skied on snow, and had attempted to master the basics of the sport by reading books and practising on grass. (That is the equivalent of trying to learn Formula One on Scalextric or preparing for a cross-channel swim in your bath.) Epitomizing the Olympic ideal, his fellow competitors provided him with equipment, a few tips and a rousing welcome when he trundled across the finish line.

Basket Case

Dennis Rodman, star forward with the Chicago Bulls, does not exactly fit the image of the stereotypical American basketball star. He dyes his cropped hair several times a week (often wearing it pink, yellow and purple to resemble a fluorescent cycling helmet), paints his nails, has various body-parts pierced and occasionally cross-dresses. Once, he turned up to a book-signing on a motorbike, dressed as a woman. He explains: 'I like bringing out the feminine side of Dennis Rodman.'

Rodman, who used to go out with Madonna, has compared himself to a reincarnated Elvis, Jimi Hendrix and even Moses, informing astounded reporters: 'I'm going to part the Red Sea and tell everyone: "Let's go and have a great time on the other side."'

He has had more than his share of run-ins with authority, including a three-game ban for throwing an ice-bag at San Antonio Spurs coach Bob Hill; a $20,000 fine for butting a referee and refusing to leave the court; and a $25,000 fine plus an eleven-game ban for kicking a TV cameraman.

His final game sounds like an event which the American TV networks will be clamouring to screen. Predicting a spectacular exit, he says: 'I'll walk off the court and take off one piece of clothing with every step. Then I'll be at about mid-court and I'll walk the rest of the way into the locker-room nude.' One can only hope that Gazza doesn't get similar ideas.

The Dry Regatta

A delightful alternative to England's famous regatta at Henley-on-Thames is staged each October at Alice Springs in Australia's Northern Territory. It is called the Henley-on-Todd Regatta, the principal difference between the Thames and the Todd being that the latter is invariably dry. But this does not prevent a series of races for canoes, including such standard events as pairs, eights and coxless fours, because all the boats taking part are bottomless. The crews' legs protrude through the holes and they simply run along the river-bed course carrying the canoes. The overall effect is rather like a Flintstones' Grand Prix.

10,000-Mile Detour

In 1983, American football fan Vince Mazzey was eagerly looking forward to seeing his favourite team, the Miami Dolphins, play in Los Angeles, 2,400 miles away. But when it came to fixing up the travel arrangements, he was horrified to learn that all direct flights between Miami and Los Angeles were fully booked. Not to be deterred, he enquired as to whether there were any alternative routes and was informed that he could always travel via London. Thus, he ended up flying from Miami to London and then back to Los Angeles, a round trip of some 12,000 miles.

A Weighty Problem

French professional wrestler Andre 'The Giant' Roussimoff was not a man to upset. He weighed over 530lb, his wrists measured more than a foot around, he took size 26 shoes and he stood 6ft 11in tall, although some 1970s promoters, billing him as 'Monster Eiffel Tower', put him at 7ft 4in. In short, he made Giant Haystacks look like Julian Clary.

Roussimoff, who was born with acromegaly (a hormonal disorder which causes the progressive enlargement of the head, face, hands, feet and chest), boasted that nobody could out-eat or out-drink him. His confidence was not misplaced. Fellow wrestler Terry Funk recounted how Roussimoff once drank 100 beers in a night, while others recalled the session when he followed endless half-nelsons with seventy-two double vodkas. The problem with a drunken Roussimoff was that it was impossible to shift him – at least, not without the aid of a crane. Thus, on the occasion when, after imbibing 119 beers, he fell asleep in the hotel bar, nobody was able to drag him to his bedroom and so he was left to sleep it off where he lay, wrapped in the cover of the grand piano.

Tough Guy Eddie

For fans of the Boston Bruins ice hockey team, it was always the highlight of the evening. As they chanted 'Hail to the Chief', their Canadian star Eddie Shore would make a grand entrance onto the ice, dressed in a matador's cloak and accompanied by a valet. Once Shore had received a fitting ovation, the valet would remove the cloak, leaving his master free to wreak havoc among the opposing players.

This he did to considerable effect, although not always legally. For Shore, who made his debut for the Bruins in 1926, was a notorious brawler, one of the toughest men on the ice. The term 'shrinking violet' was not one likely to be applied to him.

After breaking three ribs in a collision with a goalpost at New York's Madison Square Garden, he was taken to the Bruins' hotel where a doctor inspected the damage. The medic diagnosed that the injuries needed proper treatment and popped out to arrange a hospital bed. When he got back, Shore had vanished. He had caught the train to Montreal, where the following night he scored two goals and was credited with an assist against the Canadiens. On another occasion, the Montreal Maroons ganged up on him and as a result of the fracas, Shore lay unconscious on the ice for fourteen minutes. When he eventually came round, he had a broken nose, two black eyes, cuts on his cheek and over his left eye, and three broken teeth. Yet he still declared himself fit to play in the Bruins' next game. 'This is all part of hockey,' he told his open-mouthed team-mates.

Skied Backwards

At the 1952 Winter Olympics in Oslo, Greek slalom skier Antoin Miliordos had the misfortune to fall eighteen times during his run. He was so appalled by his miserable performance that he sat down and crossed the finish-line backwards. He had good reason to feel annoyed with himself, for his one-run time of 2min 26.9sec did not exactly compare favourably with that of the gold medallist, Othmar Schneider of Austria, who took only two minutes to complete *both* runs.

Billiards on Grass

Discussing sport in general, outspoken Australian Test cricketer Keith Miller said that a player's skill depended on the surface on which he was used to playing, adding: 'Even Walter Lindrum would have difficulty playing billiards on grass.'

When Australian billiards champion Lindrum read of Miller's comments, he entered into a wager that he could make a billiards break of fifty in thirty seconds on grass. So in October 1957, on a Melbourne lawn and using six jam-tins as pockets, Lindrum compiled a quick-fire break to earn himself $100 and Keith Miller's undying admiration.

Blond Ambition

Kevin Greene, key linebacker for the Pittsburgh Steelers American football team, vowed not to get his flowing blond hair cut until the Steelers had played in the Super Bowl. Despite the fact that his hair was hanging way down over his shoulders and that both his father, a colonel in the US army, and his wife Tara had begged him to have it cut all through 1995, Greene remained adamant. So it was a considerable relief to his family when the Steelers reached Super Bowl XXX against the Dallas Cowboys in January 1996.

Before the big game, Greene was in bullish mood: 'I want to win this thing before I cut these locks. The wife will be ready. I think she's going to have the scissors with her. She's going to come on the field and start chopping as soon as the game is over.' He was even considering having his hair cut during the game if opponents resorted to grabbing his mane in a bid to stop him making important plays. He was especially concerned about the Cowboys' Erik Williams: 'The only way I'll be able to keep Williams's hands out of my face is to keep a chainsaw in my back pocket . . . So there's a strong possibility I might have to be trimming it as the game is going on.'

Happily, Greene did not feel the urge to take to the field with a chainsaw, but the hair failed to provide a lucky omen and the Steelers lost. But at least his family went home happy.

Double Disaster

On 31 May 1986, fifty-two-year-old Pedro Gatica cycled from his home in Argentina to Mexico for the soccer World Cup, only to find on arrival that he couldn't afford to get in. While he was trying to haggle for a ticket, thieves stole his bike.

The Noble Art of Cow-Pat Tossing

In certain rural areas of the United States, competitors indulge in a curious show of strength. For instead of throwing the discus, they prefer to toss a dried cow-pat or 'chip' at distances of over 250 feet. Some events used to allow the pats to be moulded into a spherical, more aerodynamic shape, but in 1970, a new rule was introduced forbidding the sphericalization and demanding that all pats were 100 per cent organic. Apparently, these measures have done much to eliminate cheating in the sport.

Hairpin Bend

Ivor Brown, who with Alan Washbond won the two-man bobsleigh for the United States at the 1936 Winter Olympics, was a superstitious sort. Quite simply, he believed that his world would fall apart unless he found a hairpin on the ground every day. Fortunately for the American team, Brown's foraging had been successful for twenty-four consecutive days prior to the Olympic competition.

The 'Bear' with a Sore Head

American college football coach Paul 'Bear' Bryant (1913-83) was a tough disciplinarian. To punish one player for being late for a game, Bryant made him dig tons of manure into the cow pasture which the team used as a practice field. When Bryant himself overslept on the morning after the game, the coach agreed to dig it all back up and cart it away. He instilled such fear into his staff that when a meeting was called for 'first thing in the morning', one of his assistants slept on the office floor rather than risk being late.

As a child, Bryant craved attention and once threw a cat through an open window at a church revival meeting. The animal landed on a small girl's lap and disrupted the service. 'I got a whipping for that,' recalled Bryant later, 'and a lot of attention.' He earned his nickname as a teenager when friends dared him to wrestle a bear. A travelling sideshow had offered $50 to anyone able to last sixty seconds in the ring with the bear, but although Bryant survived the minute, he didn't collect his winnings because the promoter left town without paying. It was a lesson learned – after that, he made sure that nobody would ever again make a mug out of Paul Bryant.

The Swimmer Who Lived in a Fridge

In 1920, an Eskimo by the name of Emaku Gluco embarked on a rigorous training schedule in preparation for a bid to swim twenty-one miles across the Catalina Strait between California and the island of Santa Catalina. His training methods were decidedly unusual and made precious little attempt at acclimatization. They involved Gluco living in a refrigerator and eating only walrus meat and blubber which was specially shipped to him from the Arctic. It therefore came as no surprise when he abandoned the swim halfway across, complaining that the water was too warm.

Search Party Hunted For Skier

In the world of cross-country skiing, Mexico's Roberto Alvarez was known for one thing only – his supreme lack of ability. In view of his limited expertise, it was something of a gamble to send him to the 1988 Winter Olympics for the 50 kilometres event . . . particularly since he had never previously skied further than 20 kilometres.

His participation was suitably embarrassing. The rest of the field of sixty-one had all long been accounted for but there was still no sign of Alvarez. Officials feared that he might have got lost somewhere out on the course, and sent out a search party to find him. They need not have worried. Alvarez was merely proceeding at his own pace and eventually, to the relief of all concerned, clocked in at 3hr 22min 25.1sec, almost fifty-two minutes behind the sixtieth finisher. He could count himself fortunate that the timekeeper hadn't gone home.

The gallant Alvarez tried again in 1992, when his improved performance showed the benefit of experience. True, he still finished hopelessly last – but this time he was only just over half an hour behind the rest of the competitors.

Cri-Cri Comes a Cropper

Eugene Christophe, known to all as 'Cri-Cri', competed in eight Tours de France between 1906 and 1925. He never won, his best performances being second in 1912 and third in 1919. However, he was desperately unlucky in 1913, because he was leading the race when the front fork-stem of his bike broke on the descent from the Col du Tourmalet. With no outside assistance permitted, he had two choices – to quit the Tour or seek out the nearest blacksmith.

The majority would probably have selected the former option, but the Frenchman was not giving up without a struggle and so he carried the bike eight miles down a treacherously bumpy path to the village of St Marie de Campan, where he found a blacksmith. Under the watchful eye of Tour officials, Christophe welded the frame together with tools used for repairing horseshoes. Even then, his problems weren't over. For in addition to the time already lost, he was penalized a further three minutes for receiving 'outside assistance' when a small boy momentarily worked the bellows to keep the fire going. At that point, Christophe finally realized that it was not going to be his year.

Fatherly Concern

In 1989, Michael Bush from Phelps, New York, was arrested for trespassing after carrying a placard to school games protesting that his seventeen-year-old son was being left out of the Midlakes High American football team.

The Man Who Introduced Cheetah Racing

It seemed the perfect sport – faster than greyhound racing and with the added thrill of watching graceful big cats in action. KG Gandar Dower certainly thought so, and in 1937 he introduced cheetah racing to Britain as an exciting alternative to greyhounds.

He imported eight cats and staged highly-publicized races at Romford and Haringey. Unfortunately, he had reckoned without the natural instincts of cheetahs. They are not competitive animals, and showed little interest in racing each other and even less in pursuing that lump of rag masquerading as a hare (perhaps an electronic impala may have induced greater enthusiasm). The cats' indifference meant that the races never got going, and Mr Dower's ambitious experiment was swiftly abandoned.

The One-Armed Skier

It is difficult to imagine a more bizarre sight on the piste than that created by Canadian skier Diana Gordon-Lennox at the 1936 Winter Olympics. For not only was she wearing her customary monocle but, as the result of an accident, she was also obliged to ski both the downhill and the slalom with one arm in a plaster cast and using only one stick. Although she finished a lowly twenty-ninth overall, her plucky determination brought her a deserved ovation.

The Player Who Tackled Parked Cars

Bronko Nagurski was not content with tackling the usual twenty-stone opponent who litter an American football field – he sought a greater challenge. So between games for the Chicago Bears, he would demonstrate his colossal strength by tackling parked cars.

Born in Canada, Nagurski was discovered in 1925 by Minnesota coach Clarence 'Doc' Spears, who drove past a farm and saw a muscular young man ploughing a field – without a horse. When Spears stopped on the pretence of asking the way, he was amazed to see Nagurski use the heavy plough to point him in the right direction.

The 6ft 2in Nagurski made his debut for the Bears in 1930. In one match, the crowd had spilled onto the pitch and were being controlled by mounted police. Suddenly, Nagurski crashed through the end zone and hurtled straight into a horse, knocking the animal to the ground. He was thus able to add horses to parked cars in his list of objects successfully tackled.

Shortly afterwards, he added a third item – the brick wall which surrounded the Bears' Wrigley Field stadium. During a typically storming touchdown gallop, he fought off four tackles, rebounded off the goalposts and crashed into the wall. On returning to the huddle, he remarked: 'That last guy hit me awfully hard.' It is said that the crack in the wall is still visible.

Armadillo Racing

The mecca for devotees of armadillo racing is Fort Worth, Texas, where the annual meeting attracts entrants from a wide area of the United States. The creatures scurry along the course, hotly pursued by their human owners. One presumes that if the armadillos become too scared and roll themselves up into balls, the race is cancelled and everyone has a nice gentle game of bowls instead.

An Olympian Aged Seven

With the final of the coxed-pairs rowing at the 1900 Paris Olympics drawing nearer, the Dutch crew suddenly found they were short of one essential ingredient – a cox. Feverishly they searched for a last-minute replacement, but everybody in the vicinity with rowing experience was too heavy and would therefore have destroyed their chances. Then they hit upon the idea of forgetting about the expertise altogether. Concluding that the size of the cox was all important, they recruited a small boy, believed to be around seven years old, to steer them to victory. The boy, whose name was never recorded, did just that, to become surely the youngest ever Olympic gold medallist.

Defeat Was Hard to Take

Wilbur 'Pony' Wilson, coach of the New Jersey college basketball team Rutgers-Camden, always took defeat badly. And he had plenty of practice as his team, nicknamed the Pioneers, set up a league record of 117 successive defeats over a five-year period. In that time, Wilson lost fifty pounds in weight and became so obsessed with obtaining that elusive victory that he used to alarm his wife by yelling out the names of the players in his sleep. He was therefore probably called 'Pony' because he was a little hoarse after every game.

Finally, in January 1997, the losing run came to an end with a 77-72 triumph against Bloomfield College, but by then the hapless Wilson had been replaced. His successor, Ray Pace, insisted: 'I don't want any credit for this. The players did it for Wilbur.'

Split Personality

Big Bill Werbeniuk was one of professional snooker's greatest characters . . . and the envy of many a sportsman. For each year, the twenty-stone Canadian was allowed to set £2,000 worth of lager against his income as a tax-deductible item.

Years ago, Werbeniuk discovered that he suffered from a disease which caused his right hand to shake – hardly an attribute in a snooker player – and found that drinking vast quantities of lager was the only cure. So from then on, whenever he downed a pint it really was medicinal. He once said: 'I need six pints to get to the table, even for a practice. Then I need a pint for every frame. In a long day, I can get through twenty-five to thirty pints. Fortunately, I have a good capacity for drink.'

When competing in tournaments in Britain, Werbeniuk lived in a mobile home, complete with TV, video, stereo, kitchen, shower, two bedrooms, lounge, phone and, most importantly, lager on draught.

The side-effect of the excessive lager-intake was that it did nothing to reduce his waistline, a situation which came to a dramatic head when his trousers split during a live TV broadcast of the 1980 World Team Cup final between Canada and Wales. Werbeniuk was playing David Taylor at the time, and the noise of the tear was believed to have been heard several miles away. To make matters worse, Werbeniuk wasn't wearing any underpants – apparently they always made him feel uncomfortable. After separate appeals for calm and for needle and cotton, he left the arena for a quarter of an hour to undergo emergency repairs. There were no reports of any female spectators having to be treated for shock.

The Slow Skier

For the slalom event at the 1992 Winter Olympics, skiers took off at 40-second intervals. Sadly, the time lapse proved insufficient for Raymond Kayrouz of Lebanon, who, starting from position 129 of the 131 competitors, was so painfully slow that he was actually overtaken by the next starter, El Hassan Matha of Morocco. To compound his misery, Kayrouz then missed a gate and was disqualified.

Motivated by Fear

Dale Christensen, coach with the Libertyville High School American football team, came up with a novel way of motivating his players before a crunch game in 1994. Not for him the usual speeches or game-plans – he decided to stage an elaborate mock fight in which he appeared to be killed. Unfortunately, the bloody exercise was a touch too realistic, with the result that the players were unnerved and lost the game, and Christensen resigned. The team's senior lineman, Mike Duffy, reflected: 'The idea that we were going to die overshadowed any point he was trying to make.'

Pot-ato Black

In 1983, Gary Miller and Stuart Alliston from Humberside took a marathon 1 hour 13 minutes to complete one frame of snooker. The reason for their sloth was that they were using a potato as the cueball.

Puzzling Ban

In the autumn of 1996, Belgian agriculture minister Karel Pinxten announced a new law banning camel and ostrich racing on the nation's public roads. A sensible enough measure, one might think –

after all, an ostrich doing thirty in the middle lane could be quite a hazard, particularly if it was not displaying an adequate rear light. But as a mystified spokesman for Belgium's local authorities pointed out: 'We have no idea why we suddenly have this new law. As far as we know, no one has ever tried to race camels or ostriches in Belgium.'

The Rider Who Lost His Bearings

If one cyclist should have been accustomed to the ninety-degree-plus temperatures on the Perpignan-Nimes stage of the 1950 Tour de France, it was Abd-El Kader Zaag, who did most of his training in North Africa. But even he was feeling the effects of the intense heat and was so parched that he gratefully accepted the offer of a bottle of wine from a spectator.

Now if he had merely taken a swig, the wine might have proved beneficial but instead, he was so thirsty that he drank the entire bottle. It should, therefore, have come as little surprise when he fell off his bike a few minutes later. Realizing that he was in no fit state to continue, he decided to sleep it off at the roadside. And sure enough, within five minutes he was back in the saddle and sprinting off down the road . . . unfortunately, in the direction from which he had just come.

The Eagle Has Landed

In recent years, no competitor has encapsulated the great British sporting eccentric better than ski-jumper extraordinary, Eddie 'the Eagle' Edwards. His exploits at the 1988 Winter Olympics at Calgary, where he finished a resounding last, made the twenty-four-year-old Cheltenham plasterer with the thick beerbottle spectacles a national hero. There were TV appearances, T-shirts and records as well as the ultimate accolade – life membership of the Monster Raving Loony Party. Never was there a more deserving case.

The man described as 'Mr Magoo on skis' learned his art on the plastic ski-slopes at Gloucester. It was there that he met his girlfriend, after literally bumping into her. During his early years of competition, he travelled around Europe on a shoestring budget. He once had to stay in a scout centre for a night and helped to pay for it by washing up and chopping wood. At Turku in Finland, the only cheap accommodation he could find was the local mental hospital. He recalls: 'That was a pound a night, which was about right for a place where they were coming to the door with an axe. It was all right – they thought I was one of them!'

Competing on the 60-metre jump at St Moritz in 1986, he fell on his face breaking his jaw, his collarbone and assorted teeth. He was bloody but unbowed: 'My nose was pouring blood. I had no money to go to a hospital, so I just put a scarf around my face and carried on.'

So to Calgary. His Gloucestershire burr of an accent enchanted the Canadians and Americans, along with his frank admission that he was terrified before every jump. He said: 'There's a million and one reasons, when you stand at the top of the 90-metre jump and think, why you shouldn't go down. I remember when I did my first jump. I looked from the top and was so frightened that my bum shrivelled up like a prune.'

Serious sports journalists were eager to find out how Eddie allied his short-sightedness to ski jumping. Confessing that he often has to ask passers-by whether there is anything in front of him, he casually mentioned that his glasses always mist up when he sets off from the top of the leap. As the world's press looked on in amazement, he added: 'So I just have to hope they clear by the time I reach the bottom.'

He appeared on the prestigious *Johnny Carson Show* and quickly became a cult hero. The *Calgary Sun* said he was the biggest thing to come out of Britain since the Beatles. But not everyone was impressed, and an East German newspaper called him a 'self-publicizing clown'. East German athletes have, of course, traditionally shunned publicity. . . along with sex tests.

The sole member of the British Olympic ski-jumping team was set to compete on both the 70- and 90-metre jumps, but after Eddie had finished a predictable last on the shorter jump, Olympic officials tried to dissuade him from jumping on the 90-metre hill for his own safety.

Rob McCormack, chief of competition at the Games, said bluntly: 'The Eagle doesn't jump – he drops like a stone. In such near-perfect conditions with no wind, an eleven-year-old kid should be able to jump further.' Nevertheless, the British delegation decided he could cope, and although he lived down to expectations by finishing fifty-fifth and last, he did manage 71 metres on the 90-metre hill, only forty-seven metres behind the winner, Norway's Matti Nykaenen.

Back in Britain, Eddie's public were eagerly anticipating when they would next see him in action. In 1989, he took part in a World Cup event at Lake Placid where, to the astonishment of all concerned, he somehow finished ahead of Dutchman Gerrit Konijnenberg on 'style'. Even allowing for the fact that the Dutch aren't exactly renowned for their mountains, it was a remarkable result. Indeed, taking into account the non-finishers, Eddie's final placing was a highly creditable seventy-eighth out of eighty-three. He was beside himself with joy, and even sounded like a proper sportsman when he declared: 'I kicked some butt.'

Explaining his sudden improvement, he revealed: 'I'm going down thinking about my position, making contact, exploding on take-off, keeping my head down, getting into a good flight position. All of that is going through my mind, instead of just "Ooooooh!"'

But a week later, he broke his collarbone in practice and confessed: 'The jump was so good, and I was in such a good flight-position, that I started to panic.'

It was a comfort to know that he hadn't completely lost his old touch.

Bibliography

The Book of Sports Lists – Craig and David Brown (Arthur Barker 1983)

Boxing Encyclopedia – Barry J Hugman and Peter Arnold (TW Publications 1993)

The Breedon Book of Football Managers – Dennis Turner and Alex White (Breedon Books 1993)

Clough: A Biography – Tony Francis (Stanley Paul 1989)

The Complete Book of the Olympics – David Wallechinsky (Aurum 1996)

The Complete Book of the Winter Olympics – David Wallechinsky (Aurum 1994)

Conte Maggi's Mille Miglia – Peter Miller (Alan Sutton 1988)

The Cricket Captains of England – Alan Gibson (Cassell 1979)

Denis Compton: Cricketing Genius – Peter West (Stanley Paul 1989)

Double Century: 200 Years of Cricket in The Times – ed. Marcus Williams (Collins Willow 1985)

The Encyclopedia of World Rugby – Keith Quinn (Lochar Publishing 1991)

The Field Book of Cricket – ed. David Rayvern Allen (Pelham Books 1991)

Free As a Bird – David Hopps (Robson Books 1996)

From Sammy to Jimmy: The Official History of Somerset County Cricket Club – Peter Roebuck (Partridge Press 1991)

The Golfers – Peter Dobereiner (Collins 1982)

The Golfer Who Laughed – Phil Tresidder (Stanley Paul 1982)

Grand Prix Racing – Anthony Pritchard (Aston Publications 1991)

Grand Prix Requiem – William Court (Patrick Stephens 1992)

The Guardian Book of Cricket – ed. Matthew Engel (Pavilion 1986)

The Guinness Book of the Marathon – Roger Gynn (Guinness 1984)

Headquarters: A History of Newmarket and its Racing – Richard Onslow (Great Ouse Press 1983)

The History of Derbyshire County Cricket Club – John Shawcroft (Christopher Helm 1989)

A History of Golf – Louis T Stanley (Weidenfeld & Nicolson 1991)

The History of Horse Racing – Roger Longrigg (Macmillan 1972)

The History of Nottinghamshire County Cricket Club – Peter Wynne Thomas (Christopher Helm 1992)

The Illustrated History of Boxing – Harry Mullan (Hamlyn 1990)

The Joy of Cricket – ed. John Bright-Holmes (Secker & Warburg 1984)

Men of Steel – Peter Walsh (Robson Books 1993)

The Men in White Coats – Teresa McLean (Stanley Paul 1987)

Racing Round the Island – Bob Holliday (David & Charles 1976)

Red Roses Crest the Caps: The Story of Lancashire CCC – Eric Midwinter (Kingswood Press 1989)

The Ryder Cup: The Players – Malcolm Hamer (Kingswood Press 1992)

Sporting Profiles – Michael Parkinson (Pavilion 1995)

The Story of the Davis Cup – Alan Trengove (Stanley Paul 1985)

The Story of Steeplechasing – Elizabeth Eliot (Longmans 1957)

Tales From Far Pavilions – Allen Synge and Leo Cooper (Pavilion 1984)

Tales of the Country Eccentrics – Tom Quinn (David & Charles 1996)

The Trent Bridge Battery – Basil Haynes and John Lucas (Collins Willow 1985)

The Ultimate Encyclopedia of Golf – Ted Barrett and Michael Hobbs (Carlton Books 1995)

A Wayward Genius: The Fleetwood-Smith Story – Greg Crowden (ABC 1991)

The Who's Who of Golf – Peter Alliss (Orbis 1983)
Winners – Brian Laban (Orbis 1981)
You've Got To Be Crazy – Bob Wilson (Weidenfeld & Nicolson 1989)